Nuclear Blackmail
and Nuclear Balance

RICHARD K. BETTS

Nuclear Blackmail and Nuclear Balance

THE BROOKINGS INSTITUTION
Washington, D.C.

Library of Congress Cataloging-in-Publication data:
Betts, Richard K., 1947–
Nuclear blackmail and nuclear balance.
Includes bibliographical references and index.
1. World politics—1945– . 2. Military
history, Modern—20th century.   3. Nuclear warfare.
I. Title.
D843.B486   1987   327.1'17   87-13384
ISBN 0-8157-0936-6
ISBN 0-8157-0935-8 (pbk.)

9 8 7 6 5 4 3 2 1

THE BROOKINGS INSTITUTION is an independent organization devoted to nonpartisan research, education, and publication in economics, government, foreign policy, and the social sciences generally. Its principal purposes are to aid in the development of sound public policies and to promote public understanding of issues of national importance.

The Institution was founded on December 8, 1927, to merge the activities of the Institute for Government Research, founded in 1916, the Institute of Economics, founded in 1922, and the Robert Brookings Graduate School of Economics and Government, founded in 1924.

The Board of Trustees is responsible for the general administration of the Institution, while the immediate direction of the policies, program, and staff is vested in the President, assisted by an advisory committee of the officers and staff. The by-laws of the Institution state: "It is the function of the Trustees to make possible the conduct of scientific research, and publication, under the most favorable conditions, and to safeguard the independence of the research staff in the pursuit of their studies and in the publication of the results of such studies. It is not a part of their function to determine, control, or influence the conduct of particular investigations or the conclusions reached."

The President bears final responsibility for the decision to publish a manuscript as a Brookings book. In reaching his judgment on the competence, accuracy, and objectivity of each study, the President is advised by the director of the appropriate research program and weighs the views of a panel of expert outside readers who report to him in confidence on the quality of the work. Publication of a work signifies that it is deemed a competent treatment worthy of public consideration but does not imply endorsement of conclusions or recommendations.

The Institution maintains its position of neutrality on issues of public policy in order to safeguard the intellectual freedom of the staff. Hence interpretations or conclusions in Brookings publications should be understood to be solely those of the authors and should not be attributed to the Institution, to its trustees, officers, or other staff members, or to the organizations that support its research.

For Adela

Foreword

DOES nuclear superiority matter? Should it? How big must an advantage in the "balance" of nuclear power be for it to be meaningful? These questions have periodically bedeviled debate about U.S. defense policy, and they prompt impassioned responses on both sides of the political spectrum. Some politicians, officials, and analysts believe that nuclear weapons are good only for preventing the Soviet Union from launching a nuclear attack; others assert that they can be used effectively for political leverage and intimidation. These contrasting beliefs often play a significant background role in disputes about U.S. defense priorities and in attitudes about how American leaders should attempt to handle crises.

These questions, though important, are extraordinarily difficult to answer with confidence or precision. Prevalent views rest as often on faith or folklore as on clear evidence. Marshaling available data from declassified documents and other sources, this book takes a careful look at the role of nuclear weapons in cold war crises. Richard K. Betts, a senior fellow in the Brookings Foreign Policy Studies program, chronicles and analyzes cases in which American and Soviet leaders attempted to exploit risks of nuclear conflict in order to exert pressure on each other in international confrontations. He assesses the adequacy of common explanations for the willingness of leaders to use nuclear coercion, and he offers judgments about what to expect if such confrontations occur in the future.

The author is especially indebted to Robert Jervis, John J. Mearsheimer, Scott D. Sagan, Marc Trachtenberg, and Stephen Van Evera for exceptionally rigorous comments on the first draft of his study and for sharing illuminating documents. Robert J. Art, Barry M. Blechman, Robert R. Bowie, John Gaddis, General Andrew Goodpaster, Colin S. Gray, and Joseph S. Nye gave detailed criticisms of the manuscripts, and Bruce G. Blair, Raymond L. Garthoff, Andrew Goldberg, and Jack Snyder also provided useful comments.

Nancy Ameen assisted in gathering documentary materials, and Charles Appleby, Matthew Evangelista, and Elisa Harris provided helpful suggestions. The staffs of the Dwight D. Eisenhower and John F. Kennedy presidential libraries facilitated the author's research, particularly in processing requests to executive agencies for mandatory declassification review. The author is also grateful to David Alan Rosenberg for his pioneering work of the past decade in uncovering and arranging for the declassification of important documents. Finally, he wishes to acknowledge the support given by Adela Maria Bolet and Michael I. Handel.

This study was guided by John D. Steinbruner, director of the Brookings Foreign Policy Studies program, and William B. Quandt, acting director during 1986. At various stages, assistance in producing the manuscript was provided by Karin Burchard, Denise Dilima, Maxine J. Hill, and Christine G. Miller. The book was edited by Brenda B. Szittya, and factual sources were verified by Stephen K. Wegren. The index was prepared by Dianne Hardy.

Brookings is grateful to the Ford Foundation, the Carnegie Corporation of New York, and the John D. and Catherine T. MacArthur Foundation for financial support that made the study possible.

A few points in the book appeared in germinal form in the author's "Elusive Equivalence: The Political and Military Meaning of the Nuclear Balance," in Samuel P. Huntington, ed., *The Strategic Imperative: New Policies for American Security* (Ballinger, 1982). An early version of the second half of chapter four appeared as "A Nuclear Golden Age? The Balance Before Parity," in *International Security,* vol. 11 (Winter 1986–87).

The views in this book are those of the author and should not be ascribed to the persons or foundations acknowledged above, or to the trustees, officers, or other staff members of the Brookings Institution.

BRUCE K. MACLAURY
President

May 1987
Washington, D.C.

Contents

Now, nothing can be precluded in a military thing. Remember this: when you resort to force as the arbiter of human difficulty, you don't know where you are going; but, generally speaking, if you get deeper and deeper, there is just no limit except what is imposed by limitations of force itself. Dwight D. Eisenhower, January 12, 1955

A government that is exposed to atomic threats in peacetime readily regards them as "blackmail" whereas the threatening power is likely to call them "deterrence."
Hans Speier, in *World Politics*, April 1957

CHAPTER ONE

Risks, Threats, and Rationales

*By arranging it so that we might have to blow up the world, we would not have to. . . .
The creation of risk—usually a shared risk—is the technique of compellence that probably
best deserves the name of "brinkmanship." It is a competition in risk-taking. . . . The
perils that countries face are not as straightforward as suicide, but more like Russian
roulette.*　　　　　　　　　　　Thomas C. Schelling, *Arms and Influence*, 1966

*Whether or not atomic weapons are ever again used in warfare, the very fact of their
existence, the possibility that they could be used, will affect all future wars. In this sense
Korea was an atomic war even though no atomic weapons were used. In this sense even
the cold war is an atomic cold war. The situation is analogous to a game of chess. The
atomic queens may never be brought into play; they may never actually take one of the
opponent's pieces. But the position of the atomic queens may still have a decisive bearing
on which side can safely advance a limited-war bishop or even a cold-war pawn. The
advance of a cold-war pawn may even disclose a check of the opponent's king by a well
positioned atomic queen.*
　　　　　Paul H. Nitze, "Atoms, Strategy and Policy," *Foreign Affairs* (January 1956)

NUCLEAR WEAPONS brought American security the worst of times and the
best of times. Cursed by vulnerability to unimaginable destruction, Americans have also been blessed by "the longest sustained period in modern
Western history without war between the major powers."[1] Despite a
prolonged global contest, the only combat between the United States and
the Soviet Union has been indirect, through interventions or small wars
against each other's friends, or potential, through direct confrontations
that raised the possibility of war.

To pessimists, the superpowers' management of constant conflict without resort to war has occurred *despite* the nuclear danger: such luck cannot
last if the antagonists continue to brandish their awesomely devastating
capabilities at each other. Those who are cheered by forty-odd years of
tenuous peace resemble the man falling off the Empire State Building

---

1. Samuel P. Huntington, "Playing to Win," *National Interest*, no. 3 (Spring 1986),
p. 9. The previous "modern record" was from Waterloo to the Crimean War. Paul
Schroeder, quoted in ibid., p. 9n.

saying "so far, so good" as he passes the fortieth floor. To optimists, on the other hand, the absence of major war has been not lucky but logical; peace has endured in part *because* of nuclear weapons. By making the consequences of war apocalyptic those weapons made it unthinkable. Washington or Moscow might exploit the risk of war as they maneuvered for advantage at the margin of the conflict, but neither could dare lurch over the brink.

This book is about the role of nuclear weapons in those maneuvers at the margin and about how those weapons figured in decisionmakers' attempts to exert leverage in the crises that have peppered the more than four decades of peace between the superpowers since the bombing of Nagasaki. General stability has not ruled out the occasional danger of war. Although postwar policymakers have always wanted to avoid nuclear war, they have never made that aim their highest priority; if they had, they could have minimized the possibility by making policy declarations, military preparations, and diplomacy during crises consistent with the notion that nuclear weapons should be used for nothing but retaliation against nuclear attack. U.S. policy, however, has rested on the principle that there are interests for which the United States would make the first use of nuclear weapons rather than concede.

In crises, therefore, two aims abraded each other in U.S. leaders' deliberations and actions: preventing war and preventing political losses. One way of reducing the risk of political losses is to heighten the risk of war if the enemy presses his challenge. And one way of reducing the risk of war is to convince the enemy that any war could turn into all-out war. Thus one set of tactics is to raise the possibility that nuclear weapons could be unleashed to counter conventional military action.

When the tactic of exploiting the specter of nuclear war was used, it provoked accusations of nuclear "blackmail." Since the onset of the cold war there have been at least a dozen cases in which some sort of nuclear threat was used as a sparring tactic in tense confrontations. Both sides made use of such threats, but the United States did so more often than the Soviet Union. There is wide controversy about what to make of these incidents. How real or serious were the threats? What impact did they have on the outcomes of the crises? How did decisionmakers bring themselves to make the threats? Were the threats sensible or irresponsible? And two questions above all stand out. How did the nuclear balance of power affect the situations? Can the past serve as a guide to action in future crises, or have changes in the conditions of the superpower competition made past experience irrelevant?

One aim of this study is simply to compile and compare in one place what is known about cases of attempted nuclear coercion. The focal points are the American decision process leading to the threats and the backdrop of the nuclear balance of power. The book does not review the whole history of either nuclear strategy or various crises. Rather it considers the specific and sometimes obscure intersections of theory and practice—the instances in which official notions about nuclear strategy had a chance to come into play in leaders' responses to the complex pressures of particular confrontations. To put these ventures into context there are a few points to clarify. What exactly is meant by nuclear blackmail or coercion? Is there good reason to accord such threats any significance to begin with? What cases should be considered? What pitfalls lie in the way of analysis? Readers who have little interest in theory and are willing in advance to accept the arguments in the following chapters can skip ahead to them, but this is a tricky and controversial subject. A solid base for argument depends on some clarifications, categorizations, and caveats.

Theory and Practice

Nuclear strategy consists of ideas or war plans, developed in peacetime, to define when and how nuclear forces would be used in wartime. The principle of deterrence is that giving the adversary a window into the future, a view of what he would, or at least might, suffer if he were to provoke war, will prevent him from tempting fate. The point of deterrence is to keep the practice of war entirely theoretical. Crises, however, are twilight regions between peace and war. Indeed, the nuclear revolution encourages "the substitution of crises for wars."[2] Thus crises are the true test of deterrence, and unless deterrence fails, crises are the only realm of actual practice that counts. Crises evoke the question of whether the threats lying behind the goal of deterrence might be called to the test. How much of normal peacetime theory or strategic doctrine is applied in crisis practice, and how much is ignored or improvised?

Blackmail in Theory

"Nuclear blackmail" is a racy phrase to strategic analysts, who are apt to wince at how pejorative and evocative it seems when applied to situations that they consider in such bloodless terms as "deterrence" or "compel-

2. Stanley Hoffmann, *The State of War: Essays on the Theory and Practice of International Politics* (Praeger, 1965), p. 236 (citing Raymond Aron).

lence."[3] Blackmail is more a layman's term, but political leaders are laymen who deal more often in visceral codewords than in the sterile language of strategic theorists. Officials on both sides of the East-West conflict who have faced nuclear threats have often used the word blackmail to describe them. For anyone discomfited by nuclear pressure, aspects of the literal definition of blackmail seem quite apposite: "tribute formerly exacted . . . in return for protection or immunity from plunder. . . . Any payment extorted by intimidation or pressure, or levied by unprincipled officials . . . upon those whom they have it in their power to help or injure."[4] Anyone suspecting that official references to the adversary's blackmail are only self-serving and disingenuous would do well to recall Richard Neustadt's observation that "the tendency of bureaucratic language to create in private the same images presented to the public never should be underrated."[5]

The notion of blackmail in this study is more modest than some connotations of the word. Here it means coercion by the threat of punishment, a threat designed either to deter or to compel action by the opponent. In most of the cases included here the party attempting nuclear coercion conceived the initiative as a deterrent action, and to most people, deterrence sounds far more innocent than blackmail. A significant problem of definition, however, is that suggested by Hans Speier in one of the epigraphs to this book: the perception of whether a coercive threat represents legitimate deterrence or nasty blackmail is likely to depend on whether one is making the threat or facing it. And in one respect the most significant thing about a threat is how it is seen by its target.

When confronted by even vague and indirect nuclear pressure by the Soviets in the Suez crisis, Western officials called it blackmail. In the period of concern over a possible "missile gap," some in the United States reacted to inflated Soviet claims of superiority by referring to "the Communists' current strategy of massive nuclear blackmail."[6] Although some analysts

3. "Compellence" is coercion meant to induce desired change in enemy behavior, by forcing him to do something he does not want to do, whereas deterrence is the obverse, meant to prevent undesired change by forcing the enemy not to do something he might want to do. Thomas C. Schelling, *Arms and Influence* (Yale University Press, 1966), pp. 70–72.

4. *Oxford English Dictionary*, new edition (Oxford: Clarendon Press, 1978), vol. 1: A–B, pp. 894–95.

5. Richard E. Neustadt, *Presidential Power: The Politics of Leadership* (John Wiley and Sons, 1960), p. 139.

6. Robert Strausz-Hupé, "Nuclear Blackmail and Limited War," *Yale Review*, vol. 48 (Winter 1959), p. 175.

in the West have viewed U.S. policy in similar terms,[7] most associate the term with offensive rather than defensive threats and thus see blackmail as something attempted by Moscow rather than by Washington.[8] Yet overall, rhetoric about blackmail has come more frequently from the opposing camp.

According to A. N. Yakovlev, President Harry Truman "placed at the foundation of postwar foreign policy a strategy of nuclear blackmail."[9] In crises over the Taiwan Straits and Berlin in the 1950s both Chinese and Soviet spokesmen referred to American nuclear blackmail. In the Cuban missile crisis, wrote Anatolii Gromyko, U.S. leaders avoided direct military conflict: "Instead, they made the utmost use of techniques of political blackmail whose purpose was to convince the opposing party that should some 'undesirable' situation arise, Washington was prepared to employ both conventional and nuclear weapons without delay."[10] Indeed, the Soviets often defined the essence of U.S. deterrence policy as a whole as blackmail. Translating the word "deterrence" into the Russian language has historically been frustrating from a Western point of view.[11] This was true especially before the 1970s, as Geoffrey Jukes points out: "For their deterrence of the West, the Soviets most commonly use the word *sderzhivaniye* (restraining); for Western deterrence of them they use the word *ustrasheniye,* which comes very close to meaning 'intimidation'."[12]

7. Edward Friedman, "Nuclear Blackmail and the End of the Korean War," *Modern China,* vol. 1 (January 1975), pp. 75–91; Joseph Gerson, "Nuclear Blackmail," *Bulletin of the Atomic Scientists,* vol. 40 (May 1984), pp. 57–58. For a brief survey of definitional confusions see Jeff McMahan, "Nuclear Blackmail," in Nigel Blake and Kay Pole, eds., *Dangers of Deterrence: Philosophers on Nuclear Strategy* (London: Routledge and Kegan Paul, 1983), pp. 85–93.

8. See Arnold L. Horelick and Myron Rush, *Strategic Power and Soviet Foreign Policy* (University of Chicago Press, 1965), pp. 9–10, 12; for the postparity era, see Jack L. Watkins, "The Essence of National Defense: To Prevent Nuclear Blackmail," *Vital Speeches,* vol. 50 (October 1, 1984), pp. 738–41.

9. A. N. Yakovlev, *Ot Trumena do Reigana, doktriny i real'nosti yadernogo veka* (From Truman to Reagan: Doctrine and Realities of the Nuclear Age)(Moscow: Molodaya gvardiya, 1984), p. 14 (translation courtesy of Raymond Garthoff).

10. "The Caribbean Crisis, Part 2," translated by William Mandel from *Voprosy istorii* (Problems of History), no. 8 (1971), and reprinted in Ronald R. Pope, ed., *Soviet Views on the Cuban Missile Crisis: Myth and Reality in Foreign Policy Analysis* (University Press of America, 1982), p. 209.

11. See Peter H. Vigor, "The Semantics of Deterrence and Defense," in Michael MccGwire, Ken Booth, and John McDonnell, eds., *Soviet Naval Policy: Objectives and Constraints* (Praeger, 1975), pp. 471–78.

12. Geoffrey Jukes, "The Military Approach to Deterrence and Defense," in MccGwire, Booth, and McDonnell, eds., *Soviet Naval Policy,* p. 484.

The point that opposing sides may see the threats they pose in different ways—that what one considers an innocent deterrent, the other may see as a pernicious compellent—is important in chapter four, which assesses rationales for nuclear coercion, some of which rest on the principle that it is easier to deter than to compel. As subsequent analytical excursions unfold, it is also useful to keep in mind that emotions may have figured more prominently in decisionmakers' behavior than some documents and historical sources indicate. The word blackmail is used in the title and occasionally in the text of this book because it has been so commonly used to describe incidents dealt with in this study; it lets readers know at the outset what the book is about and reminds them later of the question of how perspective bears on judgment. In some respects, however, the term can be tendentious. To avoid entangling issues of empirical analysis and moral justification, I frequently use less pejorative terms, such as "coercion," "brinkmanship," "leverage," and especially "threat" to refer to the same phenomenon.

In one sense there is a constant nuclear threat with a whiff of blackmail inherent in standing capabilities and doctrines, but this study is concerned with specific signals in crises.[13] A threat is defined as any official suggestion that nuclear weapons may be used if the dispute is not settled on acceptable terms. Such threats can be signals of intentions—hints through public statements, diplomatic channels, or deliberate leaks about internal discussions or plans. Or they can be signaled through observable preparation or exercising of nuclear capabilities beyond normal peacetime status, indicating greater readiness to execute wartime missions. In general the latter type should seem the more potent gesture, on the principle that actions speak louder than words.

The focus of this study is on nuclear threats made by the United States. It also addresses a few Soviet uses of the tactic, but these cases were less frequent, restricted to rhetorical allusions,[14] and more often seen only as

13. The difference corresponds to Patrick M. Morgan's distinction between "general" and "immediate" deterrence, in his Deterrence: A Conceptual Analysis, 2d ed., vol. 40 (Beverly Hills: Sage Publications, 1983), pp. 28, 41. Immediate deterrence of attack arises as an issue when general deterrence fails to prevent confrontation.

14. By some measures the Russians used verbal threats as often as the Americans in earlier years. See Hannes Adomeit, "Soviet Crisis Prevention and Management: Why and When Do the Soviet Leaders Take Risks?" Orbis, vol. 30 (Spring 1986), pp. 55–56. Most of the Soviet statements, however, were directed against U.S. allies rather than Washington itself, and Soviet demonstrative uses of military capabilities were virtually all conventional rather than nuclear. Adomeit, "Soviet Crisis Prevention," pp. 57–59; and Stephen S.

bluster because the threats were usually issued after the peak of the crisis had passed.[15] Moreover, while there is a fair amount of reliable evidence about what occurred in the U.S. decision process leading to threats, virtually none is available about the Soviet side.

Threats in Practice

How significant were the attempts at nuclear coercion considered in this book? The experts disagree. There is no consensus even about what actions should be considered threats. Evidence about decisions behind the threats is fragmentary and foggy and is filtered through analysts' larger assumptions about the military and political roles of nuclear weapons. Nuclear signals were always imbedded in other major initiatives, events, and considerations, and it is hard to determine which factors dominated leaders' attention. Finally, some commentators rely on obiter dicta or use available data selectively. As a result, prevalent views have tended to overstate or understate the significance of nuclear coercion.

At one extreme are those who believe that American leaders used nuclear blackmail frequently and decisively. For example, Daniel Ellsberg claims that "*every* president from Truman to Reagan, with the possible exception of Ford, has felt compelled to consider or direct serious preparations for possible imminent U.S. initiation of tactical or strategic nuclear warfare, in the midst of an ongoing, intense, non-nuclear conflict or crisis."[16] Such assertions occasionally reflect the analyst's zealotry but have also been fueled by retrospective bravado of former presidents. Years after he left office Harry Truman claimed that in 1946 he had threatened Moscow with nuclear war if Soviet troops were not withdrawn from Iran. In 1985

Kaplan and others, *Diplomacy of Power: Soviet Armed Forces as a Political Instrument* (Brookings, 1981), pp. 54–55. Moscow did not make even verbal nuclear threats against the United States after Khrushchev's ouster. I also do not count statements in peacetime, as opposed to during crises, about general nuclear doctrine or commitments or the danger of nuclear war.

15. Francis Fukuyama, "Nuclear Shadowboxing: Soviet Intervention Threats in the Middle East," *Orbis*, vol. 25 (Fall 1981), pp. 579–605; Herbert S. Dinerstein, *The Making of a Missile Crisis: October 1962* (Johns Hopkins University Press, 1976), p. 85.

16. Daniel Ellsberg, "Introduction: Call to Mutiny," in E. P. Thompson and Dan Smith, eds., *Protest and Survive* (Monthly Review Press, 1981), p. iv (emphasis in original). See also Gerson, "Nuclear Blackmail." Arguments attributing great coercive significance to nuclear superiority are more often found on the other side of the ideological spectrum. See for example, Edward Luttwak, "The Strategic Balance 1972," *Washington Papers* 3 (Washington, D.C.: Library Press for the Georgetown Center for Strategic and International Studies, 1972), pp. 85–95; and Robert Jastrow, "Why Strategic Superiority Matters," *Commentary*, vol. 75 (March 1983), pp. 27–32.

Richard Nixon said that he had considered using nuclear weapons four times during his administration. By evidence available, these recollections were probably altogether false; they were at least exaggerated.[17] Dwight Eisenhower's memoirs also suggest more clarity and directness in the nuclear threats he made than is demonstrated by other documentary evidence of the time.

At the other extreme from observers who overemphasize the prominence of nuclear threats are those who denigrate or overlook them. "If the United States drew any political benefit from its early [nuclear] advantage," writes one essayist, "it is hard to see what it was."[18] In 1963 Secretary of Defense Robert S. McNamara argued against relying excessively on nuclear weapons by noting, as others have often done since, that U.S. superiority had not prevented the Korean War or Soviet pressure on Berlin. No nuclear threats had been made to deter North Korea before June 1950, however; indeed, Secretary of State Dean Acheson's "perimeter speech" explicitly left South Korea outside the U.S. defense line. And no one should expect normal nuclear deterrence to prevent pressure or probes; rather it is meant to prevent actual use of force. Finally, few with any sensitivity to political realities would expect nuclear threats to be relevant to revolutionary civil wars in the third world, such as the Vietnam War, or to superpower conflicts with much weaker nations where conventional instruments could be decisive. In contrast to Truman, Eisenhower, and Nixon, McGeorge Bundy, Robert McNamara, and other high-level leaders looking back from retirement tend to recall nuclear weapons playing less of a role in crises than other evidence suggests.

This study tends toward the middle ground. Nuclear threats in practice were a tentative sort of blackmail, perhaps halfway between stark blackmail and shifty bluff. Threats were never as blatant as a direct ultimatum and were usually hesitant and elliptical. They were less often a bludgeon than a crutch, something presidents reached for when they lacked confi-

17. McGeorge Bundy, "The Unimpressive Record of Atomic Diplomacy," in Gwyn Prins, ed., *The Choice: Nuclear Weapons versus Security* (London: Chatto Windus, 1984), pp. 44–45; "Nixon Says He Considered Using Atomic Weapons on 4 Occasions," *New York Times,* July 22, 1985; "An Interview with Henry A. Kissinger: 'We Were Never Close to Nuclear War,'" *Washington Post,* August 11, 1985. After checking his memory with several other top officials Kissinger reported in the latter interview, "I can safely say that there was never a concrete occasion or crisis in which the use of nuclear weapons was considered by the government."

18. Michael Mandelbaum, "International Stability and Nuclear Order: The First Nuclear Regime," in David C. Gompert and others, *Nuclear Weapons and World Politics: Alternatives for the Future* (McGraw-Hill, 1977), p. 43.

dence in the adequacy of conventional military instruments to cope with enemy moves against disputed territory. In many cases the threats were not even the principal signal emphasized in the confrontation. They were sometimes attempts at influence on the cheap. Rhetoric or alerts of the Strategic Air Command might be dangerous, but they were less expensive and easier to turn on and off than large-scale mobilization and deployment of conventional ground forces would have been.

While nuclear threats were vague, however, they were seldom transparently meaningless and easy to dismiss. Ambivalence and oscillation especially characterized leaders' thinking in these incidents. Presidents and their principal lieutenants did not think or act like pure military game theorists. The latter often focus on two-party bargaining, while top leaders must take into account numerous audiences, including domestic constituencies and allies. Indeed, what is striking about much of the record discussed in the case studies that follow in chapters two and three is the extent to which initiatives often seemed to be taken after collegial discussion that did not carefully evaluate or even address what all the possible military consequences could be, especially if the objects of the threats refused to accede to basic demands. As Irving Janis has written, official groups often spend little time worrying about how chosen policies might fail, and neglect "to work out contingency plans to cope with foreseeable setbacks."[19]

In nuclear-tinged crises decisionmakers could rarely bring themselves to face fully either set of conflicting potential consequences: the loss of political stakes if military stakes were not raised, or the results if threats failed to achieve their political purpose and military escalation occurred. In a sense, the people at the top sometimes appeared to grit their teeth, close their eyes, and forge ahead. They tried to instill cautionary uncertainty about dire risks in the minds of their adversaries, while remaining under the same uncertainty themselves.

It would be a mistake to believe that the threats surveyed in this study were so murky or muted as to be trivial. Any sort of nuclear threat in the midst of crisis, which is by definition an unstable situation, ought to be considered serious business. However indirect or tentative it may be, such a threat must be intended to raise by some degree the danger that disastrous escalation might result, and any degree is worrisome at that level of stakes. If it is not meant to raise the danger the threat has no purpose. There is also a common argument that nuclear signals were much more vague than

19. Irving L. Janis, *Victims of Groupthink: A Psychological Study of Foreign-Policy Decisions and Fiascoes* (Houghton Mifflin, 1972), p. 10.

conventional military pressure. In terms of relative significance for coercion, however, conventional threats that are ten times clearer than nuclear ones are not more impressive if conventional war is only one-tenth as bad as nuclear war.

The cases considered here could appear trivial only in hindsight. Because the crises were resolved satisfactorily, at least for the United States, the issue never arose of whether to follow through on the threats or back away ignominiously. Luckily, those instances in postwar U.S. policy of disastrous consequences from decisionmakers' avoidance of planning for the possibility of failure—for example, the Bay of Pigs and the Vietnam War after 1965—did not involve either nuclear threats or immediate confrontation with a nuclear power. Moreover, despite U.S. acceptance of reversals, retreats in those cases did not involve admissions that earlier U.S. commitments to action were bluffs.[20] In short, nuclear threats have not been discredited as bluffs, nor the cause of disaster, because they have not been called to a final test. Is that because U.S. leaders were lucky, or because the threats were too potent for the opponent to risk pressing a challenge?

Doctrine, Behavior, and Rationales

The bulk of U.S. strategic analysis and debate has focused on two functions of nuclear threats: to prevent an enemy nuclear attack, through the promise of devastating retaliation in a second strike (known as "basic," "passive," or "Type I" deterrence), and to prevent an attack by Soviet conventional forces against Western Europe, through the threat of retaliation by first use of nuclear weapons if NATO's conventional defense falters (known as "extended," "active," or "Type II" deterrence).[21] Basic deterrence has enjoyed the widest endorsement and the most analytical attention. The fundamental criticism of extended deterrence has been that development of Soviet retaliatory capability made it suicidal; once basic deterrence becomes mutual, it negates extended deterrence by definition, since the latter requires the willingness to initiate nuclear attack. Arguments to the contrary fall back on the notion that uncertainty about the rationality

20. Washington had not openly backed the Cuban exile operation, much less indicated to Moscow that it would provide whatever support would be necessary for success. Withdrawal from Vietnam occurred long after conventional escalation had already proceeded quite far, and it happened under the guise of success, several years before Saigon collapsed in 1975.

21. See Herman Kahn, *On Thermonuclear War* (Princeton University Press, 1960), pp. 126–282; Robert Endicott Osgood, *NATO: The Entangling Alliance* (University of Chicago Press, 1962), pp. 60–61, 132–34.

of the victim will suffice to deter conventional aggression directed against an interest that is vital to him.

Although policy debate for the past two decades has usually been concerned with second-strike requirements for basic deterrence, the most fundamental and vexing dilemmas in U.S. nuclear doctrine have been those posed by extended deterrence commitments to first use. And these dilemmas have been accentuated because U.S. policy has depended more than its adversaries' has on an active role for nuclear weapons. U.S. objectives were defensive, but often supported by offensive nuclear strategy meant to compensate for perceived deficiencies in conventional military power. Soviet objectives may have been aggressive, but they were usually backed by passive nuclear deterrence. In short, semantic connotations aside, Washington had a more frequent interest in nuclear blackmail than Moscow did. These points have often been confused—especially in the second half of the postwar era—as chapter five will elaborate.

While both basic and extended deterrence have been the focus of attention for strategic doctrine, they have never been tested. The cases of threats that *were* ever tested, even in a preliminary sense, fall into a broad third category related to the standard notion of extended deterrence but distinct from it: hints of nuclear first use over other issues less vital than Western Europe.[22] Official doctrine has never specified where or when nuclear first use would be mandated outside of a war in Europe; the issue would be even more controversial than the standard conception of extended deterrence. If deliberate escalation on behalf of the obviously vital interest of all of Western Europe is dubious, it would be all the more so for stakes of less importance. Yet it was only in the more marginal areas that the issue arose.

In any case, whatever nuclear leverage might apply in crises flows from the prospect that if the enemy starts conventional war, the United States will counter by starting nuclear war. But could it ever really make sense to start using nuclear weapons? If not, can the threat be credible? If not credible, can it influence the target? There are two general sets of attitudes on these cosmic questions. One tends toward *maximizing* and accepting mutual military risks to reduce political risks, the other tends toward

22. The three Berlin crises studied here are closely related to the second category but not strictly within it. Although obviously linked to the security of NATO, they involved Soviet threats against the city only, not against Western Europe as a whole. West Berlin was not even officially covered by the alliance, but by the occupying powers—the United States, Britain, and France.

minimizing one's own military risks and shifting them onto the enemy.[23] As suggested in the epigraphs from Schelling and Nitze at the beginning of the chapter, the respective metaphors for these attitudes toward nuclear maneuvering are Russian roulette and chess.

The risk-maximizing approach relies on the enemy's fear that events could get out of control and that mutual destruction could result from recklessness rather than premeditation. Credibility flows from what Schelling calls the "threat that leaves something to chance," or the enemy's fear that further pressure on his part could provoke a viscerally violent response rather than a rationally restrained one.[24] The side making nuclear threats can thus manipulate risks to advantage even if following through on the threats would prove suicidal. The wisdom of the tactic is presumed to rest on the implausibility that the target would dare take a chance on testing it, and does not depend on the wisdom of making the threat good. Thus leaders may consciously bluff in resorting to nuclear threats, or they may use the tactic without really pondering whether they would follow through. This incautious approach implicitly assumes that the enemy is not highly motivated to risk war and that an uncertain probability of disaster will suffice to dissuade him from pushing his luck in the gamble of confrontation.

The more cautious risk-minimizing alternative implicitly assumes that the enemy has a strong incentive to use force to achieve his objectives, and thus a substantial willingness to gamble on his opposition's prudence and nuclear restraint. The chess-like approach insists on thinking through the full sequence of political and military moves, and identifies the credibility of a policy with its rationality. It assumes that bluffs are dangerous, that deeds should back up words, and that a threat's efficacy flows from the plausibility of following through at acceptable cost.[25] For the action to be plausible, means should be proportional to ends, and costs to benefits. In short, leaders should not belly up to the brink of war unless they are prepared to go over it. Without protection against nuclear retaliation,

---

23. Henceforth, where not specified, "risk" refers to the military variety—the degree of uncertainty about whether disastrous damage can be avoided if the conflict intensifies.

24. Thomas C. Schelling presents many variations on these themes. See his *The Strategy of Conflict* (Oxford University Press, 1960), chaps. 2 and 8, and *Arms and Influence*, chaps. 1–3. Some "deterrent threats are a matter of resolve, impetuosity, plain obstinacy, or . . . sheer character." For brinkmanship, "there has to be some uncertainty or anticipated irrationality or it won't work." *Arms and Influence,* pp. 42, 99.

25. Paul H. Nitze, "Atoms, Strategy and Policy," *Foreign Affairs,* vol. 34 (January 1956), pp. 187–88.

though, these conditions are hard to meet. The price of the cautious approach thus is likely to be either a higher political risk (greater probability of concessions in order to arrest a slide toward war) or an ambitious military capability to make the disaster of war not mutual, but disproportionately greater by far for the enemy. The latter alternative places a higher premium on nuclear superiority.

In practice, American leaders straddled the lines between the two theoretical approaches, maneuvering at middling levels of military and political risk. As political animals they were willing to gamble rather than invite defeat, but they hedged their bets. They made their nuclear threats vague enough that they avoided being boxed into a stark choice between going ahead with escalation or being exposed as bluffers. Eisenhower and Nixon tended more toward the risk-maximizing model; Truman, Kennedy, and Carter, more in the other direction, but in all instances the politicians exhibited more flexibility and less coherence in practice than theorists do in principle. Presidents were unwilling to recognize nuclear combat as so unthinkable that they could not exploit its potential to secure international objectives, and they lacked absolute confidence that the adversaries would settle on the terms demanded.

Working both sides of the street, presidents were neither risk maximizers or minimizers as much as risk moderators, but on balance, their strategy resembled Russian roulette more often than it did chess. Since presidents never claimed that the United States could use nuclear weapons with impunity, it appears that they relied most on the incautious manipulation of risk à la Schelling and on the demonstration of political resolve rather than military capability.

Like chess, though, this is a game that two can play; hotheads or good actors are not always on one side. In a competition in risk taking, why should Americans do better at Russian roulette than Russians?[26] Indeed, in the period in which the bulk of cases occurred, Khrushchev was often seen by American leaders as recklessly adventurous, and he mentioned the danger of nuclear war over Berlin as often as U.S. presidents did. Yet the Americans were not daunted by Khrushchev's posturing, and in the end they compromised their initial objectives less than the Russians did. In a contest of resolve, a figurative game of chicken, what makes either side's will more credible than the other's? Leaders should have some substantive reason for believing that their opponent would blink first. What underlying

26. Schelling himself suggested that Americans could not manipulate risk as credibly as fanatics or totalitarians. *Arms and Influence*, pp. 42–43.

or inherent aspects of the confrontations offered grounds for presidents to think that they should have the edge?

Corresponding to the general attitudes about maximizing or minimizing risks are two sets of ideas about circumstances that could justify American first-use threats. Many risk maximizers assume that the credibility of resolve depends on the relative interests that the contenders have at stake in the dispute; risk minimizers assume that it depends on their relative military power.[27] Because the military balance has become markedly less favorable to the West than it was in the first decades of the cold war, the second explanation suggests that a nuclear threat is no longer a tactic that is safe to use, if it ever was. The first explanation, by contrast, offers grounds for relying on nuclear threats in the future, since the balance of interests between the contenders could be similar to what it was in crises of the past.

The "balance of interests" argument assumes that once both sides have the nuclear capability to inflict severe damage on each other, the balance of power—the ratio of military, especially nuclear, forces—ceases to govern a competition in risk taking.[28] If both sides have an unbearable amount to lose from going to war, then as they edge toward the brink the two sides' respective resolve to fight rather than concede flows from how much they have to lose if they back down. The aggressor in a dispute necessarily has a weaker stake in the outcome than the defender, since nations are willing to suffer more to protect what they already have than to gain something new.[29] Since the Soviets and Chinese were the presumed aggressors in the

27. Some theorists *contrast* the balance of resolve and balance of power as explanations of outcomes, but this is a confusion. As long as the crisis does not end in war, the issue is which side's resolve most impresses the other and compels accommodation before combat. The *source* of real or apparent resolve—political interests or military power—is a separate issue.

28. "Balance of power" is used in this colloquial sense rather than the academic or classical sense of the equilibrating mechanism of alliance formation in a multipolar state system. See Inis L. Claude, Jr., *Power and International Relations* (Random House, 1962).

29. Robert Jervis, "Why Nuclear Superiority Doesn't Matter," *Political Science Quarterly,* vol. 94 (Winter 1979–80), p. 628; Jervis, *The Illogic of American Nuclear Strategy* (Cornell University Press, 1984), pp. 134, 153–54; Robert E. Osgood and Robert W. Tucker, *Force, Order, and Justice* (Johns Hopkins University Press, 1967), pp. 148–49; Glenn H. Snyder and Paul Diesing, *Conflict Among Nations: Bargaining, Decision Making, and System Structure in International Crises* (Princeton University Press, 1977), pp. 456–58; Kenneth N. Waltz, "The Spread of Nuclear Weapons: More May Be Better," *Adelphi Paper* 171 (London: International Institute for Strategic Studies, Autumn 1981), p. 1; Richard Ned Lebow, "The Cuban Missile Crisis: Reading the Lessons Correctly," *Political Science Quarterly,* vol. 98 (Fall 1983), p. 448.

cases at issue, therefore, the willingness of the United States to bear the risks of war was automatically greater. Under this logic, implicitly, the issue of whether it would make sense to follow through with the threat of escalation need not arise; the balance of interests makes clear the balance of resolve, which guarantees that defensive threats will work, deterrence will hold, and the aggressor will back off first.

The "balance of power" argument assumes that if a nation will lose far more from nuclear war than it can gain or preserve, it will obviously not choose to start one, whatever else is at stake in a confrontation. Losing control of territory abroad to the enemy's conventional military initiative is less intolerable than losing the populations of cities at home to his nuclear retaliation. If basic nuclear deterrence is mutual, the only military leverage in a crisis will be conventional. So if the side that considers its conventional power to be inferior is to resist rather than retreat, exerting effective leverage requires overcoming the mutuality of deterrence and devising a way to fight a nuclear war at tolerable cost. In the age of nuclear parity, Soviet retaliatory capability makes that impossible, so most in this school now prefer to avoid reliance on first-use threats and to compensate with more powerful conventional counters to enemy moves. Many believe that overwhelming American nuclear superiority in the first two decades of the postwar era offered the possibility of destroying the Soviet Union or China while keeping damage to the United States within limits commensurate with the stakes at issue. Risks that are intolerable now were manageable then, in this view, and the loss of nuclear superiority has diminished U.S. political leverage.

The fundamental division between these two schools of thought is the attention they devote to the two sides of the nuclear brink. Each focuses on a different side: the political contest or the military one, the resolve of the contenders before war or the consequences to them during war, the diplomatic game of chicken or the nuclear crash. Devotees of the risk-maximizing approach may draw on the Napoleonic axiom that in war "the moral is to the material as three to one" to fortify their confidence that the balance of interests will make the aggressor less willing to play at Russian roulette. The risk minimizers, who see the contest as a chess game in which the prospective outcome of later military moves influences judgments in earlier maneuvers toward the brink, would take a different lesson. They would cite Clausewitz's argument that one side may surrender without a fight because of the prospect of defeat if it does fight, and that therefore if settlement results because a real combat engagement is possible, the possibility has acquired reality. . . . the overthrow of the enemy's power can be accomplished only as the result of an engagement, no matter whether it really took place or was merely offered but not accepted. . . . We are constantly brought back to the question: what, at any given stage of the war or campaign, will be the likely outcome of all the major and minor engagements that the two sides can offer one another?[30]

Analytical Issues

Nuclear blackmail presents daunting analytical challenges. The ambiguity of evidence about its use combines with the controversial nature of assumptions about how it should be evaluated to make conclusions difficult.

Cases

The following chapters consider East-West crises in which some sort of specifically nuclear threat was made by one or both sides. That principle of selection excludes a few incidents that others have considered nuclear blackmail—for example, President Nixon's dispatch of the aircraft carrier *Enterprise* to the Bay of Bengal during the Indo-Pakistani War of 1971. Not only is it doubtful, despite the reaction in India, that the dispatch of the carrier was intended as a nuclear rather than conventional signal, the act was not aimed at either of the principal adversaries, the Soviet Union or China, with whom confrontations have raised the possibility of major war.[31]

As already noted, this study is concerned with nuclear maneuvers at the margins of the basic conflict. By margins are meant those gray areas that were neither clear, central interests of one side that it would be expected to defend to the death, nor ones so obviously peripheral that no one would expect military engagement over them. Four types of crises involving the

30. Carl von Clausewitz, *On War*, Michael Howard and Peter Paret, eds. and trans. (Princeton University Press, 1976), pp. 181–82.

31. Other types of incidents are included in a related study that took a different approach. See Barry M. Blechman, Stephen S. Kaplan, and others, *Force without War: U.S. Armed Forces as a Political Instrument* (Brookings, 1978), pp. 47–48, 64–65, 98–101, 128–29.

United States and the communist powers have *not* involved nuclear threats. These include cases in which:

—the precipitating challenge was not direct military action (for example, the communist coup d'état in Czechoslovakia, 1948, or coups backed by the United States in Iran, 1953, and Guatemala, 1954);

—the direct military challenge was not by the Soviet Union or China, but by smaller adversaries supplied by them (Vietnam in the 1960s);

—sudden attacks or faits accomplis left surprised leaders without time to confer and decide on signaling before being overtaken by events (Korea, 1950; Afghanistan, 1979; Grenada, 1983);

—the attack or threat causing the crisis was against rebels in a country allied with the attacker, or at least not aligned with the opposing superpower, and lying within the intervening nation's core sphere of influence (East Germany, 1953; Hungary, 1956; Czechoslovakia, 1968; Dominican Republic, 1965).

The cases in which the United States used nuclear threats involved the convergence of two circumstances. When Soviet or Chinese military action against an American ally was considered possible and when countering such action with U.S. conventional forces alone was considered infeasible or undesirable, Washington always attempted some sort of nuclear leverage. It almost never did so when either condition was missing. The tactic was considered neither so desperate that it was reserved for contingencies of supreme importance, nor so cheap that it was used profligately in any and all East-West disputes. The Soviet Union was somewhat more reserved in its resort to nuclear saber rattling.

The cases addressed in the next two chapters are a motley assortment. They could be grouped analytically in a number of conceivable ways: chronologically; geographically; by the object of the threat; by the importance of the crisis, in terms of stakes at issue; by the severity of the crisis, in terms of how close it came to war; or by the importance of the nuclear threat in resolving the crisis. Some of those standards, however, are not relevant to the focus of this study, and some that are relevant cannot be applied well because of insufficient evidence.

Since one of the principal aims of the book is to assess the relationship of the nuclear balance of power to the use of threats, the cases are grouped loosely according to the degree of nuclear risk facing the country making the threat—that is, how much vulnerability to nuclear retaliation it faced if its first-use threat had to be executed. With one exception, the Soviet-Chinese border clashes in 1969, this criterion also overlaps with chronological order. Cases in chapter two are ones in which the side facing the threats had little if any capability to retaliate in kind. Those in chapter three are ones in which the target could contest the threat with its own nuclear deterrent.

Decisions, Effects, and Evidence

There are two fundamental sets of questions about nuclear blackmail: how and why did leaders decide to try it, and how did the threats affect the outcomes of the crises? The second may be the more important, since it bears most on whether such tactics *should* be used again: the consequences of actions are the best basis for judging whether they were wise or useful. In most cases, however, the effect of the threat on the outcomes is more obscure than the decisionmaking process. Understanding the latter may be more important for estimating whether nuclear threats *will* occur again. The incentives that drove past leaders to make such decisions may have more to do with whether future leaders do so than does the record of how the decisions turned out.

The greatest barrier to judging the efficacy of threats is that there is no reliable evidence about what leaders in Moscow or Beijing were thinking during the crises. Thus there is no way to be sure what their initial objectives were or how high a premium they placed on them, and therefore no way to be sure how much they really conceded in the outcomes of the confrontations. Nor is it possible to be sure why they conceded whatever they did, since many elements besides hints of nuclear blackmail were in play. It would be desirable to know whether U.S. nuclear leverage was determinative (forcing a change in Soviet or Chinese actions), marginally influential (combining with other factors to tilt a decision), superfluous (because the target did not really intend to do whatever the threat was meant to prevent), or counterproductive (prolonging or complicating the crisis). The only evidence available, however, is circumstantial. Finally, to the extent that threats were influential, it is uncertain whether the state of the nuclear balance of power made them so. With these caveats in mind, speculation about the effectiveness of threats in the separate case studies is still in order and is summarized briefly in chapter six.

The emphasis in the book is on decisions, usually by the United States, to attempt nuclear coercion. There is substantial data about how leaders on the American side deliberated during crises and how the nuclear balance figured in their decisions, but the evidence is tricky. Open documentary sources are incomplete and, furthermore, cannot reveal the private thoughts of top leaders.[32] Memoirs tend to recall more clarity and consistency in officials' minds than other evidence suggests existed at the time. The delicacy of the questions at issue and the lapse of time in most of the cases arouse more than the usual skepticism about how public statements or recollections may distort the truth. And there is what Stanley Hoffmann has called a "Rashomon effect" evident in how different people remember the same events.[33] For example, McGeorge Bundy recalls Averell Harriman's meeting with Nikita Khrushchev in 1959 in a manner that leads Bundy to conclude that "we can laugh off blackmail." He recalls that when the Soviet premier threatened action against Berlin, "Harriman laughed, and Khrushchev said to him, 'What are you laughing about?' 'Well, Mr. Chairman . . . that would mean nuclear war and you don't want that.' Khrushchev looked at him for a moment and said, 'You're right.'"[34] Bundy's description contrasts markedly with what is often cited from Harriman's account of the meeting—Khrushchev's statement "If you want war, you can have it. . . . Our rockets will fly automatically."[35] There is also much that indicates that some important aspects of the questions at issue were never quite cogently faced by the decisionmakers themselves. Although theorists and bureaucrats have speculated ad nauseam about nuclear strategy and the situations in which nuclear weapons could or should come into play, top political leaders have rarely dwelt on these questions at any length or in any detail, or seriously pondered in advance what to do in a crisis.[36] Nor have the circumstances of particular crises been congruent with theorists' scenarios.

Especially under the awesome pressures of a potentially nuclear confrontation, there is a natural tendency toward ambivalence and inconsis-

32. Much secret material from the Eisenhower administration is now open, but many items related to military contingency planning and nuclear weapons are exempt from declassification. At this writing some of the most pertinent materials for the Kennedy administration, especially records on the 1961 Berlin crisis, have not even been processed for filing in the John F. Kennedy Presidential Library, let alone reviewed for declassification. Hardly any secret documents for cases in the Nixon and Carter administrations have been declassified, or are likely to be for many years.

33. Stanley Hoffmann, *Gulliver's Troubles, Or the Setting of American Foreign Policy* (McGraw-Hill, 1968), p. 109. Hoffmann applied the term to nations rather than individuals.

34. McGeorge Bundy, "Risk and Opportunity: Can We Tell Them Apart," in Catherine McArdle Kelleher, Frank J. Kerr, and George H. Quester, eds., *Nuclear Deterrence: New Risks, New Opportunities* (Washington, D.C.: Pergamon-Brassey's, 1986), p. 34.

35. Quoted in Averell Harriman, "My Alarming Interview with Khrushchev," *Life* (July 8, 1959), p. 33.

36. The one president who did delve intently into operational plans and nuclear targeting options was Jimmy Carter.

tency in decisionmaking, as leaders face the tension between the twin aims of avoiding political losses and avoiding war. The first aim leads contestants to demonstrate their resolve and indicate a willingness to fight, while the second restrains them from burning bridges and encourages flexibility or ambiguity in the threats they convey. For all these reasons evidence about leaders' attitudes in the course of crisis decisionmaking is often contradictory, perhaps because officials evince shifting inclinations as their focus alternates between the two conflicting aims. Therefore, selective exploitation of available evidence can support markedly different interpretations, while a thorough and balanced presentation may appear inconclusive.

Approach

The record of what is known about nuclear signals in past crises is compiled in chapters two and three, and the cases are assessed individually. The more important case studies are the first three in chapter three: the two Berlin crises of 1958–61 and the Cuban crisis of 1962. These three involved direct confrontations between two nuclear powers over matters of central interest with no easy way for both sides to save face equally. The earlier and more numerous cases of U.S. threats against China reflect the frequency with which the Eisenhower administration used the tactic, but they do not highlight as much the dilemmas implicit in threatening a nuclear-armed adversary. Even in those cases, though, concern that the Soviet Union could intervene on behalf of the Chinese was never absent. The two examples of U.S. threats after the 1960s, though less serious or significant in many ways than the others, demonstrate that nuclear superiority is not a prerequisite for decisions to apply nuclear leverage.

Chapter four is the analytical heart of the book. It presents a comparative analysis of the two principal rationales that have been offered for U.S. attempts at nuclear coercion. Both the balance of interests and balance of power theories prove useful for explaining either the threat or the response, but neither appears adequate to account for both sides' behavior at the same time. The implication—with the balance of nuclear power offering a less plausible explanation for decisions to threaten than it does for reactions to threats—is that future attempts at nuclear leverage are not necessarily ordained to produce the same results as in the past.

Together, chapters two through four suggest that U.S. nuclear superiority in the first two decades after World War II was neither all-important nor unimportant and that leaders were ambivalent about how much they could rely on it. That superiority was lost in the decades after the Cuban missile crisis, but the significance of the change has remained uncertain because no crises comparable to the worst ones of the cold war have arisen to test it. The potential impact of parity on attempts at nuclear coercion has been obscured by several overlapping conceptual confusions and political evasions—about the definitions of superiority and parity, the standards for how they should be measured, how to make extended deterrence compatible with parity, and the cause and effect relationships between political détente and military equality. Chapter five surveys the ways in which these confusions were manifested during the period of transition into parity and explores the underlying implications for nuclear leverage. In this light, continuities between the earlier decades of the postwar era and those to come will appear as important as the apparent changes wrought by parity.

As chapter five represents the analytical bridge between the past and future, chapter six examines the lay of the land at both ends of the bridge. It summarizes the lessons of the past cases and explores the conditions that will determine whether and how nuclear blackmail could enter the contest between Washington and Moscow again. While the first part of the book shows that nuclear threats were less certain and more complex than the simple term blackmail connotes, the conclusion clarifies propositions about the future that could be inferred from a look at how the various uncertainties interact.

CHAPTER TWO

Lower-Risk Cases

The Soviets are beginning to realize for the first time that the United States would really use the atomic bomb against them in the event of war.
George C. Marshall, statement in interagency conference, October 10, 1948

Those who harbor plans for an atomic attack on the Chinese ... should not forget that the other side too has atomic and hydrogen weapons and the appropriate means to deliver them, and if the Chinese People's Republic falls victim to such an attack, the aggressor will at once get a rebuff by the same means.
Nikita Khrushchev, letter to President Eisenhower, September 19, 1958

NUCLEAR THREATS early in the postwar era were distinctive in two respects. First, hardly any were aimed directly at a nuclear opponent, and most involved regions that were of secondary importance in the global super-power contest. Most U.S. threats were against China. These threats, however, did raise the question of Soviet extended deterrence. But the only U.S. threat that involved both the Russians and the central zone of interest, Europe, occurred before the Soviet Union became a nuclear power. Second, both U.S. and Soviet threats were made by nations confident of nuclear superiority. Although there was disagreement in the United States about whether that superiority was significant enough to accomplish all the aims laid upon it, there was no meaningful dispute within government that the United States did have an overwhelming edge. Thus, as dangerous as the early nuclear threats may have been, they were easier to contemplate than were the cases to be discussed in chapter three.

The Soviet threats against Britain and France in the Suez crisis and against China in 1969 cannot be evaluated in the same way as U.S. threats because there is virtually no reliable information available on the decisions within the Kremlin. Overall, it is easier to evaluate Western decisions on U.S. threats, and Western reactions to Soviet threats. Both cases of Soviet nuclear blackmail are considered in the lower-risk category because they were directed against much weaker powers, rather than the United States.

22

The Berlin Blockade, 1948

The first possibility for the cold war to turn hot arose in 1948. In February the communists seized power in Czechoslovakia. At the end of March Soviet military authorities announced restrictions on passage of U.S. personnel through the Soviet zone of occupation in Germany. On the weekend of June 18–19, in response to currency reform in the western zones of Germany, Soviet occupation authorities closed roads to Berlin.[1] By June 24 the Soviets had closed railroad lines to the city, cut electric power flowing from East to West Berlin, and stopped food deliveries from the Soviet sector to the western enclave. Eleven months later the blockade was lifted. The dominant Western initiative in the resolution of the crisis was the successful airlift of supplies that averted the collapse of West Berlin. Indications of American preparation to go to war if necessary were a muted element in the crisis, but not absent.

How could the United States credibly prepare for war in a way that could impress the Russians? The consensus among the Western allies was that their conventional forces in Germany were far too weak to cope with a Soviet attack westward. The assumption was more certain than it should have been, given intelligence available on Soviet demobilization and the organization of their forces in Germany.[2] Even at the time some questioned the pervasive pessimism—especially General Lucius Clay, who was in charge of the American occupation. Clay, perhaps thinking of what might be accomplished with some months of American, British, and French mobilization, argued that "twenty good divisions could hold up the Russians at the Rhine"; at the time, however, twenty good divisions did not exist in Europe, and the United States had only one additional for reinforcement.[3]

Clay's optimism did not have much effect on the general anxiety, but

1. The currency reform capped a series of developments toward unification of the western occupation zones of Germany, making it more likely that they would remain independent of Soviet control. See Wilfrid Knapp, *A History of War and Peace, 1939–1965* (Oxford University Press, 1967), pp. 128–31.

2. Matthew A. Evangelista, "Stalin's Postwar Army Reappraised," *International Security*, vol. 7 (Winter 1982–83), pp. 110–38. Soon thereafter—especially after 1950—the Soviets beefed up their military posture substantially.

3. Walter Millis, ed., with collaboration of E. S. Duffield, *The Forrestal Diaries* (Viking Press, 1951), p. 460; W. Phillips Davison, *The Berlin Blockade: A Study in Cold War Politics* (Princeton University Press, 1958), p. 156.

whether or not the pessimistic consensus about the odds of stopping a Soviet attack short of the English Channel was excessive, the problem of conventional options for combat to secure West Berlin itself was hopelessly daunting. Western forces would have to forfeit the operational advantages of the defense and attack eastward to relieve the city isolated behind Soviet lines. Except for discussion of sending an armed convoy to probe down the autobahn—on the argument that the Soviets would not resist—strictly conventional war was never seriously considered to be an option. The U.S. atomic bomb was the one ace in what was assumed to be a weak military hand. The ace, however, was played rather gingerly.

Hesitant Signal

Despite the preceding events that produced the war scare of early 1948, U.S. national security authorities appear to have given astonishingly little attention to the issue of the atomic bomb's role in conflict with the USSR. During the early days of the blockade, on June 30, a high-level Defense Department meeting considered a report that a barrage balloon had been placed near British flight paths into Berlin and that the British were considering shooting it down. The report prompted an ill-informed discussion of what to do in the event of war. President Truman's top military assistant, Admiral William Leahy, favored using the A-bomb but revealed that no clear contingency plans existed. About available nuclear resources he noted that the United States did not have "very much but still we could make plans to use what we have . . . I don't know what we could do but whatever we have we could use."[4] General Hoyt Vandenberg, air force chief of staff, said that he thought his service was studying potential targets, but that he wasn't sure. Other top officials at the meeting argued about whether "a reduction of Moscow and Leningrad would be a powerful enough impact to stop a war" or whether political targets should be spared from atomic attack. The rest of the discussion "meandered."[5] Moves were already under way, nevertheless, to send a military signal to the Russians.

Four days after initial Soviet restriction of access to Berlin, and the day before the blockade was completed, Secretary of Defense James Forrestal had recommended sending American bombers to Britain (weeks earlier he

4. Samuel R. Williamson, Jr., with the collaboration of Steven L. Rearden, *The View From Above: High-Level Decisions and the Soviet-American Strategic Arms Competition, 1945–1950* (Office of the Secretary of Defense, October 1975), sanitized version, p. 104; Leahy quoted on p. 105.
5. Ibid., pp. 105–06.

had proposed sending bombers to Greece, during the civil war, for training). One B-29 squadron was already in Germany for rotational training. The Strategic Air Command (SAC) moved two additional squadrons to Labrador, to be ready to move to Europe, and put two other B-29 groups on twenty-four-hour alert.[6] Lieutenant General Curtis LeMay, commanding the U.S. Air Force in Europe, wanted two B-29 squadrons in England for operational purposes, but Clay wanted them to come to Germany first "for our immediate psychological purposes."[7]

On June 28 President Truman approved the dispatch of the planes from North America to Germany. Although British Foreign Minister Ernest Bevin immediately agreed to have two B-29 groups proceed to Britain, the U.S. decision to move them was not made for more than two weeks, in part out of concern that the British public might consider the action provocative. The fear seems unfounded. In contrast to later episodes, when they felt more vulnerable to Soviet retaliation, the British did not seem notably more skittish than Washington about nuclear threats. In anticipation of the danger to come once Moscow got its own A-bomb, Churchill even recommended an ultimatum to the Soviets to withdraw behind the Polish border or have their cities razed. On July 15 it was announced that sixty B-29s would leave for Britain. Although it was officially described as a training mission, there were leaks that the planes were atomic-capable and even hints that they carried such bombs. Neither point was true, but on the same day Forrestal approached Truman about transferring custody of atomic weapons from the Atomic Energy Commission (AEC) to the military. And by the end of the month three complete B-29 groups were in Europe.[8]

6. Gregg Herken, *The Winning Weapon: The Atomic Bomb in the Cold War, 1945–1950* (Alfred A. Knopf, 1980), pp. 257–58; J. C. Hopkins, *The Development of the Strategic Air Command, 1946–1981 (A Chronological History)* (Office of the Historian, Headquarters, Strategic Air Command, 1982), p. 13.

7. Clay cable to General Omar N. Bradley, June 19, 1948, quoted in Jean Edward Smith, ed., *The Papers of General Lucius D. Clay: Germany, 1945–1949* (Indiana University Press, 1974), vol. 2, p. 709.

8. Avi Shlaim, *The United States and the Berlin Blockade, 1948–1949: A Study in Crisis Decision-Making* (University of California Press, 1983), p. 237; Herken, *Winning Weapon*, p. 259; Millis, ed., *Forrestal Diaries*, pp. 455–58; Hopkins, *Development of Strategic Air Command*, p. 13. Churchill was out of office when he made the ultimatum recommendations to the American ambassador (before the crisis) and to Prime Minister Clement Attlee (during the blockade). "The Ambassador in the United Kingdom (Douglas) to the Under Secretary of State (Lovett)," April 17, 1948, in U.S. Department of State, *Foreign Relations of the United States, 1948* [series cited hereafter as *FRUS*], vol. 2:

The B-29 was well known as the craft that bombed Hiroshima and Nagasaki. To whatever extent the transfer was meant as tacit nuclear pressure, it was well hedged. Preparations were made for another alert in September, but the National Security Council (NSC) forbade large-scale flights over Germany or the Mediterranean and rejected use of B-29s to haul cargo in the airlift lest the Soviets misread the significance.[9] The threat was uncertain because the president wanted it to be and because it had to be.

Big Bluff?

By Forrestal's account, Western elites with whom he talked in the following two months were unanimous that the atomic bomb should be used in the event of war.[10] The one person uncertain about that prospect was the one most responsible: the president. On one hand, Truman's commitment to staying in Berlin was absolute. When Under Secretary of State Robert Lovett raised the question at the June 28 meeting Truman cut him off, saying there would be no discussion. On the other hand, the president refused to stipulate in advance what military means would be used to that end. When Secretary of the Army Kenneth Royall insistently played the strategist and questioned whether the military implications of the commitment had been sufficiently considered, Truman insistently played the politician and shot back that "we would have to deal with the situation as it developed."[11] And on June 30, Admiral Leahy told top Defense Department officials that the president "wanted to stay in Berlin as long as possible, but not to the point of shooting down a barrage balloon and starting a war for which the U.S. did not have enough soldiers."[12]

In April, before the Soviet squeeze on Berlin, the NSC had deferred the troublesome question of use of nuclear weapons in the event of war.[13] Shortly before the blockade the president had been briefed by the Joint Chiefs of Staff (JCS) on emergency war plans, which involved a nuclear counteroffensive against Soviet conventional attack. The president's re-

---

Germany and Austria (Government Printing Office, 1973), p. 895; British cabinet papers cited in "Churchill Urged Atomic Attack," *Washington Post,* January 3, 1979.

9. Steven L. Rearden, *History of the Office of the Secretary of Defense,* vol. 1: *The Formative Years, 1947–1950* (Historical Office, Office of the Secretary of Defense, 1984), p. 307; Herken, *Winning Weapon,* p. 260.

10. Millis, ed., *Forrestal Diaries,* pp. 487–89.

11. Ibid., pp. 454–55.

12. Williamson with Rearden, *View From Above,* p. 104.

13. *FRUS, 1948,* vol. 1: *General; The United Nations* (GPO, 1976), pt. 2, p. 624n.

sponse was to direct the chiefs to devise an alternate plan for strictly conventional operations, despite the nearly universal assumption that it was impossible, on grounds that the public might not stand for use of nuclear weapons, or that the weapons might be proscribed by international agreement.[14]

When Forrestal raised the custody issue on July 15 he said he was not asking for a decision on use of the bomb. The president nevertheless responded that he wanted to think carefully about the question and to ensure that there would be no delegation of his authority to make such a decision. In his bluntly colorful way Truman said he did not propose "to have some dashing lieutenant colonel decide when would be the proper time to drop one."[15] At a meeting about custody of the bomb on July 21 Royall and Secretary of the Air Force W. Stuart Symington pressed the issue, and Truman responded, "This is no time to be juggling an atom bomb around." As David Lilienthal of the AEC recounted it, Truman's words were spoken "with a sternness and solemnity that was in marked contrast to the eager-beaver attitude of some of our friends."[16] A week later, nevertheless, Forrestal told the JCS to plan on the basis that atomic bombs would be used if war broke out.[17]

On September 4 Marshal V.D. Sokolovskiy announced Soviet air maneuvers in corridors over Berlin that Western officials worried might be a threat to interfere with the airlift. According to Forrestal, at a meeting nine days later, when the question of use of the bomb was raised again, "the President said that he prayed that he would never have to make such a decision, but that if it became necessary, no one need have a misgiving but what he would do so." Thereafter Forrestal considered the question resolved, though the president did not seem to consider the decision irrevocable.[18] That same night, September 13, Truman wrote in his diary, "Forrestal, Bradley, Vandenberg . . . Symington brief me on bases, bombs, Moscow, Leningrad, etc. I have a terrible feeling afterward that we are

14. Rearden, *Formative Years*, p. 434. The Baruch plan for an International Atomic Development Authority had been tabled in the United Nations in 1946.

15. Millis, ed., *Forrestal Diaries*, p. 458.

16. David E. Lilienthal, *The Journals of David E. Lilienthal*, vol. 2: *The Atomic Energy Years 1945–1950* (Harper and Row, 1964), p. 391.

17. "Will We Use Atomic Bombs?" Notes and Excerpts from the Forrestal Diaries compiled by the NSC, p. 3, in Harry S. Truman Library, President's Secretary's File, Papers of George Elsey; declassified September 26, 1975 (Carrollton Press collection). These include portions of the diaries deleted from the published Millis edition.

18. Ibid., p. 29; cables from Murphy and Douglas to Secretary of State, September 4 and 5, 1948, in *FRUS, 1948*, vol. 2: *Germany and Austria*, pp. 1121, 1128.

very close to war. I hope not." But then Truman went on, "See Marshall at lunch and feel better although Berlin is a mess."[19]

Truman's vacillation was consistent with the ambiguity of the B-29 signal. Moreover, while U.S. conventional military power at the time was weak, so was nuclear capability. Not only did the bombers go to Europe without any nuclear ordnance; in mid-1948 only one air force unit, the 509th Bomb Group in New Mexico, and only thirty-two planes within the unit were rigged for nuclear delivery, and only twelve crews were completely trained for a nuclear combat mission. None of the B-29 reinforcements to Europe were from the 509th. The entire American atomic stockpile consisted of about fifty bombs, none assembled.[20]

These constraints aside, a SAC attack on the Soviet Union faced severe operational difficulties. Intelligence on interior targets consisted of little more than German photos of the western USSR. Problems with bombing technique such as nonvisual sighting for night attack would have to be solved. SAC would also face long flight times without fighter escort.[21] Indeed, planning called for *bomber* escort, with a high ratio of "empty" to nuclear-armed bombers, even to deliver fifty bombs.[22] Moreover, as David MacIsaac writes, General Vandenberg feared that the airlift of supplies to Berlin could be sustained *"only* by withdrawing from SAC virtually all the transport aircraft required to implement any of the pending war plans: these were the aircraft that would carry the unassembled atomic weapons and technical personnel to bases overseas. To assign them to the airlift would deny *any* atomic capability should the crisis in Berlin erupt into war."[23]

By the fall, the question of intent to use the bomb in the event of war was becoming clearer, as the NSC approved the concluding paragraphs of NSC 30.[24] By the end of the year, midway through the blockade, SAC's

19. Robert H. Ferrell, ed., *Off the Record: The Private Papers of Harry S. Truman* (Harper and Row, 1980), pp. 148–49.

20. David Alan Rosenberg, "U.S. Nuclear Stockpile, 1945 to 1950," *Bulletin of the Atomic Scientists,* vol. 38 (May 1982), pp. 28–29; Rosenberg, "The Origins of Overkill: Nuclear Weapons and American Strategy, 1945–1960," *International Security,* vol. 7 (Spring 1983), p. 14.

21. Harry R. Borowski, *A Hollow Threat: Strategic Air Power and Containment Before Korea* (Greenwood Press, 1982), pp. 103–06.

22. USAF Field Office for Atomic Energy, "Doctrine of Atomic Air Warfare," December 30, 1948; declassified 1978 (Carrollton Press collection).

23. David MacIsaac, "The Air Force and Strategic Thought, 1945–1951," International Security Studies Program Working Paper 8 (Washington, D.C.: Woodrow Wilson International Center for Scholars, June 1979), pp. 36–37 (emphasis added).

24. NSC 30, September 10, 1948, concluded: "In the event of hostilities, the National

capability had also begun to grow significantly. But even the improved emergency war plan for 1949 envisioned initial attacks against seventy cities that would produce fewer than 3 million Soviet fatalities and attacks against the Soviet hydroelectric and transportation systems that would not even begin until eight months after the start of the war. According to the Harmon Report, which assessed a prospective nuclear offensive, "The atomic offensive would not, per se, bring about capitulation."[25] In this context, was the dispatch of the B-29s a colossal nuclear bluff, a signal only of the aircraft's conventional capability, or something in between?[26] And did it matter?

One argument, made by Harry Borowski, among others, is that if Truman "had wanted to rattle his saber, he would have sent at least one squadron from the 509th"; that Soviet intelligence and deduction must have ensured that Moscow knew the groups in Europe did not have a nuclear mission; that in "deploying groups with conventional capability, Truman indicated hope for a diplomatic settlement"; and that continuation of the blockade for ten months after the bomber reinforcement implies that the move was not effective.[27] That argument is too pat and misses the point. There was certainly no intent to convey an *explicit* nuclear threat, but there hardly ever has been in any of the cases since, given the awesomeness of the idea and political leaders' universal penchant for keeping options open. It is also not realistic to assume that Truman necessarily knew or reflected about the difference in nuclear capability of separate B-29 units or that Stalin would confidently believe the difference either. Moscow was sensitive to the probability that any war could bring American nuclear strikes. Shortly before the crisis a note to the State Department from the Soviet embassy complained bitterly about a speech

---

Military Establishment must be ready to utilize promptly and effectively all appropriate means available, including atomic weapons . . . and must therefore plan accordingly." *FRUS, 1948,* vol. 1: *General; The United Nations,* pt. 2, pp. 625–28. The document did not, however, stipulate a decision firmly in advance.

25. JCS 1952/1, "Evaluation of Current Strategic Air Offensive Plans," December 21, 1948, and "Evaluation of Effect on Soviet War Effort Resulting from the Strategic Air Offensive" (the Harmon Report), May 11, 1949, in Thomas H. Etzold and John Lewis Gaddis, eds., *Containment: Documents on American Policy and Strategy, 1945–1950* (Columbia University Press, 1978), pp. 357–58, 362; Rosenberg, "U.S. Nuclear Stockpile," p. 29.

26. Given the apparent weakness of allied ground forces, the B-29s did represent a boost in conventional options. LeMay had specific war plans to send the B-29s through radar deadspots against Soviet airfields. General Curtis E. LeMay with Mackinlay Kantor, *Mission With LeMay: My Story* (Doubleday, 1965), pp. 411–12.

27. Borowski, *Hollow Threat,* pp. 126–28.

by SAC commander George Kenney concerning plans for atomic attack on the USSR.[28]

Nor is there any practical contradiction between sending a clear conventional military signal of resolve and leaving some ambiguity about whether a nuclear element was included. For diplomatic coercion in a delicate situation, ambiguity may be preferable to clarity. The view that apparent recklessness and irrevocable commitment are more effective is usually more comfortable to pure strategists than to presidents. Finally, the distinctions emphasized in arguments like Borowski's have nothing to do with the diplomatic purpose. No one in 1948 preferred war to a settlement, and no one assumed war was inevitable. Deterrence—of whatever stripe—is diplomacy.

It is fair to say, as Herken does, that with the arrival of the bombers in Europe, "only the shadow of deterrence had crossed the Atlantic."[29] But whether through arousing a specific fear or simply causing uncertainty, the aim of deterrence is to instill caution. In the dim light of crisis maneuvering, shadows can be as frightening and cautionary as the things that cast them.

The Shadow of Deterrence

Though the nuclear element in the SAC move to Europe remained ambiguous, the ambiguity was not dispelled by any Western admissions about limits of the B-29s' capabilities or mission. And although the planes did not panic Stalin into terminating the blockade, the Soviets did not raise the ante when the blockade failed to force the Western powers out of Berlin. When the airlift loosened the stranglehold on the city, the Soviets did not escalate by interdicting it as they had the ground links. If the B-29s did not force a change in Soviet policy, they were at least a symbolic statement of a limit to what Soviet actions could be taken without serious risk.[30]

Reinforcing the physical presence of the B-29s was the sharp increase in U.S. nuclear preparedness. Military contingency planning had progressed markedly by late September 1948. By December provisions had been made to enable swift transfer of atomic weapons from the AEC to the military, and more planes and crews were readied for nuclear delivery.

28. FRUS, 1948, vol. 4: Eastern Europe; The Soviet Union (GPO, 1974), pp. 886–88.

29. Herken, Winning Weapon, p. 262.

30. Shlaim, United States and the Berlin Blockade, p. 239; Davison, Berlin Blockade, p. 157.

Just before the turn of the year the White House also forbade publication of a *Saturday Evening Post* article by Rear Admiral William S. Parsons that downplayed the significance of atomic power, apparently to avoid compromising the impressiveness of nuclear deterrence.[31]

At an interagency meeting on October 10 Secretary of State George Marshall made the observation, quoted in one of the epigraphs to this chapter, that the Soviets had finally realized that the United States would use the atomic bomb against them.[32] Whether or not that was an accurate judgment of Soviet views, it reflected the development of American views. Yet it is ironic that of all the cases of nuclear threats to be discussed, the tacit signal in 1948 was among the most ambiguous and hesitant of all. The president's decision whether to use nuclear weapons against an opponent who had none seems more agonizing than that of successors who faced Soviet nuclear weapons.[33] Perhaps, since the first Berlin crisis was a novel departure in the cold war—at a time when NATO had not yet even been formed—the president's uncertainty is less surprising. At any rate, the nuclear threat of 1948 marks the crystallization of the policy of extended nuclear deterrence. It was just the shadow of deterrence at the time, but it foreshadowed clearer deterrence to come.

The Korean War, 1950–53

As the first war between the United States and communist nations in the containment era, the Korean conflict raised the question of use of

31. Williams with Rearden, *View From Above*, pp. 116, 118–19.

32. Quoted in Millis, ed., *Forrestal Diaries*, p. 502. He reiterated this point later, for example in conversation with the Norwegian foreign minister. "Memorandum of Conversation, by the Secretary of State," November 20, 1948, in *FRUS, 1948*, vol. 3: *Western Europe* (GPO, 1974), p. 281.

33. Americans have always assumed that the first Soviet nuclear detonation occurred in 1949, but there were no grounds for absolute certainly about this at the time. The "persistent but unconfirmed reports in the French press, in both 1947 and 1948, that the Russians had tested a bomb were discounted in the United States," despite the fact that the deputy foreign minister of the USSR, Andrei Vishinsky, said in 1948 that the United States had no monopoly on nuclear weapons. Americans discounted the possibility primarily because U.S. estimates did not *expect* such early results in the Soviet program. The U.S. monitoring assets to detect radioactive debris, however, were not deployed until 1949, some months before air samples over the Sea of Japan confirmed an explosion. John Prados, *The Soviet Estimate: U.S. Intelligence Analysis and Soviet Strategic Forces,* 2d ed. (Princeton University Press, 1986), pp. 18–20. Therefore, it should not have seemed beyond the realm of possibility that Moscow had developed a bomb in 1948. Since what matters for interpreting decisions is what people *believe,* however, this consideration does not seem relevant to assessing Truman's judgment.

nuclear weapons more forcefully than any of the smaller crises of the late 1940s could have. Between the Berlin blockade and the outbreak of the war the U.S. nuclear monopoly ended, but throughout the war Soviet capability to strike the United States evoked relatively little concern. The principal occasion when the United States considered nuclear use came at the end of the war, in the new Eisenhower administration. How the question figured in the initial phase, though, is also relevant, if only to show the surprising restraint in administration action after intervention by the People's Republic of China.

Crises and Conflict, 1950–52

On the evening of the first day of the war the use of atomic bombs was brought up at a high-level Blair House meeting. The president asked whether the United States could "knock out" Soviet bases in Asia, and Air Force Chief of Staff Hoyt Vandenberg replied, "It could be done if we used A-bombs." But the matter was not pursued.[34] As on Berlin, Truman did not try energetically to exploit U.S. nuclear capability. The Strategic Air Command was alerted on a standby basis twice early in the war when U.S. ground forces were on the verge of defeat—when they were squeezed into the Pusan perimeter with their backs against the sea and when Chinese intervention routed them as they approached the Yalu.[35] It is not clear that either alert was directed by political leaders, however, or that either was obtrusive enough to be noticed in Moscow or Beijing. The signal Truman did send was rhetorical and probably unintended.

On June 29, four days after North Korea invaded South Korea, a questioner at a news conference asked the president whether the United States might have to use the atomic bomb. Truman answered curtly, "No comment." A month later, asked the same question at a news conference, he replied simply, "No."[36] Since the United States was facing only North Korean forces at that point, his answer was hardly surprising. After the beginning of the United Nations forces' march north, however, China's potential role in support of the Pyongyang regime became an issue. The Chinese took measures to warn Washington against proceeding and

34. "Memorandum of Conversation, by the Ambassador at Large (Jessup)," June 25, 1950, in *FRUS, 1950*, vol. 7: *Korea* (GPO, 1976), p. 159.

35. This is reported by a former SAC commander (vice commander at the time): General Thomas S. Power, USAF (Ret.), with Albert A. Arnhym, *Design for Survival* (Coward-McCann, 1965), p. 232.

36. *Public Papers of the Presidents of the United States: Harry S. Truman, 1950* (GPO, 1965), pp. 503, 562.

pointedly indicated that they would not be deterred by the specter of the American bomb.

Chinese news media referred to possible Soviet deterrence of U.S. atomic strikes against China, but also disparaged atomic bombs as "paper tigers" and suggested that they could not be used effectively on the battlefield.[37] In late September, twelve days after the U.S. landing at Inchon, the acting chief of staff of China's People's Liberation Army, General Nieh Yen-jung, met with Indian ambassador K. M. Panikkar and told him that the PRC would intervene if American forces crossed the 38th parallel. "We know what we are in for," the general said. "The Americans can bomb us, they can destroy our industries, but they cannot defeat us on land." When Panikkar warned about the devastation of bombing, Nieh went further:

> "We have calculated all that," he said. "They may even drop atom bombs on us. What then? They may kill a few million people. Without sacrifice a nation's independence cannot be upheld." He gave some calculations of the effectiveness of atom bombs and said: "After all, China lives on the farms. What can atom bombs do there? Yes, our economic development will be put back. We may have to wait for it."[38]

In late November, massive Chinese intervention sent UN forces back down the peninsula in a desperate retreat. In a November 30 news conference Truman warned, "We will take whatever steps are necessary to meet the military situation," and was promptly asked, "Will that include the atomic bomb?" He replied, "That includes every weapon that we have." This evoked hot pursuit by the questioners: "Does that mean that there is active consideration of the use of the atomic bomb?" To which the president answered, "There has always been active consideration of its use. I don't want to see it used." Pressed again with the same question, Truman said use of the bomb "always has been" under consideration. "It is one of our weapons." And when queried about whether use would be against military or civilian targets the president said simply, "It's a matter that the military people will have to decide."[39]

Truman's remarks created a sensation in part because they followed controversial speeches by Secretary of the Navy Francis P. Matthews and

37. Melvin Gurtov and Byong-Moo Hwang, *China Under Threat: The Politics of Strategy and Diplomacy* (Johns Hopkins University Press, 1980), p. 54.

38. K. M. Panikkar, *In Two Chinas: Memoirs of a Diplomat* (London: Allen and Unwin, 1955), p. 108.

39. *Public Papers, Truman, 1950*, p. 727.

Major General Orville Anderson, commandant of the Air War College, recommending preventive war against the Soviet Union.[40] Despite a clarification by the press secretary noting that the president's remarks indicated no change in U.S. policy and that no authority to use the bomb had been delegated, diplomatic hell broke loose, as the news conference set off alarm bells abroad about the danger of World War III. The greatest debate on foreign affairs since 1945 broke out in the House of Commons, with a hundred members of Prime Minister Clement Attlee's Labour party signing a letter of protest against use of the bomb. Attlee announced that he would fly to Washington to confer. The U.S. chargé in London cabled Washington that British public opinion was "deeply troubled" that escalation in Korea could ignite "general atomic war." At the United Nations, delegates worried that the Soviet Union would use nuclear weapons outside Asia. Reaction was especially intense among third world countries. The U.S. representative reported sentiment that Washington viewed the atomic bomb as a weapon for use against "Asians but not Europeans." Indian Prime Minister Jawaharlal Nehru complained especially sharply.[41]

Ironically, Truman's offhand statement was literally correct but misleading, since internal discussions about use of the bomb were generally negative. For example, the State Department's director of policy planning, Paul Nitze, had argued that tactical use of nuclear weapons would be neither easy nor significant militarily and that use against Chinese targets would "result in the destruction of many civilians and would almost certainly bring the Soviet Union into the war." Perhaps to preempt favorable arguments he noted that the UN aegis for the war in Korea might require the international organization's approval for employment of nuclear ordnance and "that publicity attending debate of this question in the United Nations would be of military value to our adversary."[42] John Emmerson, echoing General Nieh's earlier warning, advised Dean Rusk, assistant secretary for the Far East, "that China offers few suitable A-bomb targets, in view of scattered cities, low degree of industrialization, and immense area." He also argued that the moral implications of atomic attack "would be exploited to our serious detriment," that unity of the

40. Dean Acheson, *Present at the Creation: My Years in the State Department* (W. W. Norton, 1969), p. 478. Both officials were eased out of their jobs.
41. Harry S. Truman, *Memoirs*, vol. 2: *Years of Trial and Hope* (Doubleday, 1956), pp. 395–96; *FRUS, 1950*, vol. 7: *Korea*, pp. 1296, 1300, 1334.
42. *FRUS, 1950*, vol. 7: *Korea*, pp. 1041–42.

Western position would be destroyed, and that a nuclear attack could thus lead to weakening of deterrence in Western Europe.[43]

Much of the military was skeptical of the bomb's utility in the war. In a meeting the morning after Truman's sensational press conference, Army Chief of Staff J. Lawton Collins argued that the bomb should be reserved for combat with Soviet forces and that the United States should "hold back from bombing China even if this means that our ground forces must take some punishment." The Soviets were a prominent consideration at that moment since there was serious anxiety that Chinese intervention in Korea might be a diversion preceding a Soviet attack in the West and general war. At the meeting Director of Central Intelligence Walter Bedell Smith mentioned a new estimate that "makes a much better case than previously thought for Russian plans for war soon."[44] Washington was jittery. On December 6, for example, when early-warning radar in Canada detected formations of unidentified flying objects, U.S. interceptors and air defenses were alerted, Pentagon phone lines shifted to emergency procedures, and a high official barged into Secretary of State Dean Acheson's office, recommending that important files be moved to the basement. Secretary of Defense Robert Lovett later guessed that the radar blips had been geese.[45]

Though apparently not intended as such, Truman's press conference remarks constitute a tacit threat in terms of this study. The threat did not "work," since Chinese forces did not hesitate in their offensive, perhaps because they were willing to absorb nuclear strikes, as suggested in General Nieh's September warning, or perhaps because they knew that the threat was not credible. The immediate U.S. clarification of the president's comments amounted to a retraction. Moreover, a December 7, 1950, CIA report from an espionage source described Chinese officials as "absolutely confident UN will not use the atom bomb," and British documents subsequently revealed that Donald Maclean, a Soviet spy, was privy to

43. Ibid., pp. 1098–99. "In order to obtain decisive results we should undoubtedly have to engage in atomic warfare on a wide scale. This would involve us deep in Asia and make it difficult, if not impossible, to withdraw in order to fight in another theater of war. On the other hand, should we be unable to achieve decisive results even with atomic bombing of China, the effect upon our world position, particularly as regards Western Europe and countries looking to us for protection against the Soviets, would be disastrous" (p. 1100).
44. Ibid., pp. 1279–80. Quotations on p. 1279.
45. Acheson, *Present at the Creation,* pp. 479–80.

information about Attlee's meeting with Truman in which the president made clear he had no intention of using the bomb.[46]

There were no further nuclear flaps during Truman's direction of the war. Apart from a diary entry on January 27, 1952, in which he wrote that "the proper approach now would be an ultimatum" that could lead to "all out war" destroying "Moscow, St. Petersburg [Leningrad], Vladivostok, Peking, Shanghai, Port Arthur, Dairen, Odessa, Stalingrad, and every manufacturing plant in China and the Soviet Union," there is no indication that Truman considered a nuclear option.[47] The only other nuclear signal of any sort reported was a 1952 State Department request to the CIA to arrange the spread of rumors in Korea, Japan, and China that U.S. electoral campaign pressures might make use of the atomic bomb irresistible if an armistice was not quickly concluded.[48]

Although administration signals were sparse, there was ample discussion of the option among officials. In the desperate days of December 1950 General Douglas MacArthur had requested thirty-four bombs for use against retardation targets, invasion forces, and targets of opportunity. Occasionally during the course of the war public figures such as Senators Stuart Symington and Henry Cabot Lodge—even Bernard Baruch— recommended using the bomb or threatening to do so. The army, however, remained largely opposed. Simulations of nuclear strikes in Operation Hudson Harbor in 1951 confirmed that response time to identification of troop massings was rarely sufficient to make such strikes effective. Early in the war many in the military did not want to divert weapons from the main mission of all-out war against the USSR; the American nuclear stockpile was just beginning to grow. There was also concern that militarily ineffective use of the weapons in Korean terrain would depreciate their deterrent value. (Some have suggested a bureaucratic politics motive for army opposition: Korea revalidated the need for large conventional forces, and effective use of nuclear weapons would subvert the ground forces' organizational self-interest. Such a strategic Luddism, however, is a bit

---

46. CIA report, December 7, 1950, in Harry S. Truman Library, President's Secretary's File (Carrollton Press collection); "Soviets Had Access to U.S. A-Plans in Korean War," *Washington Post,* January 3, 1981.

47. Quoted in Cass Peterson, "Truman Idea: All-Out War Over Korea," *Washington Post,* August 3, 1980.

48. "Memorandum by the Deputy Assistant Secretary of State for Public Affairs (Phillips) to the Special Assistant to the Secretary of State for Public Affairs (MacKnight)," September 3, 1952, in *FRUS, 1952–54,* vol. 15: *Korea* (GPO, 1984), pt. 1, p. 484; request to CIA mentioned in footnote.

extreme for an explanation.) There was negligible support, let alone pressure, from the civilian policy elite for nuclear attack or coercion. Secretary Acheson rejected Symington's plan to threaten the Soviets on grounds that the U.S. store of nuclear weapons was too small to worry enemies but that the idea would "frighten our allies to death."[49]

Indeed, what was most notable about Truman's strategy in the war, and most politically controversial at home, was its military restraint in general, in conventional as well as nuclear terms. The next administration was to reject limited war strategy. Two trends set the stage for Eisenhower's initiatives to end the war. While Truman was being subjected to domestic criticism for letting American forces be bled steadily without a military decision, American nuclear striking power was increasing dramatically, and the primacy of SAC in the U.S. military posture was already emerging.[50]

Deliberations, 1953

In the transition period after the 1952 election Eisenhower visited MacArthur and listened to the general's plan for using a nuclear threat to induce settlement of the conflict. Stephen Ambrose, citing an interview with Eisenhower years later, says the president-elect was "appalled" at the proposal.[51] Though certainly ambivalent at times, however, Eisenhower's subsequent role as reflected in official records belies the notion that he was a nuclear dove except in occasional moments of reflection. He considered escalation from his earliest days in office, a development that flowed logically from the administration's overall "New Look" strategy—to substitute nuclear firepower for conventional—which had its genesis in the December 1952 trip home from Korea of Eisenhower, Admiral Arthur W. Radford, and others aboard the cruiser *Helena*. Together with his secretary of state, John Foster Dulles, Eisenhower took the lead—frequently in the face of footdragging by the military chiefs inherited from

49. General Maxwell D. Taylor, U.S. Army (Ret.), *Swords and Plowshares* (W. W. Norton, 1972), p. 134; Rosemary Foot, *The Wrong War: American Policy and the Dimensions of the Korean Conflict, 1950–1953* (Cornell University Press, 1985), pp. 114–15, 155, 157, 260n; Acheson quoted on p. 116. In November 1950 the Joint Strategic Survey Committee reconsidered nuclear options, but nothing significant changed (p. 116).

50. Samuel F. Wells, Jr., "The Origins of Massive Retaliation," *Political Science Quarterly*, vol. 96 (Spring 1981), pp. 49–51: the Eisenhower New Look "refined this pattern but did not change it."

51. Sherman Adams, *Firsthand Report: The Story of the Eisenhower Administration* (Harper, 1961), p. 48; Stephen E. Ambrose, *Eisenhower*, vol. 2: *The President* (Simon and Schuster, 1984), pp. 34–35.

Truman—in developing the nuclear option as a solution to the deadlock in Korea.

One way to square the president's willingness to use nuclear coercion with the view of scholars who debunk the image of Eisenhower as nuclear adventurist—a way that also helps to explain his maneuvering in subsequent crises—is to assume that the president had nearly absolute confidence in the efficacy of a threat for deterring or coercing Beijing, so that making the threat would obviate any need to implement it. Yet Eisenhower was much clearer and more forceful in promoting nuclear plans within the secret U.S. decisionmaking process than he was in signaling them to enemies. As the following section shows, the evidence about how the threat was communicated raises questions about how clear it was to the target audiences in Beijing and Moscow.

When uncertainty about how the threat itself was delivered is juxtaposed with records of NSC discussions early in 1953, it becomes apparent that Eisenhower was interested at least as much in the potential for actually using the weapons on the battlefield as in using them for blackmail. Only after he was frustrated in his object of battlefield use and after the military role of nuclear weapons came to be reserved for a major geographical expansion of the war did Eisenhower focus on the coercive diplomatic potential of nuclear threats.[52] And only after the welcome Chinese accommodation leading to an armistice did he and Dulles come to attribute great significance to the threat as distinct from the plan to escalate.

Through the spring of 1953 leaders debated whether escalation in Korea should involve a conventional offensive, battlefield use of tactical nuclear weapons, or strikes against military targets in China. Nuclear use in one form or other dominated the planning. The record of explicit high-level deliberation over intended use of nuclear weapons in specific situations in Korea is the most extensive in the postwar era.

At a February 11, 1953, meeting of the National Security Council, Eisenhower directed that the group consider using tactical nuclear weapons in the area around Kaesong. General Omar N. Bradley, chairman of the Joint Chiefs of Staff, argued that using such weapons would be premature, although he recommended consulting the allies about ending the sanctuary enjoyed by the Chinese. Dulles sided with the president, arguing that the

---

52. As one observer argues, "The ultimatum to China was a fallback, tried only after Eisenhower finally accepted the hard truth that a quick-fix atomic strategy would not work on the Korean battlefield." Edward C. Keefer, "President Dwight D. Eisenhower and the End of the Korean War," *Diplomatic History,* vol. 10 (Summer 1986), p. 268.

special distinction between nuclear and other weapons had been used by the Soviets to their advantage and that the distinction should be broken down.[53]

In late March Eisenhower requested an estimate of the costs of a campaign that would maximize damage to Chinese forces and allow UN troops to reach and hold the waist in Korea. He asked whether such a campaign could be carried out without striking airfields in Manchuria and "indicated that the use of atomic weapons in such a campaign should depend on military judgment as to the advantage of their use on military targets." A week later Army Chief Collins noted that he was "very skeptical about the value of using atomic weapons tactically in Korea" because the communists were so thoroughly dug in across the 150-mile front that they could withstand such attack. At the same meeting Paul Nitze warned that ineffective use of nuclear weapons might "depreciate the value of our stockpile," cause problems with allies, and force Moscow to confront a decision about whether "to retaliate in kind." Collins pointedly suggested, "Before we use them we had better look to our air defense. Right now we present ideal targets for atomic weapons in Pusan and Inchon," far more vulnerable and tempting than the communist front lines.[54]

That same day the JCS sent the secretary of defense a background study and a list of six possible courses of action in Korea. Despite the lack of enthusiasm of the army, the report argued that nuclear weapons would achieve better and more cost-effective military results than conventional weapons and that their use "should be considered against military targets" and should be "planned as an adjunct to any possible . . . direct action against Communist China and Manchuria." The NSC Planning Board revised the JCS options, and the chiefs told Secretary of Defense Charles Wilson that four or five of the options required nuclear strikes "on a sufficiently large scale to ensure success. A piecemeal or limited employment . . . is not recommended." The chiefs specified what they meant in terms of scale as "extensive strategical and tactical use."[55]

53. "Memorandum of Discussion at the 131st Meeting of the National Security Council, Wednesday, February 11, 1953," in FRUS, 1952–54, vol. 15: Korea, pt. 1, p. 770.

54. "Memorandum by the Administrative Assistant to the President for National Security Matters (Cutler) to the Secretary of Defense (Wilson)," March 21, 1953, and "Memorandum of the Substance of Discussion at a Department of State–Joint Chiefs of Staff Meeting," March 27, 1953, in FRUS, 1952–54, vol. 15: Korea, pt. 1, pp. 815, 817–18.

55. James F. Schnabel and Robert J. Watson, The Joint Chiefs of Staff and National

At a March 31 NSC meeting Eisenhower brought up the nuclear question and admitted the lack of good targets in Korea, but argued that nuclear bombing could still be worthwhile.[56] Repeating earlier arguments, the president and Dulles voiced concern about how to handle the anxiety of American allies but "were in complete agreement that somehow or other the tabu which surrounds the use of atomic weapons would have to be destroyed."[57] Two days later the NSC Planning Board forwarded a review of the options, equivocated a bit more than the JCS about whether all but the lowest options would "require" nuclear use, echoed Collins's reservations about UN forces' greater vulnerability to retaliation, and noted that expending "substantial numbers" of bombs "will reduce the U.S. stockpile and global atomic capabilities."[58] A special intelligence estimate on probable communist reactions to the various options devoted one vague paragraph to the nuclear question, concluding only that use of the bomb would be seen as indicating resolve to conclude the war successfully and that "the extent of damage inflicted" would probably govern the reaction.[59]

Eisenhower once again raised the question at an NSC meeting on May 6, asking whether four recently reactivated airfields in North Korea would not be suitable targets to test "the effectiveness of an atomic bomb." General Bradley thought not, despite the president's argument that "we have got to consider the atomic bomb as simply another weapon in our arsenal." When the NSC met the following week the president again challenged army skepticism about the utility of limited nuclear strikes. General John E. Hull, vice chief of staff of the army (and soon to be commander in chief in the Far East), supported use of the weapon in large numbers outside Korea but argued that there were no good strategic targets within the country. Eisenhower was dissatisfied and insisted that nuclear ordnance was more cost effective than conventional alternatives for hitting

---

Policy, vol. 3: The Korean War, pt. 2 (Wilmington, Del.: Michael Glazier, Inc., 1979), pp. 949–61; quotations on pp. 953–54, 959–61.

56. "Memorandum of Discussion at a Special Meeting of the National Security Council on Tuesday, March 31, 1953," in FRUS, 1952–54, vol. 15: Korea, pt. 1, p. 826.

57. Ibid., p. 827.

58. NSC 147, "Analysis of Possible Courses of Action in Korea," April 2, 1953, pp. 11–14, in Dwight D. Eisenhower Library (DDEL)/White House Office Files (WHO), Office of the Special Assistant for National Security Affairs, NSC Series, Policy Papers Subseries, Box 4.

59. "Probable Communist Reactions to Certain Possible UN/US Military Courses of Action With Respect to the Korean War," April 8, 1953, in FRUS, 1952–54, vol. 15: Korea, pt. 1, p. 892. The estimate did not mention possible retaliation and said communist concessions sufficient for an armistice could not necessarily be predicted if the bomb were used.

the communist line. Faced with the problem of dug-in fortifications, he even inquired about whether earth-penetrating atomic munitions had been tested.[60] The principal division between the president and his military advisers, thus, was on the *range* of nuclear options, with the president favoring a wider variety including battlefield use, and many of the soldiers inclined to reserve the weapons for the contingency of expanding the war to Chinese territory.

At a climactic May 20 meeting of the council, Eisenhower went to unusual lengths to confirm and formalize a plan for use of nuclear weapons. He summarized the views of his military advisers that if the United States were to renew offensive action, it would be necessary to widen the war geographically and to use nuclear weapons. He then emphasized the need for absolute secrecy about the proceedings of the meeting and asked the council to agree to what then became NSC Action 794, stipulating, "If conditions arise requiring more positive action in Korea, the course of action recommended by the Joint Chiefs of Staff should be adopted as a general guide." The plan, as Eisenhower later wrote, was to mount the nuclear strikes against North Korea, Manchuria, and the Chinese coast.[61]

The president was particularly sensitive to the problem that plans to use nuclear weapons would alarm American allies, and he was reluctant to approach them about it. At the February 11 meeting he had noted that if allies objected they might be asked to provide several more divisions for a conventional offensive instead, but he had concluded by ruling out discussion of specific military plans with them. In the May 20 meeting he recommended preparing the allies gradually and subtly by informal approaches.[62] He did not need to consult directly with allies at that point, because the escalation was not planned for the near future. Eisenhower later wrote that he believed the disruptive effect of nuclear weapons use on alliance relations could be repaired over time as long as the military offensive was successful.[63]

60. "Memorandum of Discussion at the 143d Meeting of the National Security Council, Wednesday, May 6, 1953," and "Memorandum of Discussion at the 144th Meeting of the National Security Council, Wednesday, May 13, 1953," in FRUS, 1952–54, vol. 15: Korea, pt. 1, pp. 977, 1014. Hull denigrated the utility of earth-penetrating bombs.

61. "Memorandum of Discussion at the 145th Meeting of the National Security Council, Wednesday, May 20, 1953," in FRUS, 1952–54, vol. 15: Korea, pt. 1, pp. 1065, 1067–68; Dwight D. Eisenhower, The White House Years, vol. 1: Mandate for Change, 1953–1956 (Doubleday, 1963), p. 180.

62. FRUS, 1952–54, vol. 15: Korea, pt. 1, pp. 770, 1066.

63. When Eisenhower did raise the issue with British Prime Minister Winston Churchill

NSC Action 794 was not a commitment, but it was as close to a final decision as a president can come, short of the moment of execution. Eisenhower's hope, of course, was that the moment would not come because China could be induced to reach a settlement. At virtually the same time as the May 20 meeting in Washington, the nuclear plan was being translated into vague—*very* vague—diplomatic pressure on the enemy.

Faint Signals, Ambiguous Results

On May 20 Secretary Dulles began a visit to India, where he warned Nehru that if the Korean conflict was not settled, the United States would not continue to operate under military constraint. According to Sherman Adams, assistant to the president, "This message was planted deliberately in India so that it would get to the Chinese Communists."[64] By some accounts, including Eisenhower's, the warning was not a novel departure, but a reiteration. In a construction that places the events before February 22, the president's memoirs mention that the United States had "dropped the word, discreetly, of our intention" at the Panmunjom truce talks and "in the Formosa Straits area," as well.[65] Edward Keefer cites a 1965 conversation between Eisenhower and Lyndon Johnson in which, curiously, Eisenhower mentioned the government on Taiwan as a channel for one of the covert messages. Citing an interview with Eisenhower, Louis L. Gerson mentions a " 'contact' in Hong Kong" as another conduit. Although Gerson's account mentions "early 1953," it lumps the other initiatives with the message through Nehru. Adams places the nuclear warning before Stalin's death in March but appears imprecise in his recollection of timing.[66]

Other available sources do not discuss these earlier initiatives, and it is possible that the later accounts confused the timing, but there do seem to

---

several months after the armistice, at the December 1953 Bermuda Conference, he said that if hostilities in Korea resumed, the United States "would feel free to use the atomic bomb." He said that Churchill, citing Britain's vulnerability to nuclear devastation, opposed the point vehemently. *Mandate for Change*, pp. 180, 248. A Dulles memo at the time, however, said that the prime minister "quite accepted" the president's point. Quoted in Bernard Gwertzman, "Nuclear Arms: A Cool, Candid Debate," *New York Times*, July 14, 1983.

64. Adams, *Firsthand Report*, p. 48.
65. Eisenhower, *Mandate for Change*, p. 181.
66. Keefer, "President Dwight D. Eisenhower," p. 280; Robert H. Ferrell, ed., *The American Secretaries of State and Their Diplomacy*, vol. 17; Louis L. Gerson, *John Foster Dulles* (Cooper Square, 1967), p. 146; Adams, *Firsthand Report*, p. 99.

be indications that the first, vague nuclear signals occurred some time before May. As to more tangible signals, Adams asserts that nuclear-capable missiles were sent to Okinawa during the spring, and Russell Weigley writes that Eisenhower sent the 280-millimeter atomic cannon to Korea to pressure the Chinese, but such claims have been disputed.[67] Dulles linked the later armistice to the fact that the United States "had already sent the means to the theater for delivering atomic weapons. This became known to the Chinese through their good intelligence sources and in fact we were not unwilling that they should find out."[68]

Although Adams says that Dulles mentioned the nuclear option on his India visit, in the documentary record the threat of escalation is less specific. Dulles's own record of the meeting with Nehru refers to a warning "that if the armistice negotiations collapsed, the United States would probably make a stronger rather than a lesser military exertion, and that this might well extend the area of conflict. (*Note*: I assumed this would be relayed.)" Dulles did not clarify the threat in a subsequent conversation with the Indian leader.[69] Much later Dulles characterized the threat as stating "our intention to wipe out the industrial complex in Manchuria if we did not get an armistice."[70] Nehru later denied knowledge of the U.S. nuclear threat, but most accounts agree that some message did reach Beijing, probably through the Indian ambassador there. Eisenhower himself described the nuclear aspect of the 1953 threats as only thinly veiled: "to let the Communist authorities understand that, in the absence of satisfactory progress [in negotiations], we intended to move decisively without inhibition on our use of weapons."[71]

67. Adams, *Firsthand Report*, p. 48; Russell F. Weigley, *History of the United States Army*, enlarged ed. (Indiana University Press, 1984), p. 536. Weigley cites no source. Authorization to transfer weapons to military custody for deployment abroad was given in June 1953, a month before the armistice; see Rosenberg, "Origins of Overkill," p. 27. Barry M. Blechman and Robert Powell say no missiles with nuclear warheads were deployed abroad before fall 1953 (after the truce). "What in the Name of God is Strategic Superiority?" *Political Science Quarterly*, vol. 97 (Winter 1982–83), p. 592n.

68. Minutes of December 7, 1953, Bermuda meeting, cited in John Lewis Gaddis, "The Origins of Self-Deterrence: The United States and the Non-Use of Nuclear Weapons, 1945–1958," unpublished paper to appear in a future volume edited by Robert Jervis.

69. "Memorandum of Conversation by the Secretary of State," May 21, 1953, in *FRUS, 1952–54*, vol. 15: *Korea*, pt. 1, pp. 1068, 1071.

70. Quoted in Andrew H. Berding, *Dulles on Diplomacy* (Van Nostrand, 1965), p. 129.

71. *Eisenhower, Mandate for Change*, p. 181; Adams, *Firsthand Report*, pp. 48–49; Blechman and Powell, "Strategic Superiority," pp. 592, 594; David Rees, *Korea: The Limited War* (St. Martin's Press, 1964), p. 417.

The armistice ending the Korean War came in July 1953. The only evidence about the role of nuclear threats in achieving the settlement is circumstantial and has been cited selectively by those who denigrate it and by those who see it as crucial. Four separate sets of events were interacting during the six months between Eisenhower's inauguration and the peace accord: formal negotiations, changes in the political situation within the communist alliance, events on the battlefield, and informal U.S. threats. The evidence does not permit precise conclusions about the coercive efficacy of the nuclear signal. The inherently delicate nature of such an initiative makes it unlikely that clear evidence would exist. Those who made the threats, however, attributed great significance to them—at least after they happened.

On February 22, after, according to Eisenhower, the initial tacit threats were communicated, UN commander Mark Clark wrote communist commanders inquiring about the possibility of repatriating sick and wounded prisoners. American officials did not expect progress since, at the time, the issue of whether prisoners who wished not to return to China or North Korea would be sent back forcibly was the primary sticking point in the truce talks. Two days later a PRC delegation headed by China's top nuclear scientist arrived in Moscow for a visit that one State Department observer interpreted as an attempt to get Soviet support against U.S. nuclear pressure. Early in March, Stalin died. At the end of the month, the communists in Korea replied favorably to Clark's letter and agreed to repatriate the sick and wounded in Operation "Little Switch."[72] Eisenhower cited the thawing in the negotiating situation as a response to the initial U.S. threats he implied were made before Clark's letter; skeptics view it as a response to the uncertainty that Stalin's death introduced among the communists.[73]

The extreme negative view of the threat or threats is that they were not just ineffective, but counterproductive, actually prolonging the war. As early as late January, according to Edward Friedman, Chinese statements "had already treated the atomic threat as so much 'noise and bluster.'" Also, as late as April and May, the Chinese launched ground offensives in Korea. Dulles, wanting first to demonstrate U.S. superiority by dealing the PRC a military defeat, did not want the Chinese to accept a peace proposal

72. Rees, *Korea*, p. 406; Edward Rice, cited in Edward Friedman, "Nuclear Blackmail and the End of the Korean War," *Modern China*, vol. 1 (January 1975), p. 82.

73. Eisenhower, *Mandate for Change*, p. 181; Blechman and Powell, "Strategic Superiority," p. 593; Friedman, "Nuclear Blackmail," p. 78.

sponsored by India at the United Nations. The Chinese, thinking the Americans would embrace it only if they thought Beijing opposed it, therefore drew back.[74] That reasoning appears a bit tortured.

The simplest reason to doubt the threats' credibility is the months that intervened between Eisenhower's reported initial nuclear signal and the settlement at Panmunjom. According to a top American diplomat, U.S. allies in the United Nations also told the Chinese that they would restrain the Americans.[75] The counterargument, that the warning in May was decisive, is supported by correlations in the final chronology. On May 14, 1953, North Korean General Nam Il rejected United Nations Command proposals on prisoner repatriation, suggesting a continuation of deadlock. On May 25, a few days after Dulles's visit in New Delhi, the final American proposals were tabled. At the next plenary session on June 4 the communists accepted them with minor changes, and on June 8 the "Terms of Reference" were signed by both sides.[76] The communist concessions after May 22 were minor, but such details had been blocking negotiations for months.[77] Dulles asserted that the communists began negotiating more earnestly within two weeks of his visit to New Delhi. He argued that the most telling indicator was the Chinese decision *not* to terminate negotiations and dismiss the emerging settlement in June when South Korean leader Syngman Rhee provocatively released large numbers of the disputed prisoners. Less than six weeks later the truce was concluded.[78]

Ambiguity in the record is substantial. When the JCS conveyed negotiating instructions to Clark three days after the crucial May 20 NSC meeting, they told him to declare that the U.S. offer was "final," but not to present it as an ultimatum.[79] Without knowledge of Chinese delibera-

---

74. Friedman, "Nuclear Blackmail," pp. 83, 89. Friedman cites Emmett John Hughes on Dulles's opposition to conclusion of the Indian proposal, but does not cite Hughes's point that Eisenhower sharply rejected Dulles's view. Emmet John Hughes, *The Ordeal of Power: A Political Memoir of the Eisenhower Years* (Dell, 1963), pp. 91–92. Nor does Friedman cite a source for the Chinese stratagem in resisting the Indian resolution.

75. Robert Murphy, *Diplomat Among Warriors* (Doubleday, 1964), p. 360.

76. Rees, *Korea*, pp. 416–18.

77. Keefer, "President Dwight D. Eisenhower," pp. 281–82 (citing Walter G. Hermes).

78. Dulles interview in James Shepley, "How Dulles Averted War," *Life* (January 16, 1956), pp. 70–72. The accuracy of Shepley's account has been challenged. See Blechman and Powell, "Strategic Superiority," p. 592n; and Adams, *Firsthand Report*, pp. 118–19. The main criticism was overemphasis on how close the danger of implementing the threat really was. Adams denigrated Dulles's view that it was very close, but not because the threat was ineffective, rather the opposite—Eisenhower was confident that it would not be called to the test. Adams, *Firsthand Report*, p. 48.

79. Foot, *The Wrong War*, p. 210.

tions it is impossible to confirm or dismiss a linkage between the U.S. signal and the Chinese decision to conclude negotiations. The question is not necessarily whether the threat or Stalin's death was the reason; the combination of the two could have tilted a decision where neither might have alone. Nor is there any way to know whether the nuclear part of the escalatory threat would have been implemented had China remained intransigent. Clark wrote that if the Chinese had rejected the final U.S. offer based on the Indian resolution, "I was authorized to *break off* the truce talks . . . and to carry on the war in new ways never yet tried in Korea."[80] He had been told to revise his operations plan to take account of the decision to use nuclear weapons, but the initial options envisioned for escalation were conventional attacks on Yalu bridges and Manchuria.[81] Eisenhower logically would have intended to hold the nuclear option pending at least initial results of this move.

There is one more point to make about logic that may lie beneath the combined ambiguities. The May 20 NSC decision was based on a plan to use nuclear weapons against China in a general offensive that would include conventional force advances in Korea but that would not begin until the following year, after a further buildup of South Korean forces.[82] The threat so hesitantly communicated was probably motivated in large part by a desire to avoid waiting a year for the end of the war, as well as by the desire to avoid further military effort. Yet because actual implementation would not have occurred until 1954, there was a natural disincentive to making the threat clear, lest the interim make it appear hollow. Thus, as in other cases, there was a tension between the diplomatic incentives for nuclear threats and the military constraints on following through.

Uncertain efficacy of the nuclear signals aside, the record declassified two decades later makes one point clear about the U.S. decision: the president often went to great lengths in the secrecy of NSC consultations to promote explicit plans for employment of nuclear ordnance. More than once he pushed the option of tactical nuclear fires on the battlefield despite the reluctance of his JCS chairman and army chief of staff, both of whom were shortly replaced. And in the May 20 meeting Eisenhower explicitly

80. General Mark W. Clark, U.S. Army (Ret.), *From the Danube to the Yalu* (Harper, 1954), p. 267 (italics in original). The instructions from Washington came on May 23, shortly after the May 20 NSC meeting and Dulles's arrival in India.

81. Foot, *The Wrong War*, p. 209; Clark communication to Barry Blechman, cited in Blechman and Powell, "Strategic Superiority," p. 595.

82. "Memorandum of Discussion at the 145th Meeting . . . May 20, 1953," p. 1066 (see note 61).

formalized a consensus that if escalation became necessary it would involve nuclear weapons. However elliptical the threat conveyed to China, there is no evidence that it was a bluff. Indeed, in the months after the armistice the NSC had long discussions about military plans to be implemented if the communists reopened the war, and reaffirmed the intention to mount large-scale nuclear strikes against China. The principal targets were to be all forward airbases, with Eisenhower personally envisioning one atomic bomb on each field. According to the minutes, the president emphasized in a December 3, 1953, meeting that "if the Chinese Communists attacked us again we should certainly respond by hitting them hard . . . including Peiping itself."[83] Eisenhower stipulated carefully that General Hull would not have automatic authority to use nuclear weapons, but his principal concern in doing so was to ensure the acquiescence of U.S. allies. He wanted to be sure for diplomatic purposes that there was enough time between communist attack and a U.S. nuclear response to establish clearly which side had started the war.[84]

However dubious the reliability of retrospective claims may be, the two top figures of the administration claimed unequivocally that the spring 1953 threat was decisive. Some months after the truce, in his famous massive retaliation speech, Dulles attributed the end of the war to the enemy's having to face "the possibility that the fighting might, to his own great peril, soon spread beyond the limits and methods which he had selected." When asked later what had brought China to terms, Eisenhower responded simply, "Danger of an atomic war."[85]

The spring 1953 threat to the Chinese, such as it was, represented the first implementation of the massive retaliation doctrine, conceived earlier aboard the *Helena* and proclaimed by Dulles in his speech before the Council on Foreign Relations. The proclamation came several months before a case in which the doctrine faltered and a year before another in which it was partially reaffirmed.

83. "Memorandum of Discussion at the 173d Meeting of the National Security Council, Thursday, December 3, 1953," and "Memorandum of Discussion at the 179th Meeting of the National Security Council, Friday, January 8, 1954," in *FRUS, 1952–54*, vol. 15: *Korea*, pt. 2, pp. 1638, 1707. In the December 3 meeting Dulles proposed retaining an option limited "to a full atomic strike in Korea itself" as one way to reduce chances of drawing the USSR into the war (p. 1639).

84. Ibid., p. 1705.

85. Dulles speech quoted in Wells, "Origins of Massive Retaliation," p. 34; see also Shepley, "How Dulles Averted War," p. 77. Eisenhower quoted in Adams, *Firsthand Report*, p. 49.

Asian Crises, 1954–55

Crises in Indochina and the Taiwan Straits are weak cases for evaluating the political utility of nuclear weapons. In the first, the U.S. government made no attempt to exploit a threat by conveying it to the Vietminh or PRC but did consider internally the option to mount nuclear attacks. Although there were public signals in the second case, in both instances the administration compromised and accepted partial territorial losses— the partition of Vietnam and Nationalist Chinese evacuation of the Tachen Islands. "Saving" half of Indochina and the islands of Quemoy and Matsu would be cited as a success in preventing defeats on a scale otherwise anticipated, but the compromises reflect limits on the freight to be carried by nuclear blackmail.

Indochina: Developing Military Options

The Korean War had been over for less than a year when U.S. leaders had to consider military action to save the crumbling French position in Indochina. In the interim, NSC 162/2 had been approved as general policy, stipulating that "in the event of hostilities, the United States will consider nuclear weapons to be as available for use as other munitions."[86] The situation for which this commitment was most firm was general war. In Indochina, however, no Soviet or Chinese forces were directly engaged, although China was viewed as a crucial actor supplying and supporting the Vietminh. In a related document, NSC 5405, a "special weapons annex" pertaining to nuclear use was withheld during part of 1954, precluding an assumption that the weapons would automatically be employed.[87]

The first mention of using nuclear weapons in Indochina came up during the secret development of Operation Vulture, a set of contingency plans for U.S. air strikes to relieve the encircled French garrison at Dienbienphu. But Operation Vulture, which also included such purely conventional options as saturation bombing by B-29s, was never executed, and Dienbienphu fell on May 8. U.S. intervention remained under consideration for some time afterward, however, and so did the nuclear option. In late March and early April the army operations staff produced two studies

86. Quoted in Rosenberg, "Origins of Overkill," p. 31.
87. John Prados, *The Sky Would Fall: Operation Vulture: The U.S. Bombing Mission in Indochina, 1954* (Dial Press, 1983), p. 154.

envisioning nuclear strikes on Vietminh positions and supply bases around Dienbienphu involving use of one to six thirty-one-kiloton bombs to be delivered from aircraft carriers. Other army staffs and air force intelligence, however, rejected the studies as militarily unsuitable or politically counterproductive.[88]

Dulles promoted action, but JCS Chairman Arthur Radford was more of an enthusiast for intervention, although it is unclear how necessary either one thought nuclear action would be. On April 7 Radford's special assistant, and later chief of naval operations, George Anderson, reported to the State Department a Pentagon study group's conclusion that three tactical nuclear weapons could relieve the Vietminh pressure on Dienbienphu. In late May Radford reported to the secretary of defense the JCS view that if the United States intervened, it should use atomic weapons "whenever it is to our military advantage." Dulles's assistants were skeptical, echoing army views that such strikes would not reduce the requirements for large-scale intervention with ground forces, would alienate the Vietnamese and Asian neutrals, and would provoke severe European reaction.[89]

After the collapse of Dienbienphu, military attention focused on the prospect of combat with China if the United States intervened. Although there was a sharp split within the JCS, with the army especially opposed to intervention, Radford reported the chiefs' corporate position that U.S. military action should concentrate on China rather than dissipate its power by restriction to the local point of attack. Radford reiterated the need, in the event of Chinese involvement, to employ nuclear weapons "whenever advantageous" and to mount air operations against Chinese territory, while noting the chiefs' view that Indochina itself "is devoid of decisive military objectives and [that] the allocation of more than token U.S. armed forces in Indochina would be a serious diversion of limited U.S. capabilities."[90] The question of U.S. action was evolving from a limited clandestine operation against the Vietminh to relieve several thousand encircled French

88. Ronald H. Spector, *Advice and Support: The Early Years, 1941–1960* (Washington, D.C.: U.S. Army Center of Military History, 1985), pp. 200–01.

89. "Memorandum by the Counselor (MacArthur) to the Secretary of State," April 7, 1954; "Memorandum by the Joint Chiefs of Staff to the Secretary of Defense (Wilson)," May 20, 1954; and "Memorandum by the Director of the Policy Planning Staff (Bowie) to the Secretary of State," May 27, 1954, in *FRUS, 1952–54*, vol. 13: *Indochina* (GPO, 1982), pt. 1, pp. 1270–71, pt. 2, pp. 1591, 1625.

90. "Memorandum for the Secretary of Defense," May 21, 1954, and "Memorandum for the Secretary of Defense," May 26, 1954, in *The Pentagon Papers: The Defense Department History of United States Decisionmaking on Vietnam*, Senator Gravel Edition, vol. 1 (Beacon Press, 1971), pp. 510–12 (emphasis deleted).

troops into something closer to full-scale war against the second-ranking communist power.

Indochina: Decisions and Diplomacy

Eisenhower did not promote the nuclear option for Indochina as he had for Korea a year earlier. His lack of enthusiasm for direct intervention of any sort in Indochina may have reflected an appreciation of how the nature of the war differed. In 1951 he had written in his diary that "no military victory is possible in that kind of theater." Twice in late March 1954, in discussions with close associates, he considered the possibility of a covert air strike if it could be decisive and deniable, but he did not firmly embrace even this obviously nonnuclear option.[91] Dulles too went to some lengths to make clear in March that the massive retaliation doctrine that he had enunciated in January did not apply to the war against the Vietminh, but only to potential Chinese intervention.[92]

At the famous State Department meeting on April 3 at which congressional leaders were consulted about intervention, there was vigorous discussion, but apparently no mention of using nuclear weapons. The legislative representatives were far from united in enthusiasm for U.S. involvement.[93] On April 29, just over a week before the surrender at Dienbienphu, the NSC Planning Board considered a variety of questions about use of nuclear weapons. Robert Cutler's notes on the meeting reflect both the seriousness and wide-ranging uncertainties of the options:

> b. Should decision be made now as to U.S. intention to use "new weapons," on intervention, in Vietnam on military targets? Would one "new weapon" dropped on Vietminh troop concentrations in reserve behind DBP be decisive in casualties and overwhelming in psycho effect

91. George C. Herring and Richard H. Immerman, "Eisenhower, Dulles, and Dienbienphu: 'The Day We Didn't Go to War' Revisited," *Journal of American History,* vol. 71 (September 1984), p. 349.

92. Alexander L. George and Richard Smoke, *Deterrence in American Foreign Policy: Theory and Practice* (Columbia University Press, 1974), p. 255. As will be clear, Dulles did not view *tactical* nuclear weapons in the same light as those for attack on the Soviet Union or China itself.

93. Prados, *The Sky Would Fall,* pp. 96–98; Chalmers M. Roberts, "The Day We Didn't Go to War," *The Reporter,* vol. 11 (September 14, 1954), pp. 31–35; Chalmers M. Roberts, *First Rough Draft: A Journalist's Journal of Our Times* (Praeger, 1973), p. 114. Admiral Radford testified before the Senate Foreign Relations Committee in executive session on April 15, but despite the fact that the transcript was to be secret, his remarks were kept off the record. *Executive Sessions of the Senate Foreign Relations Committee (Historical Series),* vol. 6, 83 Cong. 2 sess., 1954 (GPO, 1977), pp. 217–18.

on Vietminh opposition? (Query: could one "new weapon" be loaned to France for this purpose? Could French airmen make a proper drop? Would French government dare take step?)

c. If U.S. decides that it *will* use "new weapons" on intervention

(1) Should it tell its proposed associates in regional grouping at outset? Would the effect upon them be to frighten them off?

(2) Will France and Britain take alarm, with possible repercussions on U.S. air bases overseas? . . .

d. View was expressed that U.S. use of "new weapon" in Vietnam would tend to deter Chinese aggression in retaliation, and that failure to use the "new weapon" in Vietnam would tend to increase chance of Chinese aggression in retaliation (i.e. the Chinese would feel the U.S. was afraid to use its one massive superiority).

e. View was expressed that neither USSR nor China wants a "new weapon" war now, at a time when U.S. had manifest superiority. . . . Chou En-lai is talking big to bluff the U.S.[94]

According to both Cutler's memo and Vice President Nixon's memoirs, when they met with Eisenhower the following morning the president and Nixon doubted that the bomb could be used effectively and thought conventional carrier strikes would work better, yet also wanted the possibility of offering nuclear weapons to the French kept open. Eisenhower rejected using the bomb "unilaterally," but also said it was not necessary to raise the issue with allies before securing their agreement to cooperate in intervention.[95] Interviewed years later, Eisenhower claimed that he had reacted violently at this time, saying, "You boys must be crazy. We can't use those awful things against Asians for the second time in less than ten years. My God."[96] His recollection does not seem quite consistent with Cutler's contemporary record.

The quest for allied "United Action" was the central problem in the administration's approach to intervention. In March, before the situation at Dienbienphu had become utterly desperate, Senator Symington had pressed the French prime minister about his views on use of the bomb. Pleven saw no good targets for nuclear weapons and preferred a U.S. declaration that it would defend against Chinese air attacks. At the

94. "Memorandum by the Special Assistant to the President for National Security Affairs (Cutler) to the Under Secretary of State (Smith)," April 30, 1954, in *FRUS, 1952–1954*, vol. 13: *Indochina*, pt. 2, p. 1447.

95. Ibid., p. 1447 and 1447n.

96. Quoted in Ambrose, *The President,* p. 184.

beginning of April Dulles spoke with the British ambassador and pushed "deterrent action," but in terms directed against China more than the Vietminh. He argued that if Beijing were made to see that increased Chinese activity in Southeast Asia would invite "disastrous retaliation," China might avoid dangerous initiatives. "Furthermore," the secretary explained, "the atomic balance, which is now advantageous to us, might decline over the next four years."[97]

By May, as the outpost at Dienbienphu crumbled, the French were demoralized and internally divided about bringing other countries into the conflict, the British were unenthusiastic, and negotiations with the communists were getting under way in Geneva. With the tide thus running against any major resort to force, the notion of raising nuclear strikes from the level of military contingency planning to serious consideration at the policy level would have been ridiculous.

Dulles remained interested despite the obstacles. French Foreign Minister Georges Bidault even claimed that in late April the secretary had asked whether the French would like the United States to give them two atomic bombs; Dulles denied categorically that he had made the offer.[98] In early May Dulles reported on dread in London, particularly Churchill's, of any hint of nuclear war. The British were characterized as "scared to death," "almost pathological in their fear of the H-bomb," and "almost in a panic over it." The British opposition to any nuclear use was based primarily on the danger of Soviet retaliation against Europe.[99] Dulles reviewed British opposition but at an NSC meeting he asked whether it was sensible to accept successful communist "aggression" through a Vietminh victory "even though we evaluate this loss as very serious and even though we have the military means to redeem the situation (The A-Bomb)."[100]

97. "The Chargé in France (Achilles) to the Department of State," March 5, 1954, and "Memorandum of Conversation, by the Deputy Assistant Secretary of State for Far Eastern Affairs (Drumwright)," April 2, 1954, in FRUS, 1952–54, vol. 13: Indochina, pt. 1, pp. 1096, 1217.

98. Bidault's assistant Roland de Margerie reminded the State Department of the alleged offer when coordinating a statement on Indochina in August. When confronted with Dulles's insistent denial that the conversation had taken place, de Margerie accepted that there might have been a misunderstanding. "The Ambassador in France (Dillon) to the Department of State," August 9, 1954; "The Secretary of State to the Embassy in France," August 9, 1954; and "The Ambassador in France (Dillon) to the Department of State," August 10, 1954, in FRUS, 1952–54, vol. 13: Indochina, pt. 2, pp. 1927, 1928, 1933. Bidault repeated his claim in his memoirs: Georges Bidault, Resistance: The Political Autobiography of Georges Bidault, Marianne Sinclair, trans. (Praeger, 1967), p. 196.

99. FRUS, 1952–54, vol. 13: Indochina, pt. 2, pp. 1467, 1474.

100. Quoted in Prados, The Sky Would Fall, p. 177.

Eisenhower's attitude contrasted both with his stance in deliberations about Korea the year before and with his views about the offshore islands months later. On Indochina he did not rule out the nuclear option but was certainly not inclined toward it. He also implicitly torpedoed it by casting the question in terms of the starkest version of the massive retaliation doctrine's logic. If it came to engaging China with nuclear weapons, the president said in June, the USSR would also have to be struck with full force at the same time. According to James Hagerty's diary, Eisenhower lectured the JCS, "I want you to carry this question home with you: Gain such a victory, and what do you do with it? Here would be a great area from the Elbe to Vladivostok . . . torn up and destroyed, without government, without its communications, just an area of starvation and disaster. I ask you what would the civilized world do about it? I repeat there is no victory except through our imaginations."[101]

A nuclear option for Indochina existed only in the sense that officials considered it. It did not function as a coercive signal since it never surfaced in a way that might impress Moscow, Beijing, or the Vietminh. Indeed, Washington took some care to keep its closest allies in the dark. The planning for Operation Vulture was conducted in such extraordinary secrecy that later teams of official government researchers in both the State Department and Defense Department were unable to uncover any trace of it in the records.[102]

The U.S. decision to accept the partition of Vietnam without trying any sort of nuclear blackmail, even the most indirect, helps lend significance to the cases in which nuclear threats were made. Some critics denigrate most of the other threats as being too vague to imply any commitment, thus being cost-free "throwaways." If so, one might have expected Eisenhower and Dulles to try the same move again, free from trepidation, just in case it did any good. Their decision not to bluff in Indochina weakens any assumption that other instances were bluffs.

The partition of Vietnam and the U.S. decision not to intervene were widely cited by critics at the time as evidence of the failure or inadequacy of the New Look policy.[103] The administration's inclination to rely on

---

101. Quoted in Ambrose, *The President,* p. 206.

102. *Pentagon Papers,* vol. 1, p. 97; *FRUS, 1952–54,* vol. 13: *Indochina,* pt. 2, p. 1271n.

103. See Prados, *The Sky Would Fall,* p. 199; and William W. Kaufmann, "The Requirements of Deterrence," in Kaufmann, ed., *Military Policy and National Security* (Princeton University Press, 1956), pp. 12–38.

nuclear weapons, however, was not shaken. They did not prove useful—for what in hindsight are quite obvious reasons—in dealing with internal revolutionary warfare. The decision was not so much against exploiting nuclear weapons as against commitment to any engagement at all.[104] But at a meeting in the president's office the month after Dienbienphu fell, conferees resolved, as they had after the Korean armistice, that subsequent Chinese aggression should be met with "large-scale air and naval atomic attacks on ports, airfields and military targets in mainland China." As Samuel Wells notes, "These are not the words of an administration espousing a doctrine for propaganda purposes only."[105] And in several planning exercises concerning defense of the new government of South Vietnam during the following two years, use of nuclear weapons was included as a likely option.[106]

Quemoy and Matsu: Planning

On September 3, 1954, PRC artillery launched a bombardment of the Nationalist-held outpost island of Quemoy. Two American soldiers were killed. Two months later, the Tachen Islands were bombed and a communist troop buildup opposite Taiwan continued. One hundred PRC planes raided the Tachens on January 10, 1955, and a week later several thousand communist troops overwhelmed Nationalist forces and seized the island of Ichiang, just north of the Tachens. The secretary of state and JCS chairman met with congressional leaders on January 20 to discuss whether to defend the offshore islands, but they did not discuss military options in detail and apparently did not mention nuclear weapons.[107] The

104. Although the diplomatic failure of the quest for "United Action" was the prime reason for forbearance, the reliance on nuclear options for military effectiveness may have discouraged commitment. Army Chief of Staff Matthew Ridgway opposed intervention on the ground. Seven years later, confronting similar choices in Laos, the Kennedy administration recoiled from intervention when several military leaders insisted that it might require nuclear use. Richard K. Betts, *Soldiers, Statesmen, and Cold War Crises* (Harvard University Press, 1977), pp. 21–22, 37–38, 236n.

105. Wells, "Origins of Massive Retaliation," p. 37 (first quotation from a memo of the meeting by Robert Cutler).

106. See *FRUS, 1955–57*, vol. 1: *Vietnam* (GPO, 1985), pp. 536–40, 695–700, 708, 796, 809, 820–23. At a June 1956 meeting, when an assistant secretary of state raised doubts about use of nuclear weapons in Indochina and was criticized by the JCS chairman and acting secretary of defense, Eisenhower responded by suggesting the possible deployment of Nike missiles "with small atomic warheads" to the area. "Memorandum of Discussion at the 287th Meeting of the National Security Council, Washington, June 7, 1956," in ibid., pp. 699–700.

107. "Meeting of Secretary With Congressional Leaders, January 20, 1955, 9:00 a.m.," DDEL/John Foster Dulles Papers, White House Memo Series, Box 2.

Formosa Resolution, passed by Congress at the end of January, committed the United States to defense of Formosa and the Pescadores, but did not mention the offshore islands. In the first week of February the Nationalists were evacuated from the Tachens.[108]

A week after the initial Chinese shelling of Quemoy, the JCS chairman had forwarded a long memo to the secretary of defense on policy toward the offshore islands, with views of General Hull, commander in chief in the Far East, and the separate service chiefs, including Army Chief Matthew Ridgway's sharp opposition to committing U.S. forces to protect the islands. Chief of Naval Operations Robert Carney noted that Quemoy was defensible *if* nuclear weapons were available for use. General Hull also conditioned the decision for defense on "the use of atomic weapons if necessary." On September 12, a talking paper prepared by Dulles for a National Security Council meeting noted that holding Quemoy "would probably lead to our initiating the use of atomic weapons."[109] At that meeting the president resisted recommendations to help the Nationalists bomb the mainland to relieve the PRC attacks: "We're not talking now about a limited, brush-fire war. We're talking about going to the threshold of World War III. If we attack China, we're not going to impose limits on our military actions, as in Korea."[110]

On September 17 Secretary of State Dulles mentioned to British Prime Minister Anthony Eden that Quemoy might not be defensible without resort to tactical nuclear weapons and that he therefore doubted the wisdom of commitment to hold the offshore islands. Dulles's skepticism, however, may have been meant to soothe jittery allies' nerves—as it was in the following spring, when Dulles, meeting with Australian Prime Minister Gordon Menzies, again cited in the same breath the need for nuclear weapons and the desirability of evacuating the islands if it could be done without damaging morale.[111] The issue remained open and consideration of contingencies went ahead.

In preparation for U.S. naval assistance in evacuating of the Tachens,

108. Eisenhower, *Mandate for Change*, pp. 459–70.
109. "Memorandum by the Chairman of the Joint Chiefs of Staff (Radford) to the Secretary of Defense (Wilson)," September 11, 1954, and "Memorandum Prepared by the Secretary of State," September 12, 1954, in *FRUS, 1952–54*, vol. 14: *China and Japan* (GPO, 1985), pt. 1, pp. 604, 610, 611.
110. Eisenhower, *Mandate for Change*, p. 464.
111. "Memorandum of a Conversation, Department of State, Washington, January 20, 1955, 6:30 p.m.," and "Memorandum of a Conversation, Washington, March 14, 1955, 3:05 p.m.," in *FRUS, 1955–57*, vol. 2: *China* (GPO, 1986), pp. 86–87n, 369.

rules of engagement had to be clarified. Radford cabled the commander in chief, Pacific (CINCPAC), Admiral Felix Stump, that he was authorized to strike the "source or base from which the enemy attack is launched [implicitly the PRC mainland] if necessary in defense of own forces engaged in the operation." In confirming an operations order, however, Radford specified the exception "less Atomic Annex." That annex mentioned "the use of atomic weapons in the defense of U.S. Forces should such employment be authorized by highest authority." Eisenhower's memoranda for the record on January 29 and 31 show a careful massaging of the rules.[112] On February 5, a telegram from Carney to Stump reiterated that "atomic weapons will not be employed . . . unless directed by higher authority."[113]

Secretary of State Dulles was committed to the New Look logic that *tactical* nuclear explosives, which he differentiated from "weapons of mass destruction," were to count as conventional ordnance.[114] Some attribute his view to his technical ignorance and trust in Radford's misleading advice that precision nuclear strikes could obliterate military targets with negligible collateral damage. On March 7 he explained to Senator Walter George that "the missiles we had in mind had practically no radioactive fall-out and were entirely local in effect."[115] Concerned, Dulles's aide Robert Bowie asked the CIA to estimate civilian casualties from nuclear attacks mounted against airfields and artillery opposite Quemoy. The estimate was 12 million to 14 million people. Bowie believed the figure impressed Dulles. Early in April a draft originating in Bowie's Policy Planning Staff and revised by Dulles noted the "risk of large civilian casualties through after-effects, and indeed the inhabitants of Quemoy and even Taiwan might not be immune." The draft also raised doubts whether nuclear defense of positions on the island would be in the long-term U.S. interest. The secretary's views during the second as well as first Taiwan Straits crisis, however, indicate that he was not fully dissuaded from the nuclear option.[116]

112. January 29, 1955, Radford cable to Stump and Eisenhower memos for record in DDEL/Ann Whitman File (AWF), International Series, Box 9; Atomic Annex quoted in *FRUS, 1955–57*, vol. 2: *China*, p. 165n.

113. *FRUS, 1955–57*, vol. 2: *China*, p. 225n.

114. "Memorandum of a Conversation Between the President and the Secretary of State, Washington, March 6, 1955, 5:15 p.m.," in *FRUS, 1955–57*, vol. 2: *China*, p. 337.

115. "Memorandum of a Conversation Between the Secretary of State and Senator Walter George, Department of State, Washington, March 7, 1955," in *FRUS, 1955–57*, vol. 2: *China*, p. 337.

116. Quotation from "Draft Policy Statement Prepared in the Department of State,"

On March 10 Dulles participated in a White House meeting and had an exchange with the president that Eisenhower recalled in his memoirs as follows: " 'If we defend Quemoy and Matsu,' he [Dulles] said, 'we'll have to use atomic weapons. They alone will be effective against the mainland airfields.' To this I agreed."[117] Records of this meeting and the one the following day, however, suggest that Dulles's and the president's views were more equivocal. As in earlier cases, both worried about alarming U.S. allies. At the meeting on the tenth Dulles pushed for a decision to use nuclear ordnance to offset conventional force deficiencies and argued that the need outweighed negative repercussions in Europe. The next day, however, he and the president agreed that "if possible" such use should be avoided for forty to sixty days to avoid adverse effects on European treaties then being negotiated. In a conversation with the president Dulles again mentioned the desirability of avoiding use of nuclear weapons "while the WEU [Western European Union] situation was still unsettled. After that was buttoned up he could have more freedom of action in Asia." On the eleventh Eisenhower also stipulated that initial defense of the islands be conventional and that atomic weapons should be used only "at the end," if and when such defense failed.[118] Another memo of the meeting implies that there was further discussion about dealing with the negative consequences for public opinion and alliance relations of resorting to nuclear weapons.[119]

April 8, 1955, in FRUS, 1955–57, vol. 2: China, p. 459; see also Townsend Hoopes, The Devil and John Foster Dulles (Little, Brown, 1973), pp. 277–78.

117. Eisenhower, Mandate for Change, p. 476.

118. Ambrose, The President, p. 238; "Memorandum for the Record," March 11, 1955, p. 1, and Robert Cutler, "Memorandum for the Record," March 11, 1955, p. 3, in DDEL/AWF, International Series, Box 9; quotation about WEU in "Memorandum of a Conversation Between the President and the Secretary of State, Washington, March 11, 1955, 10:45 a.m.," in FRUS, 1955–57, vol. 2: China, p. 355. See also "Memorandum of Discussion at the 240th Meeting of the National Security Council, Washington, March 10, 1955," FRUS, 1955–57, vol. 2: China, p. 349.

119. It refers to a paper bearing on interpretation of NSC 162/2 and contains a passage that refers to a deleted item by citing NSC 5501, which states: "As the fear of nuclear war grows, the United States and its allies must never allow themselves to get into the position where they must choose between (a) not responding to local aggression and (b) applying force in a way which our own people or our allies would consider entails undue risk of nuclear devastation. However, the United States cannot afford to preclude itself from using nuclear weapons even in a local situation. . . . [I]f confronted by the choice of (a) acquiescing in Communist aggression or (b) taking measures risking either general war or loss of allied support, the United States must be prepared to take these risks." "Memorandum for the Record," March 11, 1955, DDEL/WHO, Office of the Special

Some have interpreted Robert Cutler's account of the meeting of March 11 as showing that subsequent nuclear threats were only for declaratory policy and would not have been implemented.[120] That interpretation is not clear from the discussion as a whole. Nuclear strikes were discussed as a disagreeable last resort, but not as a phony diplomatic ploy. Rather the *timing* of nuclear combat was seen as a matter of diplomatic delicacy. Even the risk that fallout would endanger large civilian populations around Amoy and on Quemoy itself, or that PRC forces could regroup and attempt invasion again after nuclear attack, led the president to say that it would not be wise "to atomize the Mainland," but with the crucial qualification, "unless we are forced to do it."[121] And before the meeting on March 11 the president had affirmed to Cutler that the policy of NSC 162/2—that nuclear weapons should be "as available for use as other munitions"— remained "suited to the present situation." He demurred only from Cutler's suggestion to have the JCS make detailed estimates and plans for conventional and nuclear operations "at this time."[122]

The emphasis on avoiding use of nuclear weapons for up to two months was prompted by alliance politics, but it was facilitated by evidence that the Chinese had not yet undertaken the necessary preparations for invasion, principally a local airpower buildup. Air Force Chief of Staff Nathan Twining believed attack was not imminent.[123] On March 15 Eisenhower's assistant, then-Colonel Andrew Goodpaster, reported the views of Admiral Stump. Nationalist Chinese and U.S. conventional forces could hold the islands if the communists did not redeploy their airpower in strength. "If, however, the CHICOMS move air forces in strength into the area, the U.S. would have to be prepared to employ atomic weapons."[124] On March 24 Eisenhower declared in a National Security Council meeting that it would be "next to impossible to take out these [PRC] gun emplacements without resort to nuclear weapons," and on March 31 Dulles told a group of senators that it might be impossible to hold the islands without resorting to nuclear fires.[125]

Assistant for National Security Affairs, NSC Series, Briefing Notes Subseries, Box 17.

120. Gaddis, "Origins of Self-Deterrence," pp. 30–31.

121. Ibid., p. 31.

122. "Memorandum for the Record, by the President's Special Assistant (Cutler)," March 11, 1955, in *FRUS, 1955–57*, vol. 2: *China*, pp. 355–57 (N. B.: to be distinguished from Cutler's other March 11 memo, cited in note 118).

123. Cutler Memorandum, March 11, 1955, p. 1 (see note 118).

124. Goodpaster, "Memorandum for the President," March 15, 1955, p. 1, in DDEL/AWF, International Series, Box 9.

125. "Memorandum of Discussion of the 242d Meeting of the National Security

The president and his secretary of state were not salivating at the prospect of unleashing nuclear explosions; they hoped that the challenge in the Taiwan Straits would not come to that. It is hard, however, to read their discussion of conditions and qualifications on nuclear plans as evidence that the plans were phony. They saw nuclear attack as a last resort, but not a nonresort.

Quemoy and Matsu: Signaling

Eisenhower and Dulles made a number of public statements leaving little room for doubt—but some room—that nuclear detonations would be part of the military resistance to a Chinese invasion. As early as January, the president implied to reporters that escalation would flow inevitably from a direct military engagement.[126] On February 13 Eisenhower approved Operation Teacup, a test series for tactical nuclear weapons, and in order to use it to impress Beijing he directed that the tests be announced publicly. In a March 15 news conference Secretary Dulles reaffirmed the massive retaliation doctrine in regard to Asia: "We believe that our most effective contribution to the defense of the entire area is by a *strategic force* with a high degree of striking power. . . . U.S. policy is not to split that power up into fragments."[127] As in his famous Council on Foreign Relations speech Dulles did not specifically mention nuclear weapons, but through other language left no doubt in commentators' minds what he meant.

The next day a reporter cited Dulles's view that tactical nuclear weapons would be used in "general war" in Asia and asked Eisenhower to comment. The president responded: "Now, in any combat where these things can be used on strictly military targets and for strictly military purposes, I see no reason why they shouldn't be used just exactly as you would use a bullet or anything else." He later wrote, "I hoped this answer would have some effect in persuading the Chinese Communists of the strength of our determination."[128] Whatever the impact, the Chinese did notice. A Radio Peking broadcast accused Eisenhower of purveying the falsehood that nuclear weapons could be employed "without massacring civilians."[129]

Council, Washington, March 24, 1955," in *FRUS, 1955–57*, vol. 2: *China*, p. 390; Bennett C. Rushkoff, "Eisenhower, Dulles and the Quemoy-Matsu Crisis, 1954–1955," *Political Science Quarterly*, vol. 96 (Fall 1981), p. 478.

126. Ambrose, *The President*, p. 245; *Public Papers of the Presidents of the United States: Dwight D. Eisenhower, 1955* (GPO, 1959), p. 57.

127. "Defense Commitments in Far East and Southeast Asia," in *Department of State Bulletin*, vol. 32 (March 28, 1955), p. 526 (emphasis added).

128. *Public Papers, Eisenhower, 1955*, p. 332; Eisenhower, *Mandate for Change*, p. 477.

129. Quoted in Hoopes, *Devil and John Foster Dulles*, p. 279.

The following week, on March 23, Eisenhower's press secretary told the president that the State Department wished that he would not say anything about the crisis because the situation was too delicate. Eisenhower rejected the advice, told Hagerty not to worry, and uttered the remark cited often by revisionist scholars as evidence of Eisenhower's political genius: "If that question comes up, I'll just confuse them."[130] When asked during a news conference whether he would use nuclear weapons to defend Quemoy and Matsu, the president said he could not say in advance. But a moment earlier he had defined the difference between trivial internal political violence and war in a way that clearly envisioned use of nuclear weapons: "Now, you don't send in bombs to restore order when a riot occurs. . . . But when you get into actual war . . . *whether the war is big or not,* if you have the kind of weapon that can be limited to military use, then I know of no reason why a large explosion shouldn't be used as freely as a small explosion."[131] The interlarding of such statements with muddled equivocations can indeed serve to confuse, but it can also preserve the running room that presidents normally insist on in a crisis.

The administration, in fact, was never irrevocably committed to holding Quemoy and Matsu. The president seriously considered offering to station a U.S. Marine division and additional airpower on Taiwan to induce Chiang Kai-shek to abandon the islands. Eisenhower worried particularly about how U.S. military engagement over Quemoy and Matsu, especially with nuclear weapons, would affect both American and worldwide public opinion.[132]

The president also distinguished clearly between defending the islands per se, which he rejected, and defending against an attack that was preliminary to assault on Taiwan itself. (The Formosa Resolution also did not mention Quemoy and Matsu.) Dulles, applying a stark version of the Munich analogy, saw a linkage between the islands and Taiwan, and the president also leaned in this direction, but neither saw the connection as inevitable. On April 17 they discussed a draft paper that Eisenhower approved, envisioning a nationalist Chinese withdrawal from Quemoy and Matsu in exchange for U.S. "interdiction," a euphemism for blockade,

---

130. Eisenhower, *Mandate for Change*, pp. 477–78.

131. *Public Papers, Eisenhower, 1955*, p. 357 (emphasis added).

132. Eisenhower, *Mandate for Change*, pp. 480–81; Ambrose, *The President*, pp. 242–43. See also Leonard H. D. Gordon, "United States Opposition to Use of Force in the Taiwan Strait, 1954–1962," *Journal of American History*, vol. 72 (December 1985), pp. 637–60.

of PRC sea lanes until Beijing renounced its intention to take Taiwan by force. In order to signal the strength of U.S. commitment, the United States would station "(with public knowledge?) atomic capabilities" and additional conventional forces on Taiwan. The question mark, written in by the president on his copy of the draft, suggests that signaling to the mainland might not have been the sole motive.[133]

The question was not forced. At the Bandung Conference in late April, Chou En-Lai announced Chinese willingness to negotiate; in May he said the PRC was willing to liberate Taiwan "by peaceful means as far as this is possible."[134] Dulles, as in 1953, again touted the efficacy of brinkmanship:

Nobody . . . is able to prove mathematically that it was the policy of deterrence which brought the Korean war to an end and which kept the Chinese from sending their Red armies into Indochina, or that it has finally stopped them in Formosa. I think it is a pretty fair inference that it has.[135]

And those who denigrate the impact of the nuclear threat on Beijing cannot dismiss the possibility that it might have been implemented if the PRC had invaded.[136]

Eisenhower's stance reflected a combination of political resolve to prevent a PRC attack with military hesitation about absolute commitment to engage in nuclear combat. The tension in that combination reflects the tension between the logic of fearsome deterrence and common sense, but it was the realistic way to maximize the enemy's disincentives for war while reserving final choice in case deterrence nevertheless failed. One important reason that the president remained serene about the nuclear question is that he was among the least fearful of those in his administration that war would break out over the islands.[137] Eisenhower's confidence in

133. "Memorandum of a Conversation Between the President and the Secretary of State, Augusta, Georgia, April 17, 1955, 12:30 p.m.," in *FRUS, 1955–57*, vol. 2: *China*, pp. 494–95.

134. Rushkoff, "Eisenhower, Dulles and the Quemoy-Matsu Crisis," pp. 472–73, 476–79.

135. Shepley, "How Dulles Averted War," p. 77.

136. One analyst, for example, argues that the 1955 threat did not influence the Chinese, but notes Eisenhower's testimony that airfields and support targets had been picked for strikes if the Chinese pressed too hard. J. H. Kalicki, *The Pattern of Sino-American Crises: Political-Military Interactions in the 1950s* (Cambridge University Press, 1975), pp. 84, 149–51.

137. Eisenhower, *Mandate for Change*, pp. 477–79.

the face of other officials' anxiety was also to be manifested in the second Berlin crisis, discussed in the next chapter. And like Berlin, the contest in the Taiwan Straits was a fire that continued to smolder.

Suez, 1956

Soviet action in response to the Anglo-French-Israeli invasion of Egypt was the first case of Soviet nuclear saber-rattling in a crisis. It was also one of the few cases in which the tacit Soviet threat was to take the nuclear initiative, not, as in most other instances, to counter U.S. initiatives. The threat was veiled and directed not against the United States, but against Britain, with a nuclear force inferior to the Soviets', and nonnuclear France. The United States, however, took the initiative to become involved and countered the Soviet signal. The Soviet threat was ambiguous and consisted only of diplomatic statements, while the American counterthreat, also ambiguous, was more discreet, yet took the more tangible form of a small-scale military alert that included nuclear forces. In this sense the case became one of two opposing threats. The Soviet signal was not clearly discredited as a bluff, since the crisis was settled on terms acceptable to Moscow, but the implicit U.S. retaliatory threat reflected on its credibility.

Soviet Signals

On November 5, 1956, the Soviets issued several messages for London, Paris, Tel Aviv, Washington, and the United Nations Security Council, demanding a cease-fire in Egypt and withdrawal of foreign troops. Soviet Premier Nikolai Bulganin's note to French Premier Guy Mollet asked, "What would be the position of France if she were attacked by other states having at their disposal modern and terrible means of destruction?" To Eden he posed the same question, in one sense more cryptically and in another with greater force:

> In what position would Britain have found herself if she herself had been attacked by more powerful states possessing every kind of modern destructive weapon? And there are countries now which need not have sent a navy or air force to the coast of Britain but could have used other means, such as rocket technique. If rocket weapons had been used against Britain and France, they would probably have called this a barbarous action. Yet in what way does the inhuman attack made by

the armed forces of Britain and France on the nearly disarmed Egypt differ from this?[138]

Such rhetorical questions—especially the note to Eden that emphasized the analogy as a criticism of British intervention as much as it emphasized the Soviet capability—were scarcely direct threats of nuclear riposte on behalf of Egypt. Yet the messages were widely regarded as an ultimatum. Bulganin's note to Eden also said, "If this war is not stopped it carries the danger of turning into a third world war."[139] What was closer to an ultimatum was the Soviet initiative in the United Nations the following day to secure joint American-Soviet intervention in Egypt unless the Europeans stopped their attack within twelve hours. In this context the only explicit Soviet mention of nuclear weapons—in the note from Bulganin to Eisenhower—appears not as a threat to undertake nuclear action deliberately, but as a warning of the danger that conflict in Egypt could escalate out of control. The letter to Eisenhower referred to nuclear power only in a brief and obvious statement: "The Soviet Union and the United States are . . . the two great powers which possess . . . atomic and hydrogen weapons."[140]

American Reaction

Superpower interaction in the 1956 crisis bears some resemblance to events in another Middle East war seventeen years later. As Nixon did in 1973, Eisenhower quickly rebuffed the Soviet proposal for joint intervention, although he acted to bring pressure against his allies to halt their military action. Yet while the United States was opposing the military action of its allies, in what was the most divisive split in the history of the Western alliance, it also warned Moscow that nuclear attacks on Britain or France would draw U.S. retaliation. Although leaders in Washington regarded Bulganin's notes as bluster, they received word that the Europeans were more concerned. Eisenhower authorized his press secretary to state that if the Russians intervened or attacked U.S. allies, the United States would oppose them, and the American supreme commander in Europe,

138. Quoted in Hans Speier, "Soviet Atomic Blackmail and the North Atlantic Alliance," World Politics, vol. 9 (April 1957), pp. 318–19.
139. Quoted in Herman Finer, Dulles Over Suez: The Theory and Practice of His Diplomacy (Quadrangle Books, 1964), p. 418.
140. Ibid., p. 417.

General Alfred Gruenther, announced that if the Soviets attacked Britain or France, the USSR would be destroyed "as surely as night follows day."[141]

Eisenhower authorized alerts of the Sixth Fleet in the Mediterranean and the Atlantic Fleet. He ordered low-profile increases in military preparedness, putting units on alert and raising more ships and aircraft to ready status. He also suggested canceling some military leaves to signal Moscow "that we could not be taken by surprise."[142] These moves were aimed not just at the Middle East, however: the Soviet invasion of Hungary was under way at the same time. When intelligence confirmed the limits of Soviet military action, the president decided against any major mobilization. The only nuclear signal was a modified SAC alert to emphasize American intent to counter Soviet intervention in the Sinai. General LeMay limited the repositioning of forces to avoid giving the Soviets insights into axes of attack and general war plans, since there was no real probability of action. Yet all SAC crews were mustered, planes were loaded with weapons and fuel, and some units deployed to forward bases.[143]

As in the later case of October 1973, there are no persuasive grounds for assuming that the ambiguous nuclear elements in either superpower's signals had a meaningful impact on the outcome, because the military result on the ground—determined largely by U.S. pressure on its allies— was acceptable to both Moscow and Washington. A final cease-fire was arranged almost immediately, at midnight on November 6. Political and economic undermining of the British and French position was more obviously decisive than the Soviet threat, which some have interpreted as an attempt to divert attention from Hungary.[144] Over twenty years after the fact, Eden's public relations adviser described the Soviet nuclear threat as "twaddle."[145] Some recollections of discussions at the time, however,

141. J. M. Mackintosh, *Strategy and Tactics of Soviet Foreign Policy* (Oxford University Press, 1963), p. 188; personal communication from General Andrew Goodpaster, July 17, 1986; Gruenther quoted in Prados, *The Soviet Estimate*, p. 56.

142. Dwight D. Eisenhower, *The White House Years,* vol. 2: *Waging Peace* (Doubleday, 1965), p. 91; Charles J. V. Murphy, "Washington and the World," *Fortune* (January 1957), p. 83. Murphy's account says Eisenhower decided against cancellation of leaves.

143. Murphy, "Washington and the World," pp. 83, 210. See also John Steinbruner, "An Assessment of Nuclear Crises," in Franklyn Griffiths and John C. Polanyi, eds., *The Dangers of Nuclear War* (University of Toronto Press, 1979), p. 47n. Prados says that the alert included more than a thousand sorties by SAC bombers. *The Soviet Estimate*, p. 56.

144. Anthony Nutting, *No End of a Lesson: The Story of Suez* (London: Constable, 1967), pp. 143–44.

145. "Briton Divulges Steps to '56 Decision to Seize Suez," *New York Times,* November 25, 1979.

attribute more seriousness both to allied concern about the Soviet threat and to Eisenhower's reaction. Chester Cooper, a CIA representative in the U.S. embassy in London in 1956, writes:

> Some accounts well after the event imply that officials in London discounted the Soviet threat. But that is not the way I remember the reactions at the time. "Nuclear blackmail" rather than "diplomatic bluff" were the words I heard during the twenty-four hours following the announcement of Bulganin's message. . . .
>
> Political and military officials in London apparently felt sufficiently concerned about the Soviet warning to transmit their anxiety to the forces fighting in Egypt. Accompanying the order to cease fire at midnight, one commander remembers, was a warning that if they did not do so "there was a risk of Russian nuclear attacks on London and Paris. . . ." [French Foreign Minister Christian] Pineau apparently took Moscow's words at face value. "We have no defense against missiles," he told the Israelis. "I suggest that you do not belittle Bulganin's warning."

Cooper described his British counterparts as "ashen" after the Soviet threat, although heartened when he informed them of a U.S. Intelligence Board judgment that Moscow's ploy was a bluff.[146]

Eisenhower told a White House assistant at the time, "If those fellows start something, we may have to hit 'em—and, if necessary, with *everything* in the bucket." The president later claimed, "We just told [the Russians] that this would be . . . global war if they started it, that's all."[147]

The Soviet threat over Suez was ambiguous to begin with and inconclusive at the end. So it was again, though it was less noticed, a year later during the Syrian-Turkish crisis when Khrushchev offhandedly remarked in an October 7 interview with James Reston: "If war breaks out in the Middle East we are near Turkey and you are not. When the guns begin firing, the rockets can begin flying."[148] That sort of rhetoric was to be revived occasionally in the crises up to 1962—but not since.

---

146. Chester L. Cooper, *The Lion's Last Roar: Suez, 1956* (Harper and Row, 1978), pp. 197, 199, 200. Quotations from p. 197.

147. Quoted in Robert A. Divine, *Eisenhower and the Cold War* (Oxford University Press, 1981), p. 87.

148. Quoted in Francis Fukuyama, "Nuclear Shadowboxing: Soviet Intervention Threats in the Middle East," *Orbis,* vol. 25 (Fall 1981), p. 586.

Lebanon and the Taiwan Straits, 1958

China's renewal of pressure on Quemoy and Matsu in 1958 was generally seen as a more serious test than the first offshore islands crisis three years before. Some differences are notable. In the interim, the USSR had launched Sputnik and Khrushchev had begun his rhetorical adventures touting Soviet missile power. Thus emboldened, the Soviets became more involved in the diplomatic maneuvering of threats and counterthreats in support of their principal ally in Beijing. In addition, the threatened seizure of Quemoy and Matsu overlapped another crisis halfway around the world in Lebanon. U.S. decisionmaking in 1958, however, remained much the same as it had been in 1955. Both the elements of genuine planning for execution of a nuclear option and hesitancy about full commitment to that option were accentuated.

Lebanon

The Middle East crisis of summer 1958, beginning with a radical coup in Iraq and resulting in deployment of U.S. forces to Lebanon and British intervention in Jordan, is not generally recalled as a nuclear crisis in any significant sense. Indeed, the U.S. intervention turned out to be quite easy, and the nuclear element went unnoticed in the West. It is one of the few instances, however, in which there is any available report about the Soviet leadership's reaction to a U.S. nuclear gesture.

Just before U.S. troops landed in Lebanon a Pentagon official realized that their equipment included an Honest John rocket battery, whose introduction could prove politically explosive in the delicate situation. At the last minute it was arranged for the nuclear ordnance to be left aboard ship.[149] It is not clear that the president knew about or particularly wanted this change in deployment of what was then standard unit equipment; in his memoirs he notes the nuclear weaponry of the intervention force but does not mention that it was withdrawn upon deployment.[150] In any case, Eisenhower endorsed a nuclear signal that was of more potential significance to Moscow than tactical nuclear weapons on the ground in Lebanon would have been: he ordered SAC onto alert. Within hours more than

149. Edward Weintal and Charles Bartlett, *Facing the Brink: An Intimate Study of Crisis Diplomacy* (Scribner's, 1967), p. 4.
150. Eisenhower, *Waging Peace*, p. 286n.

1,100 aircraft were positioned for takeoff, and for several days the alert kept the show-of-force going.[151]

In recommending the alert, General Nathan F. Twining, by then the JCS chairman, noted that forward deployment of tankers to refuel the bombers would be impossible to conceal and warned that it might lead to misinterpretation of U.S. intentions. "But, far from objecting to the tanker aircraft deployment's becoming known," the president wrote subsequently, "I felt this knowledge would be desirable, as showing readiness and determination without implying any threat of aggression. The move was arranged." Eisenhower also directed Twining to "be prepared to employ, subject to my personal approval, *whatever* means might become necessary to prevent any unfriendly forces from moving into Kuwait. . . . these measures would probably bring us no closer to general war than we were already."[152] In professionals' usage general war meant nuclear war.

According to a confidant of Egypt's leader, the American resolve impressed Khrushchev. The Soviet leader told Nasser that "he thought the Americans had gone off their heads. 'Frankly,' [Khrushchev] said, 'we are not ready for a confrontation. We are not ready for World War III.' " When Nasser sought assurances, Khrushchev demurred and told him that he "would have to lean with the storm; there was no other way because Dulles could blow the whole world to pieces." The only gesture of support offered was an announcement of Soviet military maneuvers around Turkey's border. The Arabs were bitterly disappointed in the Russian faint-heartedness.[153]

The nuclear element in the U.S. response to the Middle East crisis was also noted in China. The People's Liberation Army newspaper mentioned on July 17 that "the United States openly threatened to carry out atomic warfare in Lebanon." The threat, however, did not daunt the Chinese, who at the time were also characterizing the United States as a "paper tiger." Convinced that nuclear weapons were not the determining factor in war, they also claimed powerful friends: "The socialist camp also possesses both atomic weapons and the ICBM, and is far ahead of the imperialistic nations in war potentialities."[154] Khrushchev would not

151. Hopkins, *Development of the Strategic Air Command,* p. 71.

152. Eisenhower, *Waging Peace,* pp. 276, 278 (emphasis in original).

153. Mohammed Hassanein Heikal, *The Cairo Documents* (Doubleday, 1973), pp. 133–34.

154. Quoted in Alice Langley Hsieh, *Communist China's Strategy in the Nuclear Era* (Prentice-Hall, 1962), p. 120.

remain as aloof from his allies in China as from his clients in the Middle East, but he would prove to disappoint the Chinese nonetheless.

Quemoy and Matsu: Decisions

When the second offshore islands crisis broke out on August 23, Eisenhower recalled the intent of the Formosa Resolution, which he interpreted as warranting U.S. combat commitment to the islands' defense only if a Chinese attack on them was linked to assault on Taiwan or the Pescadores. The logic of the domino theory, however, was making this danger increasingly real in the president's eyes. Loss of the islands would imperil not only Taiwan, but Japan, the Philippines, Thailand, and Vietnam. "This modern possibility that 'for want of a nail, a shoe was lost,' " wrote Eisenhower seven years later, "had led to reaffirmation of the conclusion that Quemoy and Matsu were essential to America's security."[155] Beijing, which had reasons of its own to view the offshore islands and Taiwan as a package, announced several days later, "The Chinese People's Liberation Army has determined to liberate Taiwan . . . as well as the offshore islands, and the landing on Quemoy is imminent."[156]

On August 25 the JCS advised the president that while political considerations might dictate *initial* retaliatory attacks on the PRC mainland with conventional weapons, "We will require atomic strikes . . . to effectively and quickly stop Chinese Communist aggression." Eisenhower approved a telegram to CINCPAC and the Taiwan Defense Command stipulating that initial operations would probably be only conventional but authorizing preparation "to use atomic weapons to extend deeper into Chinese Communist territory if necessary."[157]

Two days later the State Department's Far East Bureau suggested to Dulles that early use of one or two low-yield nuclear weapons against Fukien airfields might be necessary and that more extensive attacks might also be required—despite a special national intelligence estimate that

---

155. Eisenhower, *Waging Peace*, p. 294.

156. Anna Louise Strong, recognized as offering PRC views, wrote that taking Quemoy and Matsu alone "would isolate Taiwan and thus assist Dulles in his policy of building 'two Chinas,' " and might even induce United Nations intervention on Taiwan. See Hsieh, *Communist China's Strategy*, p. 128. The announcement of the invasion is quoted in John R. Thomas, "Soviet Behavior in the Quemoy Crisis of 1958," *Orbis*, vol. 6 (Spring 1962), p. 48.

157. Quoted in M. H. Halperin, *The 1958 Taiwan Straits Crisis: A Documented History (U)*, RM-4900-ISA (Santa Monica, Calif.: Rand Corporation, 1966; portions declassified 1975), pp. 109, 113.

predicted that wider strikes would draw Soviet nuclear retaliation against Taiwan, the Seventh Fleet, and possibly other U.S. assets in Asia.[158] At the end of August, as China blockaded the islands and the Chinese artillery barrages were matched with commitment of their airpower, Eisenhower said in a conference that he was considering countering an invasion attempt with tactical nuclear strikes on mainland airfields, but wanted to "reserve" the option, which might not be necessary and which could enrage world opinion. In a September 2 meeting high-level officials debated at length the conventional defensibility of Quemoy and the wisdom of relying on nuclear weapons, but the consensus was the same as it had been the previous week: nuclear use would "ultimately be necessary" if the islands were to be defended, although initial operations should be only conventional. When Dulles pressed the president on September 4 for more definite nuclear commitment—arguing that if established military doctrine did not override concerns about world opinion when the chips were down, "we must revise our defense setup"—Eisenhower was cautious, citing the possibility of Soviet nuclear retaliation against Taiwan. But, having noted that nuclear use was the essence of the issue, he reviewed with Dulles the views of the Joint Chiefs of Staff, giving special attention to the manner in which nuclear air bursts would be employed.[159]

Eisenhower's later account suggests less ambivalence on his part than other records of the time. He chose to reprint in his memoirs a memo from the September 4 meeting with Dulles that repeated the consensus of late August. To hedge against "popular revulsion against the U.S. in most of the world," the memo discussed using only small weapons and air bursts to minimize fallout and civilian casualties. But the memo concluded, "It is not certain, however, that the operation could be thus limited in scope or time, and the risk of a more extensive use of nuclear weapons, and even a risk of general war, *would have to be accepted.*"[160]

The practicability of "clean," limited nuclear strikes, however, was in question. Dulles reportedly received an Atomic Energy Commission casualty estimate similar to that of the CIA in the 1955 straits crisis: 8 million Chinese might die.[161] On November 7, well after the peak of the 1958

158. SNIE 100-9-58, in ibid., p. 184.
159. Halperin, *1958 Taiwan Straits Crisis*, pp. xi, 277–78; Ambrose, *The President*, pp. 482–83.
160. Eisenhower, *Waging Peace*, pp. 692–93 (emphasis added); see also p. 295.
161. Walter Pincus, "In '40s and '50s, Nuclear Arms Still Seen Usable," *Washington Post*, July 22, 1985.

tension, Dulles requested a military briefing on nuclear effects. Perhaps daunted by the high collateral damage estimated from attacks on airfields, the secretary asked about a more limited nuclear option against the Chinese artillery emplacements that were bombarding Quemoy. After much disagreement among the services and joint staff, the JCS told him a month later that air bursts could neutralize the artillery "with no significant radioactive fall-out implications in either the Amoy area or on Quemoy/ Taiwan."[162] Dulles's close attention to the effects of implementing the nuclear option, and his follow-up request for other variations, suggests that it was no diplomatic bluff as far as the secretary was concerned.

Ambivalence among top civil authorities magnified misapprehensions within the military bureaucracy and chain of command. Those with operational responsibility for anticipated action worried that the administration's tentativeness about use of nuclear ordnance was greater than it really was. The year before, Admiral Stump had complained to Chief of Naval Operations Arleigh Burke about the need "to stop pussy footing about use of atomic weapons. . . . In personal conversations with 2 Presidents, Diem and Chaing [sic], they have insisted that we must use our atomic weapons capability, but they both have expressed disturbing doubts about our willingness to do so," and went on, "Our weak-kneed approach to atomic play in SEATO exercises is a prime example."[163]

Stump's irritation, ironically, was displayed only months after Beijing's spokesmen had reacted with alarm to emplacement of American Matador missiles on Taiwan.[164] This irritation was compounded with anxiety in the 1958 crisis because of confusion in the communications between Washington and the field. The president's August 25 instructions for initial conventional operations were misinterpreted by Pacific Air Force headquarters as an indication that Washington envisioned an attempt at fully nonnuclear defense, a contradiction of the standard assumptions under which the New Look had been translated into naval and air force contingency planning. When the new commander in the Pacific, Admiral Harry Felt, received Eisenhower's instructions, he had to reorient himself and direct preparation of a "special nonnuclear Annex H to his Ops Plan 25–58."[165] The air force commander in the Pacific, General Lawrence

162. Quoted in Halperin, *1958 Taiwan Straits Crisis*, p. 544.
163. CINCPAC cable to CNO, Message No. 9480, August 28, 1957; declassified 1978 (Carrollton Press collection).
164. See the PRC statement quoted in Kalicki, *Pattern of Sino-American Crises*, p. 180.
165. Jacob Van Staaveren, "Air Operations in the Taiwan Crisis of 1958" (U.S. Air Force Historical Division Liaison Office, November 1962), p. 28.

Kuter, was so bitter that he argued for military noninvolvement in the conflict unless nuclear weapons were to be available. The hope in Washington was that brief conventional defense would prompt China to reverse course short of successful invasion; otherwise, the president knew, the conventional defense would provide only a preliminary pause before, and a public relations excuse for, subsequent escalation.[166] The military's misunderstanding of Eisenhower's intent was so thorough that one official service history says that Eisenhower and the JCS forbade planning for nuclear strikes.[167]

Quemoy and Matsu: Actions

Public discussion of nuclear options in 1958 was less direct than it had been in the 1954–55 case. At an August 27 news conference the president was asked about the discretion allowed to local commanders for use of nuclear weapons, and he reaffirmed that his personal approval was required. In response to a follow-up question about an exception in the case of a threat to a command he responded: "It has been a long time since I have gone through all of these directives. . . . there is one exception, but I don't believe it mentions atomic weapons . . . but I would have to make certain."[168] In fact, there was no exception for nuclear weapons, but Eisenhower's offhand remark does not appear to have been intended as a threat.[169]

In August and September the Strategic Air Command raised the strength of forces on alert on Guam and made several wings of bombers ready for possible action in the Pacific, but the alerts were soon wound down.[170] Speaking to the press on background on September 17, Secretary Dulles estimated that the military balance favored the United States over the Soviet Union, but that relative U.S. strength would erode in the future. He attributed this situation to Moscow's decision to skip a competition in long-range bombers and move to a missile force that would take time to develop. Ten days later the secretary of the air force, backed by State

166. Halperin, *1958 Taiwan Straits Crisis,* pp. 127, 139, 144, 292–93, 378–79. In some places in the text where Halperin elaborates these points there are security deletions, but the published passages affirm this interpretation.

167. Van Staaveren, "Air Operations in the Taiwan Crisis," pp. 28–29.

168. *Public Papers of the Presidents of the United States: Dwight D. Eisenhower, 1958* (GPO, 1959), p. 642.

169. Halperin, *1958 Taiwan Straits Crisis,* p. 188 and 188n.

170. Hopkins, *Development of the Strategic Air Command,* p. 72.

Department approval, stated that the United States was ready to use nuclear weapons in defense of Quemoy.[171]

By the end of September the American-designed tactics for breaking the Chinese blockade were working, the Nationalist garrison was being effectively resupplied, the Nationalist air force was giving the PRC's a licking, and the crisis seemed to be easing. Even so, the United States transferred to Quemoy 8-inch howitzers capable of firing nuclear rounds. Although no nuclear ordnance was given to the Nationalist artillerymen, the PRC reacted by stating that "U.S. imperialism has now confronted mankind with the danger of guided missile and nuclear warfare."[172]

As in previous cases, there is no clear evidence of whether U.S. nuclear threats influenced Beijing. That the crisis ended with a return to the status quo ante, a failure for the PRC, could be seen as indicating the signal's efficacy. On the other hand, previous public Chinese statements had sometimes pooh-poohed the nuclear threat. Beijing had already taken notice of the U.S. emplacement of Matador missiles on Taiwan, their test-firing in May 1958, and U.S. General Doyle's statement that those missiles would be used to counter a communist attack in the vicinity. Indeed, some interpret the initiation of the crisis as a defensive riposte to ominous U.S. actions elsewhere in Asia and in Lebanon.[173]

Barely a week before Beijing triggered the crisis, a prominent article in a PRC publication referred to Chairman Mao's declaration that "the atomic bomb is a paper tiger" and to the principle that American "atomic blackmail has never daunted the revolutionary people." At the same time, however, the article emphasized the import of *Soviet* nuclear power as a deterrent to imperialist attack.[174] Beijing's ultimate disappointment in the Soviet approach to its fraternal alliance responsibilities in the course of the crisis provides tentative support for the efficacy of U.S. nuclear signals.

Quemoy and Matsu: Soviet Involvement

The stepped-up bombardment of Quemoy and Matsu began three weeks after a secret meeting between Mao and Khrushchev. The day after the new shelling started, Khrushchev announced that he saw no interna-

171. Halperin, *1958 Taiwan Straits Crisis*, p. 16; Thomas, "Soviet Behavior in the Quemoy Crisis," pp. 55–56.

172. Tang Tsou, *The Embroilment Over Quemoy: Mao, Chiang and Dulles* (Institute of International Studies, University of Utah Press, 1959), p. 31; PRC statement quoted in Kalicki, *Pattern of Sino-American Crises*, p. 192.

173. Gurtov and Hwang, *China Under Threat*, p. 82.

174. Kalicki, *Pattern of Sino-American Crises*, pp. 186–87, 239n.

tional developments that threatened war. The first warnings to Washington as the crisis heated up did not come from top leaders or even officially in the name of the Soviet government. But on August 31, *Pravda* warned that the USSR would supply China "the necessary moral and material aid," that "any threat against the Chinese Communist regime would be interpreted in Moscow as a threat against the Soviet Union," and that "any aggression by the United States in the Far East" would lead to war elsewhere. On September 5 *Pravda* again warned that retaliation against U.S. action might not be limited to the Taiwan area.[175] The most common interpretation is that Moscow avoided any real risk and refrained from stronger or more direct threats in support of Beijing until after the crisis had passed the danger point. Certainly the Chinese felt that way at the time, although American leaders were not sure that the crisis had passed when the Soviet response became more aggressive.

On September 7 the Chinese offered to resume negotiations—the move often cited as the turning point toward easing of the crisis. The blockade continued, however, and U.S. analysts believed it was still intended to render the islands untenable. Over a week later U.S. intelligence was still pessimistic. A special national intelligence estimate suggested that the Chinese would not attempt a landing, but largely because they thought that Quemoy would collapse without invasion, from the effects of blockade. As Morton Halperin notes, "The Communists were reported to be willing to take action involving considerable risk of major conflict with the United States, and it was the unanimous view of the United States Intelligence Board that the Communists would probably fire on American ships going all the way in to Quemoy." And the estimate rejected the possibility that Beijing would accept "any negotiated settlement restoring the *status quo ante*."[176] That the crisis had eased on September 7 may not have been as clear to U.S. policymakers as some accounts based on open sources imply it should have been. Those same sources, however, use the salience of that date to explain the increase in boldness of Soviet signals, on the assumption that Moscow had convinced Beijing not to attempt an invasion and Khrushchev was willing to sound toughest when he was least worried that escalation might occur.

On September 7 Khrushchev sent a letter to Eisenhower proclaiming Soviet extended deterrence—"an attack on the People's Republic of China

175. Thomas, "Soviet Behavior in the Quemoy Crisis," p. 49; Tsou, *Embroilment Over Quemoy*, pp. 12–13, quotation on p. 13.
176. Halperin, *1958 Taiwan Straits Crisis*, pp. 423–24.

. . . is an attack on the Soviet Union"—and denigrating the reinforcement of U.S. naval power in the Pacific: "In the age of nuclear and rocket weapons . . . these once formidable warships are fit, in fact, for nothing but courtesy visits and gun salutes, and can serve as targets for the right types of rockets."[177] It is possible to infer caution in the Khrushchev letter from nuances of omission, but the omissions seem minor in light of the passages quoted above.[178] A week later the pessimistic intelligence estimate was issued. While it suggested that the Soviets might not intervene if the United States used tactical nuclear weapons in the Taiwan area, it warned that the more extensive nuclear operations against China that policymakers had decided might be necessary would probably provoke Soviet attacks on U.S. forces and bases.[179] It is not surprising, therefore, that shortly thereafter Dulles gave his background press briefing on U.S. nuclear superiority.

On September 19 another Khrushchev letter, a portion of which is an epigraph to this chapter, reminded Eisenhower to consider Soviet retaliatory power when contemplating a nuclear strike against China.[180] The CIA's view of likely Soviet action was slightly less pessimistic than that of the special estimate issued several days earlier, and Chief of Naval Operations Burke was optimistic about the Soviet question as well as about chances for neutralizing the blockade. But the confrontation was not so close to favorable settlement by the nineteenth that the top leaders could blithely dismiss the threat from Khrushchev—the most explicit yet—as empty bluster. That day Dulles assessed the situation as grave and warned that the Chinese might still be preparing an attack on the islands. Despite Burke's optimism, top U.S. officials had not yet concluded that resupply of Quemoy through the blockade could be accomplished without attacking Chinese batteries with nuclear weapons.[181]

Reassurance might have been drawn from the Soviets' failure to alert forces or undertake maneuvers in the region to counter the U.S. reinforce-

177. Quoted in Tsou, *Embroilment Over Quemoy*, p. 13.
178. Thomas ("Soviet Behavior in the Quemoy Crisis," pp. 52–54) notes that Khrushchev (1) referred to the PRC as an "ally" but did not cite the Sino-Soviet pact itself, which obliged automatic military support; and (2) denounced U.S. nuclear blackmail but did not pledge nuclear retaliation on China's behalf, instead stating confidence in China's readiness to resist.
179. Halperin, *1958 Taiwan Straits Crisis*, pp. 424–25.
180. Letter to President Eisenhower, September 19, 1958, quoted in Jonathan Trumbull Howe, *Multicrises: Sea Power and Global Politics in the Missile Age* (MIT Press, 1971), p. 249.
181. Halperin, *1958 Taiwan Straits Crisis*, pp. 429–30, 432.

ment of the Seventh Fleet, although on September 21 they did announce month-long maneuvers "with different types of modern weapons" by the Northern Fleet based in Murmansk.[182]

During the crisis the Soviets often warned about probable U.S. use of tactical nuclear weapons, and they alluded to the danger of world war. It is generally assumed today that Moscow was trying not only to warn Washington but also to induce Beijing to back off.[183] Some in Washington may have appreciated the Soviet intent at some stage—though Eisenhower believed the Soviets had purposefully instigated the crisis[184]—but not so clearly that decisionmakers were ready to dismiss the Soviet counterthreats, even after the peak of the crisis. During the crisis nuclear threats were issued by both sides, by the United States against China and by the Soviets against the United States. Only Beijing's willingness to retreat relieved Washington and Moscow of having to face the question of whether either was bluffing. To what extent that willingness was due to lack of confidence in Moscow's backing is unknown. Later, at least, the Chinese were to debunk the force of Soviet extended deterrence. According to an official statement in 1963, the Soviets were

> brazen in asserting that Soviet nuclear weapons played the decisive role in defeating the Anglo-French war of aggression against Egypt in 1956 and frustrating the plot of the U.S. armed threat against Syria in 1957 and the U.S.-British plot to send troops for intervention in Iraq in 1958. . . . It is especially ridiculous that the Soviet statement also gives all the credit to Soviet nuclear weapons for the Chinese people's victory in smashing the armed provocations of U.S. imperialism in the Taiwan Straits in 1958. . . . The Soviet leaders expressed their support for China on September 7 and 19 respectively. Although at that time the situation in the Taiwan Straits was tense, there was no possibility that a nuclear war would break out and no need for the Soviet Union to support China with its nuclear weapons. It was only when they were clear that this was the situation that the Soviet leaders expressed their support for China.[185]

182. Howe, *Multicrises*, p. 223; Thomas, "Soviet Behavior in the Quemoy Crisis," p. 58.

183. Howe, *Multicrises*, pp. 222–23.

184. Eisenhower, *Waging Peace*, p. 293.

185. "Statement by the Spokesman of the Chinese Government—A Comment on the Soviet Government's Statement of August 21," *Peking Review*, no. 36 (September 1963), p. 13.

Eisenhower's Games

When the intensified shelling of Quemoy and Matsu touched off the crisis in August, it was evident that the PRC had amassed neither landing craft nor troops sufficient for an invasion.[186] As an old army general, Eisenhower could know that as long as such concentration had not occurred, no final decision on nuclear combat was imminent. This made it easy for him to reject persistent U.S. military requests that he delegate authority to mount air operations in the event of a Chinese landing on Quemoy.[187]

Eisenhower was balancing several partially conflicting aims: demonstrating maximum resolve in the eyes of the communist capitals; reassuring friendly constituencies—domestic and allied—fearful that the United States might be recklessly stumbling into conflagration over a trivial issue; restraining military commanders anxious to ensure readiness by moving forces and plans closer to hair-trigger status; and limiting confidence of the Nationalist Chinese in the extent of American commitment to the offshore islands, to prevent Chiang Kai-shek from leveraging the United States into providing a blank check. As a result the president played several diplomatic games.

In addition to his ambiguous statements to reporters, Eisenhower told British Foreign Secretary Selwyn Lloyd on September 21 that he opposed using even tactical nuclear weapons in a limited operation[188] —despite the formal decision weeks earlier that a determined Chinese attack would require such strikes. (The statement to Lloyd was not quite duplicitous if Eisenhower was referring to the anticipated conventional "pause" phase of a defense of the islands.) The president also ordered that part of his August 25 instructions to Felt and the Taiwan Defense Command be withheld from Chiang, who thus was unaware of the readiness of a SAC B-47 squadron on Guam for nuclear missions against the mainland. At the same time Eisenhower withheld approval for a public statement of the unconditional U.S. commitment to defend the offshore islands, by use of nuclear weapons if necessary.[189]

In so often speaking out of both sides of his mouth, Eisenhower not only kept his options open but provided grounds for revisionist scholars

186. Tsou, *Embroilment Over Quemoy*, p. 10.
187. Eisenhower, *Waging Peace*, p. 299n.
188. Harold Macmillan, cited in Hoopes, *Devil and John Foster Dulles*, p. 452.
189. Halperin, *1958 Taiwan Straits Crisis*, pp. 114–15.

to discount the genuineness of nuclear threats. Recent liberal apologists for Eisenhower often claim that his statements of determination to use nuclear force were bravado and that his occasional expressions of horror about the prospect show his real reluctance. That view is hard to prove. There is no clear pattern according to the timing or the forum in which the president evinced determination or reluctance. Both attitudes show up in contemporary written records and informal conversations and in later memoirs or interviews. If Eisenhower's determination was purely an act to impress hawkish observers with his steadfastness, his reluctance could also have been an act to impress doves with his humanity. Flexibility and tacking of this sort may show that Eisenhower had not made up his mind or that he did not want to tip his hand irrevocably, but his hedging offers no more proof of bluffing than of seriousness.

Some sympathetic revisionist historians portray Eisenhower as a shrewd closet dove, who rattled his nuclear saber to keep hawks in check or to bluff his way through East-West squalls. But that interpretation seems colored by the policy disasters of subsequent administrations and also seems to confuse which of his contradictory stances were essential and which were peripheral. The revisionist interpretation is especially hard to square with Eisenhower's overall approach to the role of commander in chief. He *spoke* out of both sides of his mouth, but his *actions* to reorient U.S. war-making options were more consistent.[190] His New Look policy involved not only a change of emphasis in declared policy on nuclear weapons, but a significant institutional shift reducing restraints on nuclear forces. Unlike Truman, who left weapons under Atomic Energy Commission custody, Eisenhower transferred them to military control and oversaw their dispersion to units abroad. That decentralization involved relaxation of command and control safeguards that were not significantly tightened until after 1960. As a career military officer the president was not oblivious to the implications. While he carefully reserved formal release authority to himself, it is dubious that he would have mandated such sweeping shifts in operational posture if he had not intended that action in contingencies

190. See Robert W. Kagan's critique of the revisionist studies: "Why Like Ike?" *National Interest,* no. 4 (Summer 1986), pp. 88–94. For example, "[Ambrose's] overflowing praise for Eisenhower's quite unremarkable efforts to 'curb the arms race' is directed entirely at a modern audience. . . . Eisenhower did much talking and philosophizing about putting an end to the arms race, but his actions in office hardly fit his rhetoric, public or private . . . . for all the nasty things one might say about him, [Eisenhower] could never be accused of genuinely trying to reduce the nuclear arsenal upon which his entire defense strategy rested" (pp. 91–92).

reflect doctrinal rhetoric.[191] Moreover, the records of deliberation over Korea and Indochina make clear that Eisenhower's interest in nuclear options went beyond deterrence or signaling to militarily effective use.

In deliberations in which plans for nuclear initiatives seemed tentative because of worries about allied reactions, the president appeared concerned more with managing those reactions than with the allies' actual vulnerability. In internal discussions in which Eisenhower had less reason to dissemble than he did in public, he did not waver from the intention of nuclear first use in event of major war. As late as October 6, 1960, he responded to a National Security Council briefing on limited war by saying that he considered the concept unrealistic. The United States was unhappily wedded to reliance on nuclear weapons, and in the event of war the only sensible course would be to use them from the outset; a separation of nuclear and conventional operations would be impractical. If the Soviets were directly involved, the president said, the United States would have to strike the USSR with full force.[192]

One reason for Eisenhower's commitment to risk-maximizing reliance on nuclear force was that he saw little danger that war would occur and force the issue. Perhaps surprisingly, given that he was a professional military officer, he evinced little tendency toward "worst case" planning. On March 26, 1955, at the height of the first offshore islands crisis, he wrote in his diary,

> Lately there has been a very definite feeling among the members of the Cabinet, often openly expressed, that within a month we will actually be fighting in the Formosa Strait. It is, of course, entirely possible. . . . Nevertheless, I believe hostilities are not so imminent as is indicated by the forebodings of a number of my associates. . . . I have so often been through these periods of strain that I have become

191. In 1957 Eisenhower had apparently loosened provisions for release under emergency conditions. See Rosenberg, "Origins of Overkill," pp. 48–49; see also chap. 4, below. These exceptions, however, were almost certainly related to circumstances of Soviet attack. At the end of 1953 the president had "approved an interpretation of paragraph 39-b [in NSC 162/2] 'which made it clear that the paragraph does not constitute a decision in advance that atomic weapons will in fact be used in the event of any hostilities,' " and he reaffirmed this during the first offshore island conflict. "Memorandum for the Record, by the President's Special Assistant (Cutler)," March 11, 1955, in FRUS, 1955–57, vol. 2: China, pp. 355–56.

192. George B. Kistiakowsky, A Scientist at the White House: The Private Diary of President Eisenhower's Special Assistant for Science and Technology (Harvard University Press, 1976), p. 400.

accustomed to the fact that most of the calamities that we anticipate really never occur.[193]

At the same time, as the next chapter will underline, Eisenhower always derided the idea of limited war with the Soviet Union. Peacetime theorizing was one thing; real war was another. His disbelief that war could be limited reinforced his feeling that war was improbable, even when tension flared. Both views are implicit in the quotation from Eisenhower's January 12, 1955, press conference during the first Taiwan Straits crisis that prefaces this book. The combination also suggests why it would be a mistake to assume that Eisenhower's tendency to raise nuclear risks in crises was a bluff.

Eisenhower is the pivotal figure in this study. Whether his equivocations in use of nuclear signals were masterly or merely prudent, he moved well beyond Truman's abstemious approach to the role of nuclear weapons and established the nuclear threat as a standard tactic in confrontations. Although his successors were less comfortable with the principle of relying on nuclear force, chapter three will show that they did not reverse the pattern in practice as much as they honored it.

Soviet-Chinese Border Clashes, 1969

In March 1969 Soviet and Chinese troops entered a series of skirmishes over disputed territory on the Ussuri River and initiated history's only recorded incident of conventional combat between nuclear-armed nations.[194] Over subsequent months in 1969 Moscow issued a number of nuclear threats through unofficial sources.

In one sense, the border clashes were a reverse of the Taiwan Straits crises, with Moscow pressuring Beijing rather than supporting it. The similarities are limited, however. In the earlier instances China had no nuclear weapons—though in 1969 Chinese missiles could still not even reach many important targets in Siberia—and in 1969 the PRC had no support from any superpower. Soviet first-use threats against the Chinese in 1969 may have been more effective in the short term than second-strike retaliatory threats on their behalf had been a decade earlier. In both cases,

193. Robert H. Ferrell, ed., *The Eisenhower Diaries* (W. W. Norton, 1981), p. 296.
194. Periodic downings of American reconnaissance planes by the Soviets in the first fifteen years of the cold war hardly count as conventional engagements.

however, the long-term results appear counterproductive to Soviet interests. The first case helped to estrange the communist allies; in the second case China did not get any concessions, and the territorial status quo was preserved, but events may have pushed Beijing toward détente with Washington.

The only source available on internal Soviet deliberations in this case is the memoir of the defector Arkady Shevchenko, which may be considered suspect because of the unusual number of high-level discussions to which he claims to have been privy throughout his career. By Shevchenko's account the initial Chinese attack on Damansky Island evoked near hysteria in the Soviet Politburo. Defense Minister Andrei Grechko allegedly favored a final solution to the Chinese threat—a multimegaton attack. General Nikolai Ogarkov was more moderate. He considered a "surgical" strike on nuclear facilities but determined that it was too risky. The Politburo decided "to put out feelers through various channels" to test whether American hostility to China would prevent Washington from interfering with Soviet action.[195]

In mid-March a Chinese language broadcast by the Soviets' Radio Peace and Progress warned, "The whole world knows that the main striking force of the Soviet Armed Forces is its rocket units." The broadcast stressed that in a missile engagement the Chinese "would certainly end up in utter defeat."[196] Several months later the Soviets noted that the deputy head of the Strategic Rocket Forces had become the commander of the Far East Military District. On August 14 *Pravda* reported civil defense preparations in Kazakhstan, and at the end of the month an editorial warned that a Sino-Soviet war would bring into play "lethal armaments and modern means of delivery."[197]

A Soviet diplomat lunching with William Stearman of the State Department startled the American by asking how the United States would react to a Soviet strike against Chinese nuclear assets. The question provoked Kissinger to call a meeting of the Washington Special Action Group to begin preparing contingency plans for a Sino-Soviet war. The most active Soviet signal detected, whether intended or not, was a stand-down of the

195. Arkady N. Shevchenko, *Breaking With Moscow* (Alfred A. Knopf, 1985), pp. 164–66.
196. Quoted in Harry Gelman, *The Soviet Far East Buildup and Soviet Risk-Taking Against China*, R-2943-AF (Santa Monica, Calif.: Rand Corporation, 1982), p. 37n.
197. Ibid., pp. 37–38n; Henry Kissinger, *White House Years* (Little, Brown, 1979), p. 183. The editorial also noted, somewhat curiously given the nascent détente with Europe and the United States, that Soviet weapons in such an event "would not spare a single continent." Quoted in Gelman, *Soviet Far East Buildup*, p. 37n.

Soviet Far East Air Force, which was technically consistent with preparations to coordinate readiness for an attack. The stand-down lasted from
late August through September. In response, Director of Central Intelligence Richard Helms gave a background press briefing in which he
mentioned Soviet communications to European communists about a
possible strike against the Chinese nuclear facilities. The briefing was
disclosed by the *Washington Star,* whose correspondent had not been
invited. On September 10 a Soviet diplomat at the United Nations
mentioned to an American that military action might become inevitable if
the Chinese did not desist.[198]

In mid-September the Soviet journalist Victor Louis, universally recognized as a spokesman for policy, wrote in a London newspaper about
discussions of the possibility of war, including a Soviet plan for a strike
against China's Lop Nor nuclear testing site. The article, according to
Harry Gelman, also "cited 'well informed sources in Moscow' as asserting
that 'Russian nuclear installations stand aimed at the Chinese nuclear
facilities,' that 'the Soviet Union prefers using rockets to manpower' in
responding to border clashes, [and] that the USSR 'has a variety of rockets
to choose from.' "[199] According to Shevchenko, however, Moscow dropped
consideration of an attack when feelers produced a negative assessment.
He claims that Anatoly Dobrynin, ambassador in Washington, reported
"that the United States would not be passive regarding such a blow at
China."[200] But interest may also have cooled because the Chinese did not
press their initiative.

The PRC had reacted with numerous charges, beginning in May, of
Soviet nuclear blackmail. Though the rhetoric did not let up, the Chinese
appeared to back down on October 7 when they denied that they were
demanding return of territories seized by Russia in the previous century
and agreed to reopen border negotiations that they had broken off five
years earlier. The only Soviet compromise was to accept talks at a higher
bureaucratic level than they had wanted. In the meantime, however,
Washington had taken initial steps in the diplomatic dance that eventually
led to Sino-American rapprochement.[201]

198. Kissinger, *White House Years,* pp. 183–84, 1479n.
199. Ibid., p. 185; quotation from Gelman, *Soviet Far East Buildup,* p. 40.
200. Shevchenko, *Breaking With Moscow,* p. 166.
201. Gelman, *Soviet Far East Buildup,* p. 43; Raymond Garthoff, *Détente and
Confrontation: American-Soviet Relations from Nixon to Reagan* (Brookings, 1985), pp.
202, 211; Kissinger, *White House Years,* pp. 186, 188–89. See also Michael I. Handel,
The Diplomacy of Surprise: Hitler, Nixon, Sadat (Harvard University Center for International Affairs, 1981), chap. 4.

CHAPTER THREE

Higher-Risk Cases

We are certainly not going to fight a ground war in Europe. What good would it do to send a few more thousands or indeed even a few divisions of troops to Europe? ... with 175 Soviet divisions in that neighborhood—why in the world would we dream of fighting a ground war?   Dwight D. Eisenhower, March 11, 1959

It must not be forgotten that now the United States is not so inaccessibly distant from the Soviet Union as in the past. ... Soviet artillerymen, in case of need, can with their missile fire support the Cuban people if the aggressive forces of the Pentagon dare begin intervention against Cuba.   Nikita S. Khrushchev, July 10, 1960

ATTEMPTS at tacit nuclear blackmail were numerous in the first dozen years after World War II, but those in the brief span of 1958–62 were more serious. The inherent risks in the tactic were heightened by differences in the circumstances. In the cases of Berlin and Cuba, especially, the conflicts were direct confrontations, involved the core geographic security zones of the superpowers, and occurred after the Soviet Union had significantly increased its nuclear capability. The political costs of retreat for either side were higher than they had been in Asia, while the military costs of escalation for the United States were more daunting. Put clearly at issue was the underlying competition of credibility between the two types of nuclear deterrence—basic and extended. Where one side would use the threat of second-strike retaliation and mutual vulnerability to shield its attempt at conventional military coercion, the other would have to use the threat of nuclear first use in its attempt to turn back the conventional challenge. Over Berlin, the Soviet Union was in the former position and the United States in the latter. Over Cuba, the tables were turned. And to a degree that few casual observers appreciate, the Cuban crisis was an extension of the conflict in Berlin.

Over Berlin, the contrasts and similarities between the Eisenhower and Kennedy approaches to reliance on nuclear force were equally striking. In principle policy changed significantly, but in practice it did not. Kennedy's team considered Eisenhower's relaxed attitude toward Soviet pressure

82

complacent and his risk-maximizing brand of military strategy dangerous, so the new administration began to move formal doctrine from massive retaliation to flexible response. In practice, Kennedy's reliance on a massive nuclear threat turned out to be almost as great as Eisenhower's.

The Middle East War of 1973 and the Persian Gulf crisis of 1980 were perhaps less central than the crises of the early 1960s, with the nuclear element less of a factor in the unfolding of events. But these last two instances are significant because they occurred in the context not only of appreciable Soviet retaliatory capability, but of generally acknowledged parity of nuclear striking power.

The Berlin Deadline Crisis, 1958–59

At the end of 1953, Eisenhower's first year in office, five years after the first Berlin crisis and five years before the second, the National Security Council applied the New Look to Berlin contingency planning: "If all measures short of the use of force fail to regain access to Berlin, the Western powers should use limited military force to attempt to reopen access to Berlin. If determined Soviet opposition should develop, the Western powers should not undertake to commit additional forces to meet such opposition in an effort to hold Berlin, but would have to resort to general war."[1] Despite changes in the strategic balance over the rest of the decade Eisenhower was to reaffirm that formulation virtually wholesale when the contingency loomed again. During the 1948 blockade, when the United States had a monopoly on nuclear power, Truman had agonized over exploiting even the shadow of nuclear blackmail toward Moscow. A decade later, in the face of Soviet nuclear capability, Eisenhower agonized less and relied more on the U.S. nuclear threat.

Background

Eisenhower remained wedded to the New Look reliance on nuclear force even as his administration came to accept "sufficiency" as a standard for U.S. nuclear striking power, rather than a decisive "superiority" that

1. NSC 173, Report to the National Security Council by the NSC Planning Board, "United States Policy and Courses of Action to Counter Possible Soviet or Satellite Action Against Berlin," December 1, 1953, pp. 12–13, in Dwight D. Eisenhower Library (DDEL)/ White House Office Files (WHO), Office of the Special Assistant for National Security Affairs, NSC Series, Policy Papers Subseries, Box 8.

might prevent massive damage to the American homeland. Although the navy and even Secretary of State John Foster Dulles had joined the army in promoting improved limited war options, the president refused to revise policy when it came to the defense of western Europe.[2]

The Soviets, meanwhile, were themselves maneuvering amidst changes in the strategic equation. In 1955 the Federal Republic of Germany had been integrated in NATO despite Soviet efforts to head off West German rearmament. Within two years Moscow faced not only the addition of a German army to the Western defense force, but the prospect of conditional German access to tactical nuclear weapons. "Dual key" arrangements gave U.S. commanders nominal control over warheads, although in practice such American control was for some time rather tenuous.[3] In April 1957, as part of the sparring over such issues, a note from Khrushchev to the government in Bonn "threatened to turn Germany into a nuclear grave-yard."[4] Because of these concerns, some have argued that preventing German access to nuclear weapons was a motive behind Soviet initiation of the second Berlin crisis. That issue was an important part of the background, but my study focuses on the actual demands presented for territorial and political adjustment.

In late 1958, Moscow set off the crisis by announcing its intention, within six months, to conclude a peace treaty with the German Democratic Republic that would effectively revoke the rights of World War II occupiers in Berlin. The Soviet note to Washington on November 27 also warned, "Methods of blackmail and reckless threats of force will be least of all appropriate in solving such a problem as the Berlin question . . . but can only bring the situation to the danger point. But only madmen can go to the length of unleashing another world war over the preservation of privileges of occupiers in West Berlin."[5]

2. David Alan Rosenberg, "The Origins of Overkill: Nuclear Weapons and American Strategy, 1945–1960," *International Security,* vol. 7 (Spring 1983), p. 54.

3. U.S. congressmen inspecting units in Europe in 1960 "found fighter aircraft loaded with nuclear bombs sitting on the edge of runways with German pilots inside the cockpits and starter plugs inserted. The embodiment of control was an American officer somewhere in the vicinity with a revolver. The enraged committee precipitated the installation of radio locks called permissive action links." John D. Steinbruner, *The Cybernetic Theory of Decision: New Dimensions of Political Analysis* (Princeton University Press, 1974), p. 182.

4. Karl F. Spielmann, *The Political Utility of Strategic Superiority: A Preliminary Investigation Into the Soviet View,* IDA Paper P-1349 (Institute for Defense Analyses, May 1979), p. 62. Rhetoric of this sort, disjoined from a specific crisis, is not considered a case of threat in this study, just as peacetime American declarations about first-use doctrine are not.

5. "Note by the Government of the Union of Soviet Socialist Republics to the

The Western powers were not absolutely rigid in their attitude toward possible arrangements in Berlin, much to West German Chancellor Konrad Adenauer's alarm. The day before the Soviet note even Dulles suggested the possibility of some compromise.[6] On the essential issue of West Berlin's independence from East Germany, however, Washington was to be unyielding. Eisenhower's task was to convince Khrushchev that he was dealing with a leader ultimately willing to undertake what the Soviet note had said "only madmen" could contemplate.

Decisions

On December 11 Tass announced that it would view "any attempt to force a way into Berlin" as an attack on East Germany that would mobilize the Warsaw Pact and raise the possibility of nuclear war.[7] On the same day Eisenhower met with Vice President Richard Nixon and a dozen others. In his memoirs he recalled saying: "In this gamble we are not going to be betting white chips, building up the pot gradually and fearfully. Khrushchev should know that when we decide to act, our whole stack will be in the pot." The role of nuclear blue chips was implicit in a late January meeting in which conventional force preparations were discussed and in consultations and public statements in the first part of March. At the January meeting a debate ensued between Dulles and the Joint Chiefs of Staff about the scale of military action that would be necessary when and if the East Germans blocked a ground convoy to Berlin. The chiefs wanted to move with a full division, Dulles with less. Eisenhower took Dulles's side and directed that a smaller force be used, but not because of unwillingness to rely on escalation. His reasoning was that a division was bigger than needed for a probe but too small to be good for anything more than a show of force.[8]

The president constantly and explicitly denied any hope of restricting a war in Europe to conventional combat. He used muddled terms in public but was frank with select members of Congress in private. Most pertinently,

---

Government of the United States of America on the Situation in Berlin, November 27, 1958," in Wolfgang Heidelmeyer and Guenter Hindrichs, eds., *Documents on Berlin: 1943–1963* (Munich: R. Oldenbourg Verlag, 1963), p. 195.

6. Roger Morgan, *The United States and West Germany, 1945–1973: A Study in Alliance Politics* (Oxford University Press, 1974), p. 89.

7. Quoted in Robert M. Slusser, "The Berlin Crises of 1958–59 and 1961," in Barry M. Blechman, Stephen S. Kaplan, and others, *Force without War: U.S. Armed Forces as a Political Instrument* (Brookings, 1978), p. 367.

8. Dwight D. Eisenhower, *The White House Years*, vol. 2: *Waging Peace, 1956–1961* (Doubleday, 1965), pp. 338–41. Quote on pp. 338–39.

he insisted on continuing his planned reduction of army manpower by 30,000. In meetings on March 6 senators and representatives roundly criticized the reduction as inconsistent with preparations to fight over Berlin. In response Eisenhower argued essentially that it was necessary to rely on deterrence, that the Soviets were bluffing and would back down in the face of Western resolve, but that if miscalculation led to war it must be general war—meaning all-out nuclear engagement. Formerly top secret records of these meetings are worth quoting at length. Numerous passages in these records remain classified (those parts are marked by the word "deletion" in quotations below), but from the context of lines preceding and following them, several appear obviously to refer to use of nuclear weapons. In a morning meeting, Senator Lyndon Johnson

> pointed out the seeming inconsistency of the current force reductions. . . . To this the president answered . . . that when we reach the acute crisis period, it will be necessary to engage in general war to protect our rights. He cited examples in the past of Communist tactics in which they have maintained a strong bluff to the last moment and then backed out. . . . The President admitted the possibility that this firm position could conceivably bring about a miscalculation and therefore general war. . . .[9]

In a meeting at the end of the day Representative Carl Vinson echoed Johnson's view that reducing forces contradicted readiness to fight. Eisenhower argued that the Soviets counted on easy success "through economic measures. They desire us to overreact." The president "went on to assert that Berlin should not throw us off balance and render us hysterical. We are going to live with this type of crisis for years." When Senator Richard Russell warned about the danger of facing a ground war, Eisenhower reiterated the high-stakes poker metaphor: "the President expressed his basic philosophy of the necessity for the U.S. to be willing to 'push its whole stack of chips into the pot' when such becomes necessary. [Deletion] The President, Senator Russell, and Mr. Vinson agreed that if war comes, it will be an all-out war."[10]

9. John S. D. Eisenhower, "Memorandum of Conference With the President, March 6, 1959, 10:30 AM," March 6, 1959, p. 6, in DDEL/WHO, Office of the Staff Secretary, International Series, Box 6.

10. John S. D. Eisenhower, "Memorandum of Conference With the President, March 6, 1959, 5:00 PM," March 7, 1959, pp. 3–5, in DDEL/WHO, Office of the Staff Secretary, International Series, Box 6.

Senator J. William Fulbright raised the question of whether nuclear weapons would be used if limited harassment by the East Germans led to a small fire fight.

> The President here admitted that our course of action is not entirely clear. . . . If the situation as it faces the U.S. is serious, the President remarked [deletion] the President would recommend to congress that we go into general war. With haste, Senator Russell assured the President that consultation with Congress would not be necessary, but that the initiative is his and Congress will support it.[11]

When Russell asked again about increasing military forces Eisenhower again refused, saying that mobilization "would probably provide us two or three more divisions with which to counter the Soviet force of 175. This makes no sense. He expressed the conviction that the actual decision to go to all-out war will not come, but if it does come, we must have the crust to follow through."[12]

Fulbright introduced the issue of domestic politics, saying his constituents were asking why the army was being cut. In response the president cited the large expenditures on intercontinental ballistic missiles, implying that enhanced nuclear striking power compensated for the cuts. Vinson summed up the meeting by accepting "our great military capability and the futility of considering limited action in the Berlin crisis," and noting that "we are ready to 'cross the bridge' if necessary."[13]

Elsewhere Eisenhower had less success in developing a consensus against striving for a limited war option. Even Dulles, the lieutenant most identified with brinkmanship (and just then leaving office because of his final illness), thought it might be wise to delay the ground force reductions, but the president yet again refused.[14] More substantial objections arose in Congress when Acting Secretary of State Christian Herter testified in secret Senate Foreign Relations Committee hearings on March 10. He argued the futility of war with conventional weapons against the legendary 175 Soviet divisions, and observed, "We are in a good position to meet what may be the ultimate threat." Queried immediately by Senator Mike Mansfield about whether that remark referred to "nuclear bombing," Herter replied,

11. Ibid., pp. 5–6.
12. Ibid., p. 6.
13. Ibid., pp. 9–10.
14. A. J. Goodpaster, "Memorandum of Conference With the President, March 9, 1959," March 10, 1959, p. 1, in DDEL/Ann Whitman File (AWF), DDE Diaries, Box 29.

"It would have to come to that. . . . If there is an overt act of war there. . . . We would have to make it perfectly clear that this is going to all-out war."[15]

Senator Wayne Morse declared himself "aghast." Assistant Secretary of State Livingston Merchant inadvertently stepped further into controversy when he tried to smooth anxiety by stating the deterrent rationale—that if Moscow were convinced that "we are prepared to retaliate with everything we have . . . the Russians will go to the brink and pull back"—but linked the point to contingency planning for a limited Soviet attack on a U.S. convoy. Committee Chairman J. William Fulbright reacted sharply, trying to pin Merchant down on whether nuclear response to any sort of attack had been definitely determined by the administration. Weaving a bit, Merchant sought refuge in the impossibility of making precise judgments in advance of the fateful moment of decision. Pressed again to clarify, Merchant denied that Herter and he envisioned "an unlimited response to a limited probe," but failed to mollify the nervous legislators. Senator Bourke Hickenlooper tried to rescue him by emphasizing the danger of discussing U.S. war plans in committee. Senator Russell Long, nevertheless, again brought up the foolishness of cutting back infantry just when access to Berlin was threatened, saying, "It looks like we are just telling these folks that the only thing in the world we can do is resort to a war of extermination."[16]

Signals

Eisenhower's staunch reaffirmations of the massive retaliation principle alternated with muddy equivocations, especially in public. His commitment to general war rather than surrender Berlin did not mean that he saw no utility in conventional capabilities. Indeed, if the massive retaliation doctrine was conceived in the absolute sense that alarmed some critics, the administration should have pushed harder for the 1956 "Radford Plan" to cut manpower by 800,000 and reduce the army in Europe to small nuclear task forces and would not have promoted German rearmament.[17] But while conventional forces were not just a pure tripwire, neither were they meant to cope with a large and determined Soviet assault. In terms of

15. *Executive Sessions of the Senate Foreign Relations Committee (Historical Series)*, vol. 11, 86 Cong. 1 sess., 1959 (Government Printing Office, 1982), pp. 220–21.

16. Ibid., pp. 225, 229, 231, 233–34.

17. The abortive Radford Plan undermined Adenauer and German rearmament when it leaked just as conscription legislation of dubious popularity was coming up in the Bundestag. James L. Richardson, *Germany and the Atlantic Alliance: The Interaction of Strategy and Politics* (Harvard University Press, 1966), pp. 40–42.

the simpler conception of massive retaliation Eisenhower's signals on Berlin can be seen as logically contradictory, but in practical terms they were complementary.

In late January the president directed the Joint Chiefs of Staff to bring units in Europe up to strength with quick filler replacements "to show the Soviets that we meant business. . . . it was certain that the Soviets would detect the movements and probably interpret them correctly as evidence of our determination." He also authorized other military preparations in Berlin meant to be observed by the Soviets but to be discreet enough to avoid public alarm in the West.[18] In pure strategic terms the efficacy of these preparations should have been neutralized by the overall force reduction program: a few white chips were being pushed into the pot while more were being pulled out. Practically, however, even if the filling of units was inconsistent with other conventional signals, in combination with the massive retaliation stance it presented a diffuse statement of U.S. military preparedness for war. In any case, dubious logic could contribute to the uncertainty component of deterrence, keeping Moscow guessing.

The president also kept the Western public guessing, in order to avert hysteria about nuclear war, which would cause political difficulty within the alliance and thereby weaken the nuclear threat to the USSR. At a February 25 press conference Eisenhower mentioned vague plans for defense of Berlin and did not emphasize massive retaliation. On March 8, however, a newspaper reported Defense Secretary Neil McElroy's rejection of army proposals to increase conventional forces and noted his statement that restricting military engagement over Berlin to a limited war would be hard.[19]

On March 11, the day after Herter's and Merchant's grilling in the secret Senate committee session, the president danced back and forth around the same questions in another press conference. Asked about delaying the cuts in the army and marine corps, he made the stark statement that serves as an epigraph to the chapter about not fighting "a ground war in Europe." When a questioner picked up immediately on the implication, however, and asked whether the United States would resort to nuclear war to defend Berlin, Eisenhower responded, "Well, I don't know how you could free anything with nuclear weapons," but then added that the United

18. Eisenhower, *Waging Peace*, pp. 340–41.
19. Slusser, "The Berlin Crises of 1958–59 and 1961," p. 373; Jack M. Schick, *The Berlin Crisis: 1958–1962* (University of Pennsylvania Press, 1971), p. 52n.

States and its allies were firmly committed to maintaining their rights in Berlin.[20]

Pressed again on the ground force reductions, Eisenhower said that an army of 870,000 was not a small one, but then reiterated how nonsensical a conventional war in Europe would be. To "enforce" Western will, he noted, "You have got to go to other means," and if military engagement exceeded a brush fire, "you have got to think in much, much bigger terms." The press was unwilling to let the confusion ride, and the president was unwilling to resolve it. Asked if he had in mind an intermediate response between conventional and nuclear war, Eisenhower replied, "I didn't say that nuclear war is a complete impossibility. I said it couldn't as I see it free anything." And after citing nuclear war as "a self-defeating thing for all of us," he reaffirmed that the West would do "what is necessary" to back up its rights and responsibilities.[21]

If the president's footwork seems nonchalant, it could have been because the crisis was easing. Shortly before, Moscow had backed off from the six-month deadline on the ultimatum issued in November.[22] The public storm over the problem was far from over, though, and Eisenhower gave a rare televised address on March 16. For the umpteenth time he rejected bolstering conventional forces and argued that strategic power enabled the United States "to rapidly apply necessary force to any area of trouble."[23] While the president had spoken publicly in muddled terms about military options throughout the crisis period, he had also remained consistent and clear about commitment to defense of West Berlin.

The deadline crisis passed, but however Khrushchev may have taken note of Eisenhower's strategic signals, they did not settle the issue. The Soviet leader professed readiness to face the danger of nuclear escalation. In a June meeting he ranted to Averell Harriman about "talk of maintaining your position in Berlin with force. That is bluff. If you send in tanks, they will burn and make no mistake about it." Khrushchev also warned that in the event of such action, Soviet missiles would "fly automatically."[24]

20. Press conference, March 11, 1959, in *Public Papers of the Presidents of the United States: Dwight D. Eisenhower, 1959* (GPO, 1960), pp. 244–45. Quotation on p. 245.

21. Ibid., pp. 249, 252.

22. Thomas W. Wolfe, *Soviet Power and Europe, 1945–1970* (Johns Hopkins University Press, 1970), p. 91n.

23. Quoted in Slusser, "The Berlin Crises of 1958–59 and 1961," p. 375.

24. Quoted in Hannes Adomeit, *Soviet Risk-Taking and Crisis Behavior: A Theoretical and Empirical Analysis* (London: Allen and Unwin, 1982), p. 255; and Wolfe, *Soviet Power and Europe*, p. 93.

As with the Tass statement of December 11, 1958, Khrushchev's rhetoric implies that Soviet leaders saw—or claimed to see—the relationships between military initiative and response, and between conventional and nuclear interaction, in a fashion that reversed Eisenhower's formulation. The American president spoke of nuclear escalation as a Western initiative to counter Soviet military action against West Berlin; the Soviet premier spoke of nuclear retaliation as an Eastern move to counter U.S. military action against East Germany. Actually, though, both leaders seemed to view the crucial distinction as between peace and war, between settling demands short of resort to force and moving into military conflict undifferentiated by types of weapons involved. Khrushchev's temporary cutback in conventional forces around this time also mimicked the logic of the American New Look.

Two things are notable about the similarities in the attitudes of the chief executives. First, each presented his own side as the defender of stability and the other side as the one that would initiate military hostilities if the dispute came to war. Thus two issues—the nature of the status quo and the identity of the aggressor—that must be clear if the "balance of interests" theory is to serve as an explanation for the logic of American brinkmanship were muddled; this point will be elaborated in chapter four. Second, Eisenhower's and Khrushchev's undifferentiated view of war, blurring the break between conventional and nuclear combat, contrasts markedly with the fine theoretical distinctions that became so crucial in the development of U.S. strategy after the 1950s.

To one adulatory biographer, Eisenhower's handling of the crisis was a masterpiece of political and diplomatic finesse: "He gave Khrushchev the room to retreat, he mollified his allies, he kept the JCS . . . and the other hawks in check, he kept the risks at a minimum level, he satisfied the public that his response was appropriate, and he kept the Democrats from throwing billions of dollars to the DOD. His most basic strategy was to simply deny that there was a crisis."[25] That facile encomium may be comforting, but in the luxury of hindsight it ignores two crucial points. The notion that risks were low was far from clear to all before the fact. The risks in fact were mixed. The logic of massive retaliation was to reduce the risk that war would occur by raising the risk that it would be apocalyptic if it did. And Eisenhower did not resolve the problem, if indeed the problem was not a "crisis"; the Soviet challenge to West Berlin remained

25. Stephen E. Ambrose, *Eisenhower*, vol. 2: *The President* (Simon and Schuster, 1984), pp. 517–18.

unsettled. Perhaps his manipulation of uncertainty was a bit too masterly. Whatever sobering effect Eisenhower's signals might have had, they did not stop Khrushchev from probing the next president's resolve.

The Berlin Aide-Mémoire Crisis, 1961

The debate in the United States about the massive retaliation doctrine highlighted the growing consciousness of its dangers, and Soviet leaders took comfort from the American critics' sensitivities. Marshal V. D. Sokolovskiy later wrote of the conclusion to which American analysts were driven by the end of the 1950s: "While previously the United States could, with almost complete immunity, threaten the unrestrained use of nuclear weapons . . . the changed balance of power has made it dangerous to engage in 'nuclear blackmail' and to risk the security of the country."[26] The American administration that followed Eisenhower's was also populated by figures who had been prominent in the analytical attack on the credibility of massive retaliation. The course of the third Berlin crisis, however, was to show both sides' leaders that less had changed than they thought.

On the second day of the Vienna summit meeting between John Kennedy and Khrushchev, June 4, 1961, the Soviet premier handed the new president an aide mémoire on Berlin. It restated the points of the November 1958 note to Eisenhower, demanding neutralization of Berlin and specifying six months as the time within which negotiations to implement peace treaties should be held. If Washington and Bonn would not cooperate, Moscow would sign a separate treaty with East Germany that, in the words of the aide mémoire, "will also mean the liquidation of the occupation regime in West Berlin with all the resulting consequences. Specifically, the question of using land, water, and air communications across the territory of the German Democratic Republic will have to be settled in no other way than through appropriate agreements with the German Democratic Republic."[27] In Khrushchev's first speech after the summit he "stressed his intention of 'freeing' West Berlin from its 'occupation regime,'" and East German chief Walter Ulbricht "announced that

---

26. V. D. Sokolovskiy, *Soviet Military Strategy*, 3d ed., Harriet Fast Scott, ed. and trans. (Crane, Russak, 1975), pp. 56–57.

27. Quoted in Jean Edward Smith, *The Defense of Berlin* (Johns Hopkins University Press, 1963), p. 233; see also p. 232.

the treaty would soon enable him to close West Berlin's refugee centers, radio station and Tempelhof Airport."[28] President Kennedy reportedly decided that if Khrushchev was serious, "the prospects for nuclear war were now very real."[29]

Khrushchev had been making increasingly vigorous claims about the power of Soviet nuclear forces. Several times in 1960 he touted the vulnerability of the U.S. interior, not in terms of first-strike options, but in terms of deterrence. As Kennedy prepared to assume office, Khrushchev's report to the Communist party announced: "The present correlation of forces in the international arena enables the socialist camp . . . for the first time in history, to set themselves the entirely realistic task of forcing the imperialists, under threat of seeing their system destroyed . . . to refrain from unleashing a world war."[30] And at the Vienna summit the premier hammered the point that any combat over Berlin would be started by the Americans. "Obviously," recounted one of the new president's closest assistants, "he did not believe that Kennedy would start a nuclear war over traffic controls on the *autobahn*."[31]

To admit the reality of Soviet basic deterrence meant to deny the viability of American extended deterrence; if Moscow could deter a U.S. first strike, then, by definition, Washington could not launch such a strike. This fundamental problem was especially relevant to Berlin. Although Western conventional military power might be improved enough to defend West Germany, capability to attack eastward to liberate West Berlin would remain out of the question. Furthermore, the objective stake the United States had in the city was far less than its stake in Western Europe as a whole, and did not rationally warrant nuclear war even if defense of NATO territory did. As Khrushchev said near the height of the crisis, the Western powers' contention that they would fight to preserve freedom in the city "is a fairy tale. There are 2,200,000 people living in West Berlin. But if a war is unleashed, hundreds of millions might perish. What sensible person would find such arguments of the imperialists convincing?"[32]

Kennedy had come to office as a critic of massive retaliation, but also promising in his inaugural address to "pay any price, bear any burden"

28. Theodore C. Sorensen, *Kennedy* (Harper and Row, 1965), p. 586.
29. Ibid., p. 549.
30. Quoted in Adomeit, *Soviet Risk-Taking*, pp. 224–25.
31. Sorensen, *Kennedy*, p. 587.
32. Quoted in Robert M. Slusser, *The Berlin Crisis of 1961: Soviet-American Relations and the Struggle for Power in the Kremlin, June–September 1961* (Johns Hopkins University Press, 1973), pp. 125–26.

for the defense of liberty.[33] While wavering more than Eisenhower on the doctrine behind military commitment to Berlin, he would not waver on the commitment. Thus against his will he came to feel compelled, in effect, to show that he might not be a "sensible person," in Khrushchev's terms, when it came to nuclear war. And the signals he would ultimately send on this score were less ambiguous than Eisenhower's a few years earlier.

Facing the Dearth of Alternatives

Three weeks after the June meeting in Vienna, former Secretary of State Dean Acheson submitted a report to the president. As Arthur Schlesinger describes it, Acheson's conclusion was that Khrushchev had initiated the third Berlin crisis because his fear of nuclear war had abated. The essential task, therefore, was to convince him that the United States would indeed prefer nuclear war to a retreat from the status quo.[34] Although the president would come to act on this basis, the notion did not sit well with the more nuclear-nervous cast of the new administration.

The American elite was also not absolutely united in an unyielding stance over Berlin. In the previous Berlin crisis, Senators Fulbright and Mansfield had advocated compromise, and in June 1961 Mansfield, by then the majority leader in the Senate, proposed demilitarizing Berlin as a free city under the United Nations. A free city solution of a different sort was part of the Soviet proposal. In opposing existing U.S. policy Mansfield emphasized that it "carries the ultimate implication of American willingness to pledge the lives and fortunes of every man, woman, and child in the nation to Berlin's defense."[35] He submitted a memo to Kennedy advocating careful planning for limitation of any necessary use of force.[36]

Kennedy, who was already receiving reports on contingency planning from the Pentagon, established a special interagency task force, virtually all of whose substantive documents on operational contingency plans

---

33. *Public Papers of the Presidents of the United States: John F. Kennedy, 1961* (GPO, 1962), p. 1.

34. Arthur M. Schlesinger, Jr., *A Thousand Days: John F. Kennedy in the White House* (Houghton Mifflin, 1965), pp. 381–82. In an earlier draft Acheson endorsed flexible response, but the sections entitled "Nuclear Forces" remain classified. "A Review of North Atlantic Problems for the Future," March 1961, in John F. Kennedy Library (JFKL)/ National Security Files (NSF), Regional Security Series, Box 220; deleted sections on nuclear forces on pp. 6–9, 53–61.

35. Smith, *Defense of Berlin*, pp. 202–03, 238–39; Mansfield quoted on p. 238.

36. Senator Mike Mansfield, Memorandum for the President, "Berlin," June 23, 1961, in JFKL/President's Office Files (POF), Countries Series, Box 117.

remain classified.[37] NATO and JCS plans reportedly called for small probes down the autobahn, to be followed by use of nuclear weapons if unsuccessful, and the president reacted negatively: "We go immediately from a rather small military action to one where nuclear weapons are exchanged, which of course means . . . we are also destroying this country."[38] Other sources deny that the supreme allied commander in Europe, Lauris Norstad, was wedded to the automatic escalation in the contingency plan, and it certainly contradicted the strategic preferences of the president's closest military adviser, Maxwell Taylor.[39] But the fact remained that no conventional options were being offered that could be decisive against Soviet resistance.

In early May, McNamara had opposed proposals from the services for a budget supplement of more than $2.6 billion to increase conventional forces, and recommended adding less than $400 million to the fiscal year 1962 budget.[40] On May 25, nine days before Khrushchev presented the aide mémoire, the president chose a much larger increase—$3.4 billion.[41] If there was logic relevant to Berlin implicit in McNamara's earlier budget recommendation, it was that even a larger conventional buildup would not provide the means to liberate West Berlin by force, and, most importantly, that nuclear means might be usable without precipitating complete holocaust. The latter idea was explicitly reflected in McNamara's evolving controlled response counterforce doctrine[42]—a doctrine for which he never manifested genuine enthusiasm and from which his own thinking

37. Some documents have been sanitized, but without publishing sensitive portions. For example, in two reports, one from McNamara and one from Army General Wheeler and Chief of Naval Operations Burke, in White House files, about 90 percent of the contents are deleted. Earle Wheeler and Arleigh Burke, Memorandum for the Secretary of Defense, "Berlin," April 28, 1961, appendix A, and Robert S. McNamara, Memorandum for the President, "Military Planning for Possible Berlin Crisis," May 5, 1961, in JFKL/ NSF, Countries Series, Box 81.

38. Quoted in Schlesinger, A Thousand Days, pp. 587–88 (ellipsis in original).

39. See Richard K. Betts, Soldiers, Statesmen, and Cold War Crises (Harvard University Press, 1977), pp. 107, 253n.

40. McNamara, Memorandum for the President, "Reappraisal of Capabilities of Conventional Forces," May 10, 1961, pp. 1–3, in JFKL/NSF, Departments and Agencies Series, Box 273.

41. Wolfe, Soviet Power and Europe, p. 94.

42. "Counterforce" doctrine concentrates targeting plans against the enemy's military capabilities, especially his offensive nuclear forces. In contrast, "countervalue" targeting aims at civilian assets—population, industry, and economic infrastructure. "Controlled response" refers to the development of varied options for limiting the scale of nuclear attacks and for excluding certain classes of targets.

would depart soon after it was formally adopted, but a doctrine whose greatest moment in the sun coincided with the last Berlin crisis. Yet as in most cases addressed in this study, doctrine in principle was not completely congruent with the specific circumstances in practice.

Planning: Doctrine vs. Contingency

Contingency planning for the 1961 Berlin crisis was seminal. It was the first serious exercise in elaborating and applying the logic of flexible response. Much of the planning took place under the direction of Paul Nitze, then assistant secretary of defense for international security affairs. Nitze had been, in his 1956 *Foreign Affairs* article, among the first to articulate a rationale for discriminating and graduated nuclear options.[43] The ideas were annealed in the crucible of the 1961 crisis. Nitze's responsibility did not allow his thinking to stop with deterrence and thus to be satisfied with a gamble on brinkmanship. Mandated to provide implementable military options, he had to look hard at prospective steps toward the nuclear brink and beyond. With that responsibility and experience it is perhaps not surprising that in the following decade Nitze became the principal expositor of concerns about the loss of U.S. escalation dominance.

The Berlin flexible response planning yielded complex options for the use of force, beginning with small-scale conventional actions and ranging upward.[44] The hope was that calibrating response to provocation would allow the West to contest limited Soviet military pressures on West Berlin without lurching immediately into large-scale war. The possibility of most concern, however, remained decisive action by the East to absorb the city. Nuclear options were integral to dealing with that end of the continuum of challenges, and large-scale nuclear war was the ultimate focus on the continuum of options. According to Richard Barnett, the presidential directive finally approved, National Security Action Memorandum 109, ordered:

> If, despite Allied use of substantial non-nuclear forces, the Soviets continue to encroach upon our vital interests, then the Allies should use nuclear weapons, starting with one of the following courses of action but continuing through C below if necessary: A. Selective nuclear attacks for the primary purpose of demonstrating the will to use nuclear

43. Paul Nitze, "Atoms, Strategy and Policy," *Foreign Affairs,* vol. 34 (January 1956).
44. See Schick, *Berlin Crisis,* pp. 149–52.

weapons. B. Limited tactical employment of nuclear weapons to achieve in addition significant tactical advantage such as preservation of the integrity of Allied forces committed, or to extend pressure toward the objective. C. General Nuclear War.[45]

Given the dissatisfaction with Eisenhower's old approach, how was "General Nuclear War" to be made an acceptable option?

The new Kennedy crew set about modifying massive retaliation in the first year of the administration, but the process of preparing discriminating counterforce options took time—in defining the details of the new doctrine in principle and in translating it into military organizational practice. Problems in both parts of this adjustment indicate that it could not have offered a new option in time for the most critical phase of the crisis.

One adjustment, which was intended to allow the Soviets the choice of limiting a nuclear exchange, was to remove Moscow from the roster of initial nuclear targets. That decision, however, was not made until late 1961, after the peak of the crisis, and the order was not implemented until well into 1962. In another adjustment, the Single Integrated Operational Plan (SIOP) was revised to incorporate several options for limiting attacks on the Soviet interior, providing more flexibility than the standing war plan (SIOP-62), which involved a full-scale assault on the USSR, Warsaw Pact countries, and China, with fatalities numbering in the hundreds of millions. Although the JCS resisted the revision, they approved it in 1961 and officially adopted it in January 1962, but even the designation of targets necessary for reprogramming the plan was not completed until June—ten months after the Berlin Wall went up. The revised plan, SIOP-63, did not go into effect until August 1962.[46]

In early July 1961 Carl Kaysen warned McGeorge Bundy about a dangerous lag in planning. He reported that he had discussed "the initial response of the Joint Chiefs [deletion] in connection with Berlin [deletion]. . . .The planning for [deletion] which might be relevant to the Berlin crisis

45. Richard J. Barnett, *The Alliance: America, Europe, Japan: Makers of the Postwar World* (Simon and Schuster, 1983), p. 231. The passage is allegedly a direct quotation, although the source of the document is not indicated.

46. Fred Kaplan, *The Wizards of Armageddon* (Simon and Schuster, 1983), p. 269; Desmond Ball, *Politics and Force Levels: The Strategic Missile Program of the Kennedy Administration* (University of California Press, 1980), pp. 139n, 191; Scott Sagan, article forthcoming in *International Security*. In the SIOP programming process lags of up to two years have been known to occur between instruction by the Secretary of Defense and final implementation. Sagan has informed me that the option to withhold all weapons from Moscow targets may not even have been in effect until the later SIOP-64.

has not begun. Rowen is drafting a request for such planning . . . but I think this should be considered as an urgent matter at higher levels."[47] In light of the existing SIOP oriented to massive retaliation, the existence of plans for use of tactical nuclear weapons, and Kaysen's memorandum for the record of the same day, the security deletions above must have referred to nuclear counterforce options. Kaysen reported that in talking with Maxwell Taylor, the military representative of the president, "I tried to convey the importance of adding some option to the SIOP which is relevant to a war which might break out in relation to Berlin. Taylor seemed confident that the appropriate planning would be done. . . . I am not sure I got across the point about the general war aspect of Berlin planning."[48] That month McGeorge Bundy warned the president that the nuclear war plan was still "'dangerously rigid,' and that it 'may leave you with very little choice as to how you face the moment of thermonuclear truth.'"[49]

Construction of the Berlin Wall in mid-August marked the beginning of the tensest phase of the crisis. Although ultimately the wall helped ease the crisis because it solved one of the communists' problems, the population exodus, U.S. decisionmakers feared it might be the first ratchet in a sequence leading to forcible action against the Western presence in the city. According to Arthur Schlesinger, the president remarked "that there was one chance out of five of a nuclear exchange."[50] Nevertheless, despite the continuing lack of a ready nuclear war plan for less than all-out assault on the East, Kennedy dispatched the U.S. First Battle Group in a convoy to reinforce the West Berlin garrison—a move he feared could be intercepted, precipitating conflict. When this did not happen, many in the government assumed that a showdown might come in October, when Khrushchev was expected to call a German peace conference[51]—again, before SAC would be ready for discriminating attack.

Another problem in applying the counterforce doctrine if the moment of decision had arrived during the crisis was the continuing uncertainty

47. Carl Kaysen, "Memorandum for Mr. Bundy," July 3, 1961, in JFKL/NSF, Meetings and Memoranda Series, Box 320.

48. Carl Kaysen, Memorandum for the Record, "Conversation with General Taylor, July 3, 1961, 1:30 P.M.," July 3, 1961, in JFKL/NSF, Meetings and Memoranda Series, Box 320.

49. Gregg Herken, *Counsels of War* (Alfred A. Knopf, 1985), p. 158. A handwritten outline labeled "JFK's Berlin Agenda," apparently from July 21, 1961, notes "Nuclear War—its flexibility. (Schelling Memo.)," JFKL/NSF, Countries Series, Box 81.

50. Schlesinger, *A Thousand Days*, p. 395.

51. Sorensen, *Kennedy*, pp. 586, 595.

about the number of Soviet intercontinental ballistic missiles. The allegation of a "missile gap" favoring the USSR had been a staple of Kennedy's campaign, but it was cast into doubt from the early days of the administration. It was not definitively debunked, however, until much later in the year. As of late summer there was still disagreement within the intelligence community about whether the Soviets had only a few operational ICBMs or as many as 125. The CIA reported on September 6 that the earlier estimate of 50–100 operational ICBMs as of mid-1961 "is probably too high," but that the estimate was still "under urgent review." And while the CIA memorandum cited Soviet counterforce capability as only "limited" in the coming few months, it also said that Soviet forces "pose a grave threat to U.S. urban areas," and that Soviet medium-range missiles put NATO allies at risk.[52]

A coterie of civilian analysts that McNamara brought into the Pentagon believed that a discriminating counterforce strike was feasible; the delicate planning for this option is discussed below. The regular intelligence bureaucracy's persisting uncertainty about the Soviet target base, however, stood in the way of the internal government consensus that would, practically, have been necessary for top leaders even to begin to think that they might confidently resort to such an option. Together with the military bureaucracy's inability to implement the appropriate changes in SAC's operational repertoire until many months after the turning point of the crisis, the lack of internal consensus about the target intelligence makes clear that a counterforce option different from Eisenhower's could have been relevant to a potential fourth Berlin crisis, but not to the one that Kennedy actually faced. Timing problems apart, there were reasons that the luster of the administration's new nuclear doctrine, so treasured by some of the newly influential analysts, faded in the eyes of responsible political officials.

No evidence comparable to that for Eisenhower is available about President Kennedy's own view of what he would actually do if West Berlin were cut off. From what *is* available, it appears that he stopped further short of firm decision than Eisenhower did. Such a stance would be

52. CIA Memorandum, "Current Status of Soviet and Satellite Military Forces and Indications of Military Intentions," September 6, 1961, p. 5, in JFKL/POF, Countries Series, Box 117. The intelligence dispute in mid-1961 pitted high air force estimates (300 Soviet ICBMs) against low navy estimates (10 or fewer), with CIA, the army, and the State Department in the middle (50 to 100). John Prados, *The Soviet Estimate: U.S. Intelligence Analysis and Soviet Strategic Forces,* 2d ed. (Princeton University Press, 1986), p. 117.

consistent with the overall difference in the two presidents' operating styles—Eisenhower being more formal and organized in his internal approach to policy while somewhat more muddled in public rhetoric, with Kennedy, in a sense, the reverse.

If war had appeared both possible and imminent, reluctance on Kennedy's part to make a firm decision about the nature of ultimate military response would seem reckless, especially when he was undertaking potentially escalatory responses such as the dramatically visible reinforcement of the West Berlin garrison in August. As in the previous crisis, however, the administration had reason to believe that although war was possible, it was not imminent. The aide mémoire constituted political warning of war, but no Soviet military preparations consistent with strategic warning took place. As of early September Soviet conventional forces in the area remained at normal readiness levels.[53] Moreover, the anticipated military challenge was a blockade, which the allies would have to break, or an assault on West Berlin, but not an attack on West Germany. There were also indications that Moscow would not press the ultimatum. In late August, for example, a CIA source—an East European official—claimed that the Polish delegation at a Warsaw Pact meeting had convinced Khrushchev not to set a real deadline for the German peace treaty; Warsaw Pact members could thus assume that public rhetoric citing the end of 1961 was only a "tactical measure in negotiations with the West."[54]

In this context planning about major conflict in terms of future rather than immediate options was reasonable. While it is unclear how involved the president himself was in the planning, there was substantial activity among mid-level staffs and consultants. In one late summer crisis simulation Thomas Schelling proposed a nuclear warning shot over some isolated location in the USSR. Other advisers rejected the idea on various grounds— as timorous, indecisive, reckless, or counterproductive.[55] In the fall, options for graduated escalation on the battlefield were discussed with allies, although the details of the later phase involving tactical nuclear weapons were not settled.[56]

A more awesomely ambitious option, generated in the Office of the

---

53. CIA, "Current Status of Soviet and Satellite Military Forces," p. 6. On the distinction between political and strategic warning, see Richard K. Betts, *Surprise Attack: Lessons for Defense Planning* (Brookings, 1982), pp. 4–5.

54. Cable from Bundy to McHugh, August 21, 1961, in JFKL/POF, Countries Series, Box 117.

55. Herken, *Counsels of War*, pp. 158–59.

56. Kaplan, *Wizards of Armageddon*, pp. 302–03.

Secretary of Defense (OSD) outside the military planning process, was a discriminating attack against Soviet nuclear forces. Although the intelligence community had not yet quite resolved the issue of how many Soviet ICBMs were deployed, reconnaissance data had convinced some civilian analysts and officials that the counterforce target base—bombers, missiles, air defense and warning nets, and command and control nodes—was adequately identified and vulnerable to relatively "clean" strikes. The Soviets needed hours to arm, fuel, and ready their missiles to fire, and their bombers were not on alert. Large holes in detection systems for tactical early warning might let a number of U.S. bombers sneak through at low altitudes. This sort of option was discussed by a few high civilian officials and consultants early in 1961. Detailed preliminary analysis to support such a hypothetical attack, more discrete than yet envisioned in the SIOP, evolved under the auspices of civilian analysts.[57]

By mid-September intelligence estimates had settled on the low number of Soviet ICBMs, and more detailed studies on the first-strike counterforce option had been done. The chairman of the JCS, however, lobbied hard against the notion of shifting the nuclear war plan toward a finely tuned counterforce strike. In a lengthy briefing on the SIOP given to the president on September 13, General Lyman Lemnitzer emphasized the "grave risks" in executing a lesser part of the plan, the impracticality of minimizing Soviet casualties without sparing some military targets or reducing their damage expectancy, and the fragility of U.S. command, control, and communications under nuclear wartime conditions. The briefing concluded, "The ability to defeat the enemy must not be lost by the introduction into the SIOP of an excessive number of options which would contribute to confusion and lower our assurance of success under the most adverse circumstances."[58]

In any case, when the discriminating counterforce option developed in OSD was discussed among high-level officials the response was unfavor-

---

57. The preceding and following paragraphs are based on ibid., pp. 294–301, and Herken, *Counsels of War*, pp. 159–60. Kaplan describes the plan as relying on a limited number of U.S. bombers. Herken cites Carl Kaysen as saying it would have expended the whole U.S. long-range nuclear inventory. Given the normal tendency of operational planning to add elements as the process unfolds, the plan may have metamorphosed from small to large versions between spring and fall.

58. "Briefing for the President by the Chairman, Joint Chiefs of Staff on the Joint Chiefs of Staff Single Integrated Operational Plan, 1962 (SIOP-62)," September 15, 1961, declassified August 15, 1986, pp. 16–19 (document to be reprinted in *International Security*).

able. Moral questions aside, even a very effective first strike could not eliminate all Soviet retaliatory power. Although there were few Soviet ICBMs to target, the large number of medium-range and short-range systems—whose locations were not all certain—meant that enough might well survive to kill tens of millions of Western Europeans. And enough Soviet intercontinental capability would survive, by the range of estimates developed by the OSD planners, to kill between 2 and 15 million Americans. The overall uncertainties about how efficiently the plan would work in practice, as distinct from the sterile bounds of a game-theoretic frame of reference, also loomed much larger. Paul Nitze was reported to be especially opposed.

Given the grave doubts at this level, it is virtually certain that the president, by experience and responsibility the one necessarily most attuned to political realities, would have considered both the material and moral costs prohibitive. However bad the alternative might seem, the range of choice would still be far greater than it would be if a *Soviet* nuclear attack appeared imminent. Furthermore, there are reasons to doubt the actual feasibility of the first-strike option as conceived. The premise of the plan appears to have been that Soviet forces could be caught on the ground in their normal nonalert status. This assumption is inconsistent with the only plausible circumstances in which a president might conceivably order nuclear attack—the outbreak of conventional war at Soviet initiative. That problem will be explored further in chapter four. Not surprisingly, contingency planners also discussed numerous nonnuclear options for dealing with a Soviet squeeze on West Berlin. Nevertheless, despite all the reasons for reservation, the U.S. response to the aide mémoire wound up leaning on nuclear power.

Maneuvering: Action and Rhetoric

In the summer of 1961 Washington and Moscow dueled over Berlin with escalating rhetoric and actions. At the end of the first week in July Khrushchev suspended Soviet troop reductions and announced an increase in defense spending that matched Kennedy's increase of late May. He also warned, "It is best for those who are thinking of war not to imagine that distances will save them."[59] The next day, for the first time in five years,

---

59. Quoted in Slusser, *Berlin Crisis of 1961*, p. 54. The absolute amount of the Soviet budget increase (3,144 million rubles) roughly equaled the U.S. figure ($3.4 billion), but in terms of figures Khrushchev used for the whole Soviet military budget (12,399 million rubles) it represented a boost of one-third. Ibid., p. 55; see also Raymond L. Garthoff,

the Soviet Air Force Day celebration showed off new planes, including a jet bomber. On July 25 Kennedy countered in a dramatic television speech, elaborating on his military budget increase. He announced an increase of military manpower of over 200,000, a reserve call-up, and significant increases in the draft. Measures in the speech related to nuclear war preparation included a significant upgrading of strategic bomber alert status and a request for over $200 million for civil defense. On August 8 the president announced postponement of the retirement of 270 B-47 bombers.[60]

Kennedy had already decided to accelerate the Polaris and Minuteman programs and at the end of March had called for a breathtakingly high 50 percent rate of ground alert for SAC, which was attained by July. About 250 heavy and 450 medium bombers were regularly poised for takeoff within fifteen minutes, and by late summer 12 B-52s were always on airborne alert, a sharp contrast to the normal situation in subsequent years of about 30 percent ground alert and no airborne alert. The move to high day-to-day alert levels may explain why there was apparently no special increase at the peak of the crisis.[61] On August 17, four days after the wall began going up in Berlin, foreign attachés were invited, for the first time since World War II, to observe Soviet military maneuvers, which included simulated use of tactical nuclear weapons.[62]

During the summer Kennedy gave an interview to the *New York Post*, after he had just met with the JCS, in which he said that only fools believed in victory in a nuclear war. Then echoing Acheson's logic, however, he said that he feared Khrushchev might see reluctance to face nuclear war as evidence of U.S. timidity; therefore, it might be necessary someday to demonstrate American preparedness to go as far as nuclear war. At the moment, however, he did not want to scare or provoke Moscow, so he wanted measured response rather than crash mobilization.[63]

Despite the change in military doctrine, Kennedy's stance differed little

Soviet Military Policy: A Historical Analysis (Praeger, 1966), p. 115. The official Soviet figure for their total defense budget has always been grossly understated.

60. Garthoff, *Soviet Military Policy,* p. 116; Slusser, *Berlin Crisis of 1961,* p. 80; Arnold L. Horelick and Myron Rush, *Strategic Power and Soviet Foreign Policy* (University of Chicago Press, 1965), p. 124; Wolfe, *Soviet Power and Europe,* p. 94.

61. J. C. Hopkins, *The Development of the Strategic Air Command, 1946–1981 (A Chronological History)* (Office of the Historian, Headquarters, Strategic Air Command, 1982), pp. 96, 98; "Blue Strategic Forces," paper in collection for NATO Planning Conference, September 8–11, 1961.

62. Garthoff, *Soviet Military Policy,* p. 116.

63. Schlesinger, *A Thousand Days,* p. 391.

from Eisenhower's, except for the bolstering of conventional forces. At a news conference on August 10, a reporter asked what would happen if combat erupted over Berlin: would it remain conventional or escalate to use of nuclear weapons? Kennedy said simply, "Well, we are hopeful that we would be able to reach peaceful solutions to these problems."[64] Whereas Eisenhower's response under similar circumstances two years earlier had been muddled, Kennedy's was evasive. The net significance was similar.

On September 7 Paul Nitze gave a speech implicitly articulating the options both for use of tactical nuclear weapons and for general counter-force:

> We are not particularly impressed with the Soviet threat to develop nuclear weapons in the 100-megaton range. We are not interested in arms of a terroristic nature, but rather our nuclear capability is tailored to specific tasks.
>
> We have a tremendous variety of warheads which gives us the flexibility we require to conduct nuclear actions from the level of large-scale destruction down to mere demolition work. . . . the number of delivery vehicles of all types which the United States possesses provides the flexibility for virtually all modes and levels of warfare.[65]

By late September new reconnaissance satellites had produced enough film to bring the estimated number of operational Soviet ICBMs down to a handful; the downward revision was reported in the open press by Joseph Alsop.[66] At that time Nitze became the agent for what may have been the first directly transmitted nuclear warning to Moscow. He lunched with the Soviet ambassador and told him that Washington knew the intercontinental missile gap favored the United States. On October 6, President Kennedy met with Foreign Minister Andrei A. Gromyko. Some have suggested that he confronted him with the evidence of Soviet weakness in ICBMs;[67] whether he did is unknown.

American leaders gave signals that were intentionally ambiguous about whether they envisioned the possibility of anything remotely like an easy nuclear war. They did so for several reasons. First, those at the top did not believe it and were not committed to the option. Second, while they wanted to convince the Soviets of U.S. advantage, they did not want to induce

64. *Public Papers, Kennedy, 1961*, p. 558.
65. Quoted in Slusser, *Berlin Crisis of 1961*, p. 223.
66. Philip J. Klass, *Secret Sentries in Space* (Random House, 1971), pp. 66, 106–07.
67. Ball, *Politics and Force Levels*, p. 98, citing Klass.

panic, or to provoke a Soviet ICBM crash program any sooner than necessary. Third, if U.S. reliance on a nuclear first strike were telegraphed too insistently to Moscow, it would logically become less feasible, since the Soviets might take measures to forestall a surprise operation. And, finally, clear indication of a first-strike strategy would be provocative not only to Moscow, but also in the West. So U.S. nuclear warnings, while more factually detailed than comparable Soviet rhetoric, remained indirect.

At a press conference on October 11 the president pressed home the buildup of U.S. military power, mentioning his orders for a 50 percent increase in the number of alert bombers and Polaris submarines to be on firing stations and the doubling of production capacity for Minuteman ICBMs, as well as other nuclear programs. Khrushchev seemed unimpressed by the U.S. signals, however, when he gave a speech a week later and referred again to the shift in power favoring the East. Thereupon the top U.S. leaders caucused and decided to amplify the nuclear message in a carefully planned speech by Deputy Secretary of Defense Roswell Gilpatric. The rationale for using Gilpatric was supposedly that he was a high enough official to demonstrate the seriousness of the policy, but not high enough to be provocative.[68]

Follow-up briefings for allies were scheduled deliberately to include "some whom we knew were penetrated, so as to reinforce and confirm through Soviet intelligence channels the message carried openly through the Gilpatric speech."[69] The same rationale had applied to the emphasis on nuclear options in contingency planning. Secretary of State Dean Rusk revealed that "for reasons which I cannot specify, we assumed that the Soviet Union would become fully informed of these contingencies and would take such possibilities into full account in their decisions."[70]

Gilpatric's speech on October 21 ticked off the count of U.S. bombers, submarines, carrier strike forces, and theater nuclear forces favoring the United States. He noted: "The total number of our delivery vehicles, tactical as well as strategic, is in the tens of thousands; and of course, we have more than one warhead for each vehicle." Gilpatric also emphasized U.S. second-strike capability ("at least as extensive as what the Soviets can deliver by striking first"), but not to the exclusion of a U.S. first-strike option. The next day in a television interview Rusk denied Khrushchev's

68. Ibid., p. 97; Roger Hilsman, *To Move a Nation: The Politics of Foreign Policy in the Administration of John F. Kennedy* (Doubleday, 1967), p. 163.

69. Hilsman, *To Move a Nation*, pp. 163–64.

70. Dean Rusk, letter to Marc Trachtenberg, January 25, 1984, quoted with permission.

claim that strategic parity existed. While denying equality of capability, however, he also noted, "There is an ability to inflict very great damage on both sides."[71]

These were hefty declarations of superior U.S. nuclear power, but not blunt claims of capability to wage nuclear war at a cost "acceptable" to the United States. Thus continuing Soviet claims of a big nuclear capacity were not necessarily transparently desperate bluster, especially if seen in terms of a countervalue deterrent against a U.S. first strike. Two days after the Gilpatric speech Soviet Defense Minister Rodion Malinovsky replied by reemphasizing the import of individual Soviet weapons' explosive power. He said that American estimates assumed "a warhead of only five megatons. But . . . we have nuclear warheads with yields ranging from 20 to 30 to 100 megatons."[72] In the last week of October the Russians tested two huge weapons in the Arctic—thirty and fifty-eight megatons.[73]

Soviet Views

For more than a year before the Vienna summit Khrushchev had been moving toward his own version of a New Look, planning to scale down conventional troop strength and build up missile power. About half of the planned troop cuts had been made before they were halted in spring 1961. Leaders in the West do not appear to have attributed great significance to this shift. Kennedy moved in the opposite direction, since the conventional wisdom in the West remained that Soviet conventional forces were overwhelmingly superior. Indeed, it was after the initial increments to the Kennedy defense budget that Khrushchev reversed course and announced his own budget increase. In any case, the Soviet plan to scale down manpower was logically consistent with a basic stance of military deterrence, in terms of war in Europe, as cover for leverage on Berlin. Reduced offensive capacity for invading West Germany would not to the same extent reduce defensive capacity for containing a Western attack to relieve the encircled city.

In March 1961 *Pravda* quoted Khrushchev as saying that in war, neither side could be expected "to concede defeat before resorting to the use of all weapons, even the most devastating ones."[74] In a speech soon after delivery of the aide mémoire turned up the burner on Berlin, Khrushchev stressed

71. Quoted in Slusser, *Berlin Crisis of 1961*, pp. 372–73, 375.
72. Ibid., pp. 91, 385.
73. Klass, *Secret Sentries*, pp. 70–71.
74. Quoted in Wolfe, *Soviet Power and Europe*, p. 145n.

the important burden on Soviet nuclear forces for deterring Western attack.[75] On July 2 he told British Ambassador Sir Frank Roberts that six Soviet hydrogen bombs "would be quite enough to annihilate the British Isles and nine would take care of France."[76] Of Kennedy's July 25 address, the premier charged that it amounted to a preliminary declaration of war and warned that if Western countries were thinking of shooting their way into Berlin, they should consider the Soviet superiority in military forces and geographic proximity to the battle area.[77]

Appearing on television on August 7, Khrushchev dismissed the possibility of limited war over Berlin, much as Eisenhower had, saying a clash would escalate rapidly. "But if the U.S. leaders appreciate the nature of modern war involving the use of thermonuclear weapons," the premier asked, "then why do they inflame the atmosphere, as President Kennedy did in his speech?"[78] Two days later he boasted falsely of having weapons with yields greater than a hundred megatons, noted that the USSR had placed astronauts in space, and said, "We can replace them with other loads that can be directed to any place on earth."[79]

Khrushchev referred to Dulles's old policy of "barefaced atomic blackmail," admitted that Soviet retaliatory power in that period had been insufficient, and averred that "now the situation has radically changed." He relied heavily on the "Hostage Europe" deterrent and later recalled Adenauer's frequent admissions that West Germany would be the first to be destroyed in a third world war: "For him to be making public statements like that was a great achievement on our part. Not only were we keeping our number one enemy in line, but Adenauer was helping us to keep our other enemies in line, too."[80]

In July, major Soviet preparations in civil defense got under way, and the summer was punctuated by Soviet statements about the inevitability of nuclear escalation in war. At the end of August Moscow deferred release of active service personnel to the reserves and announced the resumption of nuclear testing. On September 10, ICBM firings into the Pacific for the

75. Slusser, *Berlin Crisis of 1961*, p. 17.

76. Joe Ritchie, "Soviet Atomic Threat Reported," *Washington Post*, August 18, 1979.

77. Schlesinger, *A Thousand Days*, p. 392; Khrushchev quoted in Adomeit, *Soviet Risk-Taking*, pp. 254–55.

78. Quoted in Slusser, *Berlin Crisis of 1961*, p. 110; see also Smith, *Defense of Berlin*, p. 254.

79. Klass, *Secret Sentries*, p. 62.

80. Strobe Talbott, ed. and trans., *Khrushchev Remembers* (Little, Brown, 1970), p. 517.

following month were announced. On October 17 Khrushchev announced multimegaton tests, but at the same time he lifted the deadline for the peace treaty.[81]

The standard interpretation of Khrushchev's nuclear rhetoric was that it was a bluff, attempting to exploit potential but undeployed capabilities for political coercion. In this light, the autumn messages from Washington about U.S. knowledge of the actual weakness of deployed Soviet forces may well have been effective—especially when the Soviet installation of missiles in Cuba a year later is considered. But if Khrushchev's statements and U.S. estimates are taken together, two simple points seem clear. First, Khrushchev banked on a finite deterrent, which threatened losses disproportionate to the tangible value of West Berlin. Second, even if claims of nuclear capability were inflated, that finite deterrent did exist, as chapter four makes clear. In these terms the Soviet position resembled the logic of proportional deterrence, at least the capacity to "tear off an arm," that has been the underlying rationale in French nuclear doctrine.

Could it be, ironically, that Moscow took the Kennedy administration's backing away from Eisenhower's reliance on nuclear weapons at face value, while the administration, when pressed, did not? While hard-headed cost-benefit analysis and careful calculation of material trade-offs became the hallmark of formal defense planning under Kennedy, it did not characterize Berlin policy. U.S. strategy came down to threatening nuclear war if the people of West Berlin—only a fraction of those who would be killed in such a war—were absorbed into East Germany. Joseph Alsop claims that when he asked Kennedy later how he would have handled the Berlin challenge if the missile gap had actually been in Soviet favor, the president asked him "not to pursue the subject; whenever he began to think about it, he said, he had too much trouble sleeping."[82]

Kennedy never had to face an ultimate decision. On Berlin, both sides may have been bluffing, but Moscow folded first. The American victory was far from clear and uncompromising, but in giving up the demand for a separate treaty and revocation of occupation rights in Berlin, the Soviets conceded more from their opening position than did the Americans. Erection of the wall solved the problem of accelerating depopulation in East Germany, but the wall was a fallback for the Russians, not a solution

81. Slusser, *Berlin Crisis of 1961*, pp. 65, 157, 161–62, 196; Horelick and Rush, *Soviet Strategic Power*, p. 125; Garthoff, *Soviet Military Policy*, pp. 117–19.

82. Joseph Alsop, Comment, in *Foreign Policy*, no. 16 (Fall 1974), p. 87.

to their demands in the aide mémoire.[83] Indeed, the wall's appearance did not end the crisis, which intensified as it went up and lasted more than two more months. Nor can one really say that Moscow "won" in preventing West German acquisition of nuclear weapons, which some analysts believe was what the crisis was really about. Autonomous German nuclear weapons had never been more than a hypothetical possibility, and Soviet threats and deadlines were not directed to this issue. As to dual-key nuclear weapons under joint German and American control, they existed before, during, and after the crisis and have ever since.

Given the evidence of Kennedy's lack of confidence in a U.S. nuclear option, the Kremlin's accommodation in the face of U.S. resolve might be attributed to the "balance of interests"—the notion that a power defending territory has inherently more credible determination than the one threatening to take it—or to the principle that compellence is harder than deterrence. If so, however, the logic did not apply to the United States a year later in Cuba when the shoe was on the other foot.

The Cuban Missile Crisis, 1962

The role of nuclear weapons in the Cuban crisis was indirect and, in the *retrospective* views of some participants, negligible. Yet the case is a major one for several reasons. First, the missile crisis was the epochal military confrontation of the cold war. In the view of all observers, whatever their differences, the superpowers have never been closer to the nuclear brink. Second, the crisis was *about* the nuclear balance. Kennedy himself saw it as "the first direct test" between the superpowers that focused on nuclear weapons themselves.[84] If not for the importance of U.S. nuclear superiority, why did the Russians put missiles in Cuba secretly and lie about it? If not for the importance of the balance, why did the United States trot to the brink of war to prevent the change? It is widely acknowledged that the domestic political vulnerability of the Kennedy administration and the symbolic significance of the Soviet emplacement were key motives behind the U.S. reaction. If they were really *all* that brought the administration to teeter at the brink, however, U.S. policy was either cynical or reckless.

83. Garthoff, *Soviet Military Policy*, p. 119.

84. McGeorge Bundy, "The Presidency and the Peace," *Foreign Affairs*, vol. 42 (April 1964), p. 359.

Finally, the issues in the Cuban crisis were intimately entangled with those concerning Berlin. Indeed, Cuba was tacitly a fourth Berlin crisis.

Power, Rights, Resolve: Sources of the Crisis

The Cuban crisis can be considered in two ways, depending on whether one focuses on the missiles' significance for Cuba or on their importance for Europe. Viewed in the first way, the Soviet action was an attempt to provide extended deterrence to an ally that it could not protect using conventional military capabilities—Havana was as vulnerable as West Berlin. Viewed in the second way, the crisis was over a Soviet attempt to change the nuclear balance of power so that renewed confrontation over Berlin would find Moscow with a more persuasive deterrent against U.S. escalatory threats. In the first sense the competition in credibility was between potential Soviet nuclear first use and U.S. retaliatory nuclear deterrence; in the second sense the sides were reversed.

Considering the crisis in both these ways at once involves some controversial analogies and arguments about subjective factors affecting the interests and resolve of both sides. Available data make it comparatively easy to characterize the U.S. position but limit assessment of the Soviet side to assertions based on logic. Considering the interlocking aspects of the Cuban and European issues, this section presents an argument developed more generally in chapter four that there was more logical symmetry in how both sides perceived their interests than is usually assumed by American analysts. Since there was relative comparability not only in the two sides' interests but in their conventional military options on Cuba and Berlin, the difference in their resolve should be attributable to something else—in part, perhaps, to the asymmetry of nuclear power.

Khrushchev's memoirs cite two motives for the Soviet emplacement of the missiles: to deter U.S. military action against Cuba and to equalize "what the West likes to call 'the balance of power.'"[85] The first would aim to enforce Moscow's extended deterrent, the second to negate Washington's. The implications are tricky, because many Western observers deny any analogy between the Soviet role in Cuba and the American role in Europe—not only in the 1962 crisis, but also on such issues as deployment of U.S. intermediate-range nuclear forces for NATO in the 1950s and

---

85. Talbott, ed. and trans., *Khrushchev Remembers*, p. 494. Anastas Mikoyan told a closed meeting of communist ambassadors that the Soviet deployment was motivated by the asymmetry in nuclear power. Zbigniew Brzezinski, "How the Cold War Was Played," *Foreign Affairs*, vol. 51 (October 1972), p. 193.

again in the 1980s. Although differences between the two situations do mitigate the analogy, the question of whether some meaningful symmetry in the regional issues exists is central. Some analogy does exist, despite the fact that Washington militantly assumed or acted as if it did not. And while there might be a theoretical inconsistency in Soviet hopes that their extended deterrence for Cuba would work, while that of the United States for Berlin would not, both aims could have coexisted in Khrushchev's mind. Therefore it is not crucial to determine which of the two was the "real" Soviet motive. Americans usually focus on the challenge to the balance of power, but those who focus on defense of Cuba can cite evidence such as Khrushchev's July 10, 1960, statement that serves as an epigraph to this chapter, as well as his remark on June 3 of that year: "The Soviet Union does not need bases for missiles in Cuba, for it is enough to press a button here to launch missiles to any part of the world."[86] Those statements preceded the discrediting of the missile gap. In the course of the following two years the U.S.-backed exile invasion attempt at the Bay of Pigs and the continuation of covert paramilitary actions in Operation Mongoose signaled the potential danger of a more decisive U.S. attack on the Castro regime,[87] and the unfolding of the Berlin crisis invalidated the reliability of Moscow's finite nuclear deterrent against U.S. first use.

Others argue that the character of the Soviet deployment in 1962 was inconsistent with defense of Cuba—that troops, tactical nuclear weapons, or short-range missiles would have been more appropriate. The medium-range ballistic missiles (MRBMs) could hit Washington, and the intermediate-range ballistic missiles (IRBMs) must have been meant for strikes against SAC bases.[88] But if one looks at the impracticality of a Soviet conventional defense of Cuba and takes as a model U.S. doctrine that

86. Interview, June 3, 1960, and speech, July 10, 1960, quoted in Herbert S. Dinerstein, *The Making of a Missile Crisis: October 1962* (John Hopkins University Press, 1976), pp. 80, 82.

87. This program began with President Kennedy's November 30, 1961, directive to "use our available assets . . . to help Cuba overthrow the Communist regime." On January 19, 1962, Robert Kennedy told CIA officials that "a solution to the Cuban problem today carried top priority. . . . No time, money, effort—or manpower is to be spared." Both quoted in *Alleged Assassination Plots Involving Foreign Leaders,* an interim report of the Senate Select Committee to Study Governmental Operations with Respect to Intelligence Activities, 94 Cong. 1 sess. (GPO, 1975), pp. 139, 141.

88. Arthur M. Schlesinger, Jr., *Robert Kennedy and His Times* (Houghton Mifflin, 1978), pp. 503–04; Horelick and Rush, *Soviet Strategic Power,* p. 131. Horelick and Rush note that even for MRBMs to strike close-in targets (in the Florida area) related to a U.S. invasion force, they would require a special high-lofting trajectory.

based deterrence in Europe on nuclear attacks on the Soviet interior (stipulated as an early response by Eisenhower and as a last resort by his successors), there is no incongruity in the Soviet move. Moscow had more than enough incentives for increasing nuclear capability against the United States. Dean Rusk put the case simply during discussion of the Soviet motive at the first major caucus of U.S. leaders in the crisis: "One thing Mr. Khrushchev may have in mind is that . . . he knows that we have a substantial nuclear superiority, but he also knows that we don't really live under fear of his nuclear weapons to the extent that . . . he has to live under fear of ours."[89]

Soviet rhetoric after mid-1961 had backed off from bluffs of superiority and claimed only strategic parity, but Khrushchev argued that equality in strategic forces should mean equality in political rights.[90] He also made threats that he pointedly avoided fulfilling when challenged in October 1962. A Soviet statement in February 1962 asked, "By what right and by what law does the U.S. government organize and direct aggression against another country accusing it of having established a social system and a state different from what the United States wanted? . . . If the United States threatens Cuba, then let it draw conclusions regarding countries where American military bases are located."[91] Later in the year Moscow continued to proclaim extended deterrence on behalf of Havana:

> There is no need for the Soviet Union to shift its weapons for the repulsion of aggression, for a retaliatory blow, to any other country, for instance Cuba. . . . the Soviet Union has so powerful rockets to carry these nuclear warheads that there is no need to search for sites for them beyond the boundaries of the Soviet Union. . . . one cannot now attack Cuba and expect that the aggressor will be free from punishment. If this attack is made, this will be the beginning of the unleashing of war.[92]

In the course of the crisis American leaders mightily resisted the notion that Soviet military presence in Cuba was as legitimate as that of the United States in Europe, but almost as if they were protesting too much. At the

89. Transcript, "Off-the-Record [sic] Meeting on Cuba, October 16, 1962, 11:50 A.M.–12:57 P.M." (hereafter, "morning"), p. 14, in JFKL (special collection in care of staff). Large excerpts from this and the "evening" document cited below are reprinted in "White House Tapes and Minutes of the Cuban Missile Crisis: The ExCom Meetings October 1962," *International Security*, vol. 10 (Summer 1985), pp. 164–203.

90. Horelick and Rush, *Soviet Strategic Power*, p. 87.

91. Quoted in Dinerstein, *Making of a Missile Crisis*, p. 167.

92. "Text of Soviet Statement Saying That Any U.S. Attack on Cuba Would Mean War," *New York Times*, September 12, 1962.

initial meeting, the president ruminated, "It's just as if we suddenly began to put a major number of MRBMs in Turkey. Now that'd be goddam dangerous, I would think." At that point McGeorge Bundy, whose jaw must have dropped at the absentmindedness of the president's remark, reminded him, "Well we *did,* Mr. President." Kennedy's lame response was, "Yeah, but that was five years ago. . . . that was during a different period then."[93] Earlier, Eisenhower had privately admitted concern about plans to place U.S. IRBMs in Europe precisely because of the analogy. Referring to the then-hypothetical situation, "If Mexico or Cuba had been penetrated by the Communists, and then began getting arms and missiles from them," Eisenhower wondered whether the United States "were not simply being provocative, since Eastern Europe is an area of dispute in a political sense."[94]

The decisionmakers in 1962 were well aware of the analogy between U.S. Jupiter missiles in Turkey and Soviet missiles in Cuba but preoccupied with finding ways to deny it. At an October 18 meeting the conferees' tortured reasoning led them to agree that the difference lay in a universal understanding "that sensitive areas, such as Berlin, Iran, or Laos, should not be turned into missile bases, and that missile installations only be established pursuant to open military alliances, such as NATO."[95]

Though lawyers can construct some legal case for any policy, it is hard to imagine a detached observer, a man from Mars, as it were, believing that Soviet deployments in Cuba, with the permission of that country's government, were less legitimate than American nuclear deployments

---

93. "Off-the-Record Meeting on Cuba, October 16, 1962, 6:30–7:55 P.M." (hereafter, "evening"), p. 26, in JFKL (special collection in care of staff). In what would be a telling offhand revelation of the assumed double standard if it clearly referred to the Soviets, Kennedy noted that what bothered him about the missile move was that "it makes them look like they're coequal with us." Ibid., p. 14. This would sound rather curious in the later age of parity. The context is ambiguous, however, and the language could be referring to the Cubans. Also, it should be noted that Kennedy and his lieutenants were confused about when U.S. missiles were actually emplaced in Turkey. Although decisions to proceed were made in 1959 and 1961, missiles were not operational until 1962, and the final arrangement—turning over control of the bases to Turkey—was not complete until October 22, 1962, the day of Kennedy's television speech announcing the quarantine of Cuba. The full story of this phenomenal misunderstanding is being prepared by Murray Marder.

94. "Memorandum of Conference with the President, June 16, 1959," June 19, 1959, p. 1, in DDEL/WHO, Office of the Staff Secretary, Subject Series, State Department Subseries, Box 3. Eisenhower was referring to plans, never implemented, to put additional IRBMs in Greece.

95. Frank A. Sieverts, "The Cuban Crisis, 1962" (a secret 1963 history of the crisis deliberations), pp. 49–50, in JFKL/NSF, Countries Series, Box 49.

adjacent to the USSR. Denial of the symmetry of justification may be based on arguments against moral equivalence of the superpowers, but it becomes less credible when it is based on international law or convention. Violation of the Monroe Doctrine was cited,[96] but it is not clear why that hoary policy would have any more international legal standing than Moscow's initiative to conclude a World War II peace treaty with East Germany. That Moscow was attacking the status quo might be cited to fix responsibility for the crisis. But while it was clear to Americans that the Soviets were responsible for threatening to upset the status quo, there is more to the issue. In Cuba, stationing the missiles was subverting the military status quo to *preserve* the political status quo, the Cuban revolutionary regime. It resembled the U.S. movement of IRBMs to Europe to preserve the political status quo in Berlin.

One argument against symmetry is that the stakes in Cuba were far more vital to Washington than the stakes in Berlin were to Moscow, so American resolve should have been stronger in both cases. Another objection is that Cuba lay within the recognized U.S. sphere of influence. These criticisms are dubious as long as the comparison is with the status of Berlin rather than with defense of NATO as a whole. As Khrushchev noted, West Berlin contained fewer than 3 million people; it was a bone in his throat because it lay anomalously inside East Germany, Moscow's most vital satellite; and its link with the West was a relic of the wartime provisional occupation agreement. Cuba was much larger, both in territory and in population, and was a significant interest for Moscow because it was the only example apart from China or North Vietnam of a communist state formed on the Marxist model of revolution, not by the Soviet army. There is no clear reason that loss of West Berlin would necessarily appear more damaging to the West than loss of Cuba would to the East.

Decisions

Interpretations of the Cuban crisis written after the fact have tended to assess the outcome as inevitable: the Soviets simply had to swallow the fact that they had no choice but to capitulate to American diktat. During the crisis, however, U.S. leaders made no such assumption. While a majority of the Executive Committee of the NSC (the so-called Ex Com) favored U.S. air attack on the missiles in Cuba, the president worried that the

---

96. George W. Ball, *The Past Has Another Pattern: Memoirs* (W. W. Norton, 1982), p. 289.

Soviets would respond by striking the Jupiters in Turkey.[97] McNamara expected a Soviet response somewhere in the world and suggested using a SAC airborne alert to deter it, despite other risks that such an alert would raise.[98] In this way American deterrence and compellence were linked. SAC's deterrence of Soviet "horizontal" escalation in another region guarded the flank of U.S. conventional military compellence against Cuba.

The principal preoccupation was retaliation against Berlin. The Cuban and Berlin conflicts were intertwined in Khrushchev's maneuvering for months before the October crises.[99] At the first emergency meeting on October 16 to assess discovery of the missiles, Rusk mentioned a report "that high Soviet officials were saying, 'We'll trade Cuba for Berlin.'" Later in the meeting he speculated that the Russians might be trying to provoke the United States to take the first move against Cuba so that they could then move against Berlin.[100] Four days later a special intelligence estimate said that American use of force against Cuba would probably lead the Soviets to retaliate in Berlin "with major harassments . . . even a blockade," but that in no case would Moscow initiate general war.[101]

If the imbalance of conventional forces in the Caribbean was the determinant of the outcome in Cuba, as is often asserted, there is no good explanation for why the Soviets did not counter the U.S. naval blockade with a blockade of Berlin, where the conventional imbalance was reversed. One could assume that the Soviet presidium was simply more cautious than the Kennedy administration, although the assumption seems inconsistent with the original Soviet gamble on putting the missiles in Cuba. Otherwise it is hard to avoid the conclusion that the imbalance of nuclear power—U.S. superiority—was an influence. Soviet concern about the nuclear balance was reflected in the decision for the missile deployment in the first place.

What is remarkable, in terms of the logic of strategy, though not perhaps in terms of psychology, is the apparently disjointed or careless quality of

97. Robert F. Kennedy, *Thirteen Days: A Memoir of the Cuban Missile Crisis* (W. W. Norton, 1969), pp. 74, 77.

98. Off-the-Record transcript (evening), pp. 9–10.

99. See Alexander L. George, "The Cuban Missile Crisis, 1962," in George, David K. Hall, and William E. Simons, *The Limits of Coercive Diplomacy: Laos, Cuba, Vietnam* (Little, Brown, 1971), pp. 98–99.

100. Off-the-Record transcript (morning), pp. 9, 15.

101. SNIE 11-19-62, "Major Consequences of Certain US Courses of Action on Cuba," October 20, 1962, pp. 9–10 (Carrollton Press collection). The estimate also asserted that Soviet response was *more* likely if U.S. action was limited than if it included invasion and occupation of Cuba.

U.S. deliberations over the logical relationships between the potential military significance of the Soviet missiles in Cuba, the import of the existing overall nuclear balance, the probability of war and escalation, choices for U.S. military action in the event of major war, and prospective costs of such actions. A brief review of the poorly integrated views on these questions reveals why so many participants' later denigration of the salience of the indirect U.S. nuclear threat in the crisis should lack conviction.

In terms of strictly military implications, contemporary estimates were that the Cuban deployment would have increased Soviet land-based missile first-strike capability by 40 percent and that including the Cuban missiles in a Soviet first strike would reduce surviving American weapons "by about 30 percent, and would thus leave only about 15 percent of the number in our pre-attack force."[102] Yet such estimates did not weigh heavily in deliberations. Although some officials worried about reduction of tactical warning time, the Ex Com paid scant attention to calculations; emphasis was placed on the political and symbolic import of the deployment in Cuba. At the second October 16 meeting the president observed of the new Cuban missiles, "I would think that our risks increase," but then asked, "What difference does it make? *They've got enough to blow us up now anyway.* I think it's just a question of. . . . After all this is a political struggle as much as military."[103]

At the same time, decisionmakers lacked clear confidence in U.S. ability to prevail without eventually having to escalate. On the sixteenth Rusk said, "I think we'll be facing a situation that could well lead to general war."[104] That same day Secretary of Defense Robert McNamara warned that once the Cuban missiles were operational a U.S. strike could not be sure to prevent some from being launched and triggering holocaust. Nevertheless, on October 27—after the CIA had reported some of the missiles to be operational and the FBI had reported destruction of documents by Soviet diplomats in apparent preparation for war—McNamara said a U.S. attack was then "almost inevitable."[105] Thus even McNamara,

---

102. The actual increase would have been about 80 percent. The NIE at the time estimated seventy-five operational Soviet ICBMs, although the actual number was forty-four. The balance of total nuclear launchers capable of hitting the superpower homelands was 1,778 U.S. vs. 316–342 Soviet (including 20–40 in Cuba). Raymond L. Garthoff, "The Meaning of the Missiles," *Washington Quarterly,* vol. 5 (Autumn 1982), pp. 77–79; quotation from Garthoff's October 27, 1962, memorandum, reprinted in ibid., pp. 78–79.

103. Off-the-Record transcript (evening), p. 15 (emphasis added; ellipsis in original).

104. Off-the-Record transcript (morning), p. 10.

105. Barton J. Bernstein, "The Cuban Missile Crisis: Trading the Jupiters in Turkey?"

who was among the more conservative advisers regarding the use of force, was willing to accept what he believed was a serious risk that nuclear war would result.[106] The president himself later claimed to believe that the odds of war were "somewhere between one out of three and even."[107]

If war had come, hawkish folklore suggests that leaders had reason for confidence in U.S. first-strike capability against the USSR. And at the October 16 meeting McNamara suggested threatening Moscow with what amounted to all-out preemption, telling them that "if there is ever *any indication* that they're [missiles in Cuba] *to be* launched against this country, we will respond not only against Cuba, but we will respond directly against the Soviet Union, with a *full* nuclear strike."[108] The president's public warning in his October 22 television address, however, was of a full *retaliatory* strike.

Even if the since-vaunted U.S. first-strike capability in the early 1960s was impressive—and there are grounds for estimating that it was far less than perfect—the leaders who counted took little comfort in it.[109] As the one who counted most—the president—had said on the first day, "They've got enough to blow us up now anyway." Rusk said later, "We did not count missiles on either side," and McNamara affirmed, "It was not a slide-rule calculation."[110]

As Marc Trachtenberg points out, there was no discussion at the October 16 meetings of what would happen if war occurred, no reference to estimates of damage to the United States. "It was as though all the key concepts associated with the administration's formal nuclear strategy, as

---

Political Science Quarterly, vol. 95 (Spring 1980), p. 112; Marc Trachtenberg, "The Influence of Nuclear Weapons in the Cuban Missile Crisis," *International Security,* vol. 10 (Summer 1985), pp. 141–42.

106. Trachtenberg, "Influence of Nuclear Weapons," p. 142.

107. Quoted in Sorensen, *Kennedy,* p. 705. Kennedy appears to have had a penchant for citing numerical odds; recall his estimate in summer 1961 of a 20 percent chance of nuclear war. This reflects the point that despite the chess-like reasoning that characterized the attitudes of limited-war theorists in the administration, the president's approach remained more similar to Russian roulette.

108. Off-the-Record transcript (evening), p. 47 (emphasis added).

109. "United States strategic forces, despite their numerical superiority, were still under development, and their actual capabilities inherently constrained any serious temptation for pre-emptive war against the Soviet Union. The early missile systems had a number of technical imperfections and the more developed bomber force was still constrained by the imperfectly developed organization of strategic attack capability. A decisive, disarming strike against all Soviet strategic forces could not be undertaken with the confidence a rational decision-maker would require." John Steinbruner, "An Assessment of Nuclear Crises," in Franklyn Griffiths and John C. Polanyi, eds., *The Dangers of Nuclear War* (University of Toronto Press, 1979), p. 37. See chapter four below.

110. Quoted in Herken, *Counsels of War,* p. 167.

set out for example just a few months earlier in McNamara's famous Ann Arbor speech—in fact, the whole idea of controlled and discriminate general war—in the final analysis counted for very little," even though discussions evinced fear that "peace was hanging on a thread."[111]

Fred Kaplan reports a meeting sometime during the two weeks of crisis in which Dean Acheson recommended attacking the missiles in Cuba. When asked what the Soviets would do, he guessed that they would retaliate against U.S. missiles in Turkey, which would then require the Americans to destroy a missile base in the USSR. Then what? "'That's when we *hope*,' he answered, 'that cooler heads will prevail and they'll stop and talk.'"[112] This is the only available report of discussions of nuclear war scenarios in the crisis decision process, and it scarcely testifies to well-honed plans or hedging. In terms of risk-minimizing standards for decisionmaking on war and peace, the reality appears frightening: U.S. leaders felt required to take what they saw as a high risk of nuclear war without examining how it would be undertaken or waged to advantage and without confidence that the consequences could be "acceptable." And as it turned out, the only palpable signals in the crisis of readiness for nuclear war were American, not Soviet.

The Dogs of War: Growling and Cowering

As the crisis burgeoned, U.S. nuclear forces went on alert. *Polaris* submarines sped out of port, and military forces around the world moved to the higher alert level of Defense Condition (DEFCON)-3. SAC increased readiness—battle staffs went on duty around the clock, all leaves were canceled, and personnel were recalled. One hundred and thirty-six Atlas and Titan ICBMs were prepared for firing, B-47s were dispersed, bomber and tanker ground alert increased, a large and continuous B-52 airborne alert was instituted, with one-eighth of the force in the air at all times, and all launchers were armed. On October 24 SAC ratcheted up to DEFCON-2—the level just one notch below deployment for combat. By the end of the crisis the SAC systems alone ready to execute the SIOP, irrespective of navy and other air force weapons, included almost 2,000 launchers and over 7,000 megatons—more than the total explosive power in the U.S. inventory today.[113] The Ex Com, however, decided against undertaking

111. Trachtenberg, "Influence of Nuclear Weapons," pp. 147–48, 152.
112. Kaplan, *Wizards of Armageddon*, p. 305 (emphasis added).
113. Hopkins, *Development of the Strategic Air Command*, p. 106; Scott D. Sagan, "Nuclear Alerts and Crisis Management," *International Security*, vol. 9 (Spring 1985), pp. 108–10; "The U.S. Air Force Response to the Cuban Crisis" (USAF Headquarters,

any civil defense crash program, which would have been consistent.[114]

Conventional forces were being prepared to invade Cuba, and the combination of this process with the heightened alert threatened Soviet retaliatory capability at sea. The U.S. Navy was tracking Soviet submarines around a wide area, which amplified the signal of the SAC alert posture. Although they had ordered these operations in the blockade area,[115] members of the Ex Com may not have appreciated how extensively such operations were being mounted elsewhere in the world or may not have pondered their significance.[116] Given the commitment to counterforce targeting and the general military preparation for war, it would have been peculiar to expect the navy *not* to be doing the tracking, in the absence of special orders to refrain, but as the other evidence suggests, decisionmakers might not have been thinking carefully about all these matters.

Even if this amplification of the signal of nuclear war preparations was inadvertent, it could have affected Soviet judgments. In addition there were two signals definitely unintended by the leadership. One was SAC commander Thomas Power's dispatch of an *uncoded* message to the Pentagon "emphasizing the full strength of SAC's alert force."[117] Another was accidental but, in tandem with the previous one, could have seemed ominous to Moscow. On October 27, the navigation system of a U-2 on an air-sampling flight failed, and the plane went off course and penetrated Soviet territory. As Kennedy worried, Moscow might have been expected to read this as a possible final reconnaissance for a U.S. nuclear strike. In his letter accompanying the Soviet decision to withdraw the missiles from

---

n.d.), pp. 7–8. JCS plans for invasion of Cuba were not revised to remove use of tactical weapons from the operation until October 31, after the crisis had turned down. "The U.S. Air Force Response to the Cuban Crisis," p. 11.

114. "Summary Record of NSC Executive Committee Meeting No. 6, October 26, 1962, 10:00 A.M.," p. 1, in JFKL/NSF, Meetings and Memoranda Series, Boxes 316–17.

115. Kennedy, *Thirteen Days,* pp. 61–62, 69–70, 77.

116. Sagan, "Nuclear Alerts," pp. 112–18; Steinbruner, "Assessment of Nuclear Crises," p. 38; George, Hall, and Simons, *Limits of Coercive Diplomacy,* pp. 112–14. Graham Allison says the Ex Com did not find out until October 24. Graham T. Allison, *Essence of Decision: Explaining the Cuban Missile Crisis* (Little, Brown, 1971), p. 138. Such tracking occurs in normal peacetime but probably surged during the crisis. The day before the crisis broke, however, an intelligence bulletin, marked "For the President Only," reported that a Soviet submarine surfaced south of Japan and complained about interference from the U.S. ships that had it under surveillance. Notes appended to CIA, "The President's Intelligence Checklist," October 15, 1962, in JFKL/NSF, Meetings and Memoranda Series, Box 313. The placement of the bulletin in the files indicates that it was reviewed in the October 21 NSC meeting.

117. Sagan, "Nuclear Alerts," p. 108.

Cuba, Khrushchev referred to the incident, noting that the U-2 "could be easily taken for a nuclear bomber, which might push us to a fateful step."[118]

Whatever their perceptions or calculations, the Soviets neither prepared for "a fateful step" in response to the U.S. nuclear alert, nor undertook significant conventional military preparations in Europe.[119] As Air Force General David Burchinal put it, Khrushchev never even put any bombers on alert: "We had a gun at his head and he didn't move a muscle."[120] Soviet observers were well aware of the U.S. counterforce doctrine and prevalent views of American strategists about how reciprocal fear of surprise attack increases temptations in crisis to strike first.[121] The remarkable Soviet nonalert was equivalent to a threatened dog's rolling over belly-up.

Understanding Nuclear Coercion: Now and Then

Some arguments about national security are never resolved because ideological differences prevent analytical agreement. Disputes over whether U.S. nuclear superiority played a significant role in Cuba have continued ever since the crisis, but they cut across divisions between hawks and doves. Both Paul Nitze and Bernard Brodie, for example, placed great emphasis on the Soviet failure to counter the pressure against Cuba by exploiting their conventional superiority against Berlin as evidence of the nuclear impact.[122] Most of the senior participants, however, came to argue to the contrary. Twenty years after the crisis Dean Rusk, Robert Mc-Namara, George Ball, Roswell Gilpatric, Theodore Sorensen, and Mc-George Bundy wrote:

American nuclear superiority was not in our view a critical factor, for

118. Quoted in Allison, *Essence of Decision,* p. 141. See also Sagan, "Nuclear Alerts," pp. 118–21.

119. Kennedy, *Thirteen Days,* p. 58; and, for example, CIA Memorandum, "The Crisis: USSR/Cuba," October 24, 1962, and "Summary Record of NSC Executive Committee Meeting No. 5, October 25, 1962, 5:00 P.M.," p. 1, in JFKL/NSF, Meetings and Memoranda Series, Box 315.

120. "We got everything we had, in the strategic forces . . . counted down and ready and aimed and we made damn sure they saw it without anybody saying a word about it." Burchinal oral history interview, quoted in Trachtenberg, "Influence of Nuclear Weapons," pp. 157, 161.

121. See Soviet statements cited in Trachtenberg, "Influence of Nuclear Weapons," p. 159.

122. Paul Nitze, "Foreword," in Donald G. Brennan, *Arms Treaties With Moscow: Unequal Terms Unevenly Applied?* (New York: National Strategy Information Center, 1975), p. xi; Bernard Brodie, "What Price Conventional Capabilities in Europe?" in Henry A. Kissinger, ed., *Problems of National Strategy* (Praeger, 1965), p. 324.

the fundamental and controlling reason that nuclear war, already in 1962, would have been an unexampled catastrophe for both sides; the balance of terror so eloquently described by Winston Churchill seven years earlier was in full operation. No one of us ever reviewed the nuclear balance for comfort in those hard weeks.[123]

Maxwell Taylor, also looking back two decades later, argued against the relevance of the nuclear balance with a more comforting twist:

> During the EXCOMM discussion I never heard an expression of fear of nuclear escalation on the part of any of my colleagues. If at any time we were sitting on the edge of Armageddon, as nonparticipants have sometimes alleged, we were too unobservant to notice it. . . . Our great superiority in nuclear weapons contributed little to the outcome of the Cuba crisis. In this situation the stakes involved were far too small for either party to risk a resort to nuclear weapons.[124]

In light of the actual record these recollections—perhaps dimmed by time, conceivably colored subconsciously by subsequent developments—appear to be half-truths. It is indeed apparent that the senior policymakers did not dwell on the quality of the nuclear balance and that discussions were not constantly dominated by fear of escalation, but the danger of nuclear war *was* asserted at various times, especially by the president and secretaries of state and defense. The way to square the record and the recollections is to figure that anxiety about the danger of escalation was intermittent, or a genuflection to awareness of the hypothetical possibility, while visceral confidence that the Soviets would have to blink was overriding. Or as Arthur Schlesinger put it, remembering the concern about nuclear war during the crisis, "one lobe of the brain had to recognize the ghastly possibility; another found it quite inconceivable."[125]

Some of those participants who denigrated the role of American nuclear leverage after the fact did not do so at the time. On October 26, 1962, Taylor wrote to McNamara, "We have the *strategic advantage in our general war capabilities.* . . . This is no time to run scared." And a few months after the crisis McNamara testified in Congress that Khrushchev "knew without any question whatsoever that he faced the full military

123. Dean Rusk and others, "The Lessons of the Cuban Missile Crisis," *Time* (September 27, 1982), p. 85.

124. Maxwell D. Taylor, "Reflections on a Grim October," *Washington Post*, October 5, 1982.

125. Schlesinger, *Robert Kennedy and His Times*, p. 529.

power of the United States, including its nuclear weapons." If this was a throwaway line, McNamara went to unnecessary lengths to drive the point home: "We faced that night the possibility of launching nuclear weapons and Khrushchev knew it, and that is the reason, and the only reason, why he withdrew those weapons."[126]

There is another interpretation that would make the disjunction between rhetoric and belief appear less disingenuous. Just as they were ambivalent about whether there was a real danger of war, the leadership during the crisis may have held both contradictory positions about U.S. nuclear superiority—that it was and was not meaningful. Distracted by multiple problems and responsibilities and averse to confronting hard choices before the moment when they could no longer be avoided, high officials may have recognized one sort of cold logic at some times while feeling some vague confidence in the value of numerical superiority at others. This notion would be alien to the rationalistic tradition in deterrence theory, but not to psychological approaches to decision theory.

U.S. leaders may not have recognized, agreed about, or relied consciously on an advantage inherent in numerical nuclear superiority. But they acted as if they did. To sum up, the existence of indirect nuclear threats and the direct relevance of U.S. nuclear superiority in the Cuban crisis can be inferred from three facts. First, the United States assumed that the Soviet missile deployments were intolerable, an assumption that, even if grounded solely in concern about their symbolic impact, testifies to the political salience of change in the balance of nuclear power. Second, the United States was willing to exploit conventional superiority in the Caribbean despite the analogous Soviet option to do the same against Berlin, an action that would have pushed subsequent moves in the confrontation toward the higher nuclear level of military power. Third, the United States prepared its nuclear striking forces for war, and the Soviets did not respond. In addition, recent testimony by Fidel Castro strongly implies that the Soviets told him that their nuclear inferiority was the reason that they had to bow to U.S. demands and remove their missiles from the island.[127]

The civilian principals in the Cuban crisis agreed on a risky coercive response and believed at some points in their deliberations that appreciable danger of war was real, even though their discussions show that they were

---

126. Taylor and McNamara quoted in Trachtenberg, "Influence of Nuclear Weapons," pp. 139n, 141 (emphasis added).

127. Interviews cited in Tad Szulc, Fidel: A Critical Portrait (Morrow, 1986), pp. 582–83, 585.

not confident in the damage-limiting capability of U.S. nuclear forces. Others would claim, however, that they *should* have been confident, because parity did *not* exist, and thus risks were not really great. The next case, the 1973 Middle East War, was one in which making a nuclear threat might be seen as posing acceptable risks because war between the super-powers was not likely. But in 1973 the old cushion of U.S. nuclear superiority—whether or not it had really been valuable in the past—was all but gone.

The Middle East War, 1973

By the early 1970s it was universally agreed that nuclear parity had arrived; the notion was implicitly codified in the SALT I agreement. Some would later argue that the United States retained a waning margin of superiority for several more years, but that argument is correct only in terms of technical edges in various static indexes of nuclear power. For example, in 1973 U.S. forces had a small advantage in throwweight; the Soviets, an even smaller advantage in number of delivery vehicles. The United States had a large superiority in the number of warheads; the Soviets, a small edge in equivalent megatonnage.[128] Superior accuracy and reliability were also generally attributed to the United States in the early 1970s. Although hawks would later note such advantages when criticizing trends in the nuclear balance in the later part of the decade, virtually no one in 1973 was saying that the Soviet nuclear force was inferior to the American.

Decisions

Toward the end of the October War in the Middle East, as a second cease-fire unraveled and Israel appeared to be threatening to collapse Egypt's defense completely, Moscow sent an urgent message to Washing-ton. The letter, which arrived on the night of October 24, proposed joint superpower intervention to reinstitute the cease-fire they had arranged, and threatened to consider unilateral action if the United States refused to participate. Within an hour a meeting of the Washington Special Action Group (WSAG), with the president absent, convened in the White House Situation Room.

128. Donald H. Rumsfeld, *Annual Defense Department Report Fiscal Year 1978* (GPO, 1977), p. 61.

By October 12, U.S. intelligence had ascertained that all seven Soviet airborne divisions were on alert. Some critics have charged that this detection could not have been a direct cause of the American alert that emerged from the WSAG meeting, because as Secretary of Defense Schlesinger noted in an October 27 press conference, the alert had been in effect since much earlier in the war. Some accounts, however, claim that the Soviet alert was heightened for some fraction of the airborne units on the twenty-fourth.[129]

While Soviet military measures on the twenty-third and twenty-fourth were not the primary precipitant of the U.S. decision, they contributed to the sense of urgency. In addition to the Soviet alert of the divisions, a special airborne command post was established in the southern USSR, several airborne garrisons prepared to move, transport planes started some loading, air force units were alerted, much of Soviet airlift capacity could not be located by U.S. intelligence, intercepted messages indicated that Soviet flight plans for the twenty-fifth were being changed, and traffic in some communications nets was surging.[130]

The consensus in the late night WSAG meeting of October 24 was that the U.S. answer to Brezhnev's note would lack impact unless tangible evidence of response reached Moscow before the written reply. The conferees thus decided on a U.S. military alert even before finishing a draft of the reply. "We all agreed," according to Kissinger, "that any increase in readiness would have to go at least to DefCon III before the Soviets would notice it." About an hour later they decided that more was needed. The Eighty-second Airborne Division was alerted "for possible movement," and additional aircraft carriers were ordered to the eastern Mediterranean.[131] Some units in Europe and the Mediterranean had been on a higher than normal readiness footing throughout the war. What the WSAG decision did was to put all U.S. units in the world at DEFCON-3. Although the nuclear component of the shift was what attracted most attention when

129. Raymond L. Garthoff, *Détente and Confrontation: American-Soviet Relations from Nixon to Reagan* (Brookings, 1985), pp. 377, 378n; Galia Golan, *Yom Kippur and After: The Soviet Union and the Middle East Crisis* (Cambridge University Press, 1977), p. 122; Golan debunks other indicators as well (pp. 122–24).

130. Barry M. Blechman and Douglas M. Hart, "The Political Utility of Nuclear Weapons: The 1973 Middle East Crisis," *International Security*, vol. 7 (Summer 1982), pp. 136–37; Douglas M. Hart, "Soviet Approaches to Crisis Management: The Military Dimension," *Survival*, vol. 26 (September–October, 1984), p. 216. Raymond Garthoff believes these accounts overstate the certainty of the indicators.

131. Henry Kissinger, *Years of Upheaval* (Little, Brown, 1982), pp. 587–89.

it was unexpectedly splashed across headlines the next day, the principal elements of the signal were conventional—the alert of the Eighty-second Airborne and the naval movements.

Some years later, Kissinger is alleged to have said that the DEFCON-3 move was not one he would have dared repeat in the late 1970s, given the shift in the strategic balance. To many the remark seems exaggerated, since the change in the balance in the 1970s was only between degrees of roughness in rough parity, not enough to make any meaningful difference in a risk estimate, and Kissinger had no better reason for any confidence in U.S. superiority earlier in the decade than he would have at its end. Indeed, Kissinger's public remarks at the time of the crisis made not the remotest suggestion of U.S. nuclear advantage and referred only to the awesome danger of mutual annihilation. The possible inconsistency in Kissinger's views during and after the crisis compares curiously with the same question about those of some participants in the 1962 missile crisis decision. McNamara and Taylor later claimed to have seen no relevance in numerical U.S. nuclear advantage, despite statements to the contrary at the time. In Kissinger's case the difference is reversed.

One indication that Kissinger did draw some comfort from the nuclear balance at the time of the crisis is the recollection of one of his principal staff assistants whose own views about strategy and the balance are in the mold of mutual assured destruction and who thus has no psychological incentive to color his recollection to attribute value to whatever U.S. nuclear edge might have been perceived at the time. The assistant said that Kissinger did have the nuclear balance on his mind during the 1973 crisis and at one point remarked, "This is the last time we'll ever be able to get away with this."[132]

In any case, if conferees in the WSAG sensed some significance in a marginal U.S. nuclear advantage, it could not have seemed more than a remote and trivial one. And although surprisingly little attention was paid in 1962 to what sort of engagement would follow if the Soviets were not cowed by U.S. action, no attention at all was given to that question in 1973. Given the lack of time, U.S. leaders did not even think about what military moves they would make if the Russians were not deterred by the alert.[133] The U.S. threat in 1973 was not developed in terms of a calibrated judgment about material costs and benefits to the two sides, but was an example of manipulation of risk, the "threat that leaves something to

132. Personal conversation, May 17, 1983.
133. Blechman and Hart, "Political Utility of Nuclear Weapons," p. 151.

chance," an exploitation of the danger that the crisis could slip out of control and into mutual catastrophe.[134] At worst it was meaningless vis-à-vis the ostensible targets, the Soviet leaders, and meant rather to play in domestic politics by giving the appearance that the administration was being tough on the Soviets while it was actually doing what Moscow wanted—squeezing the Israelis.

Signals

Large portions of U.S. intercontinental forces are ready to launch during peacetime, when SAC's standard status is DEFCON-4. With the global alert, tankers dispersed and undertook operations that went beyond routine, while ICBMs went onto a slightly higher footing and some ballistic missile submarines sailed out of port.[135] Perhaps most visible was the recall of SAC B-52s from Guam. The bombers had been left there as a deterrent against North Vietnam despite congressional prohibition of bombing in Indochina. In Kissinger's words, "Now we used the opportunity to end this empty game and in the process give the Soviets another indication that we were assembling our forces for a showdown."[136]

The main problem with using the higher alert, especially its nuclear element, as a signal was that it seemed transparently inappropriate. The Soviets were not threatening to attack American or allied territory, only to interpose forces on their ally's territory and at Cairo's invitation to enforce an agreed truce; indeed, they were asking Washington to act as a partner in peacekeeping. And coinciding as it did with an epochal American constitutional crisis, the height of the Watergate scandal, with the "Saturday Night Massacre" less than a week in the past, the immediate reaction at home was to question whether the alert was a domestic ploy to divert attention. That it was is unlikely, but Watergate did figure in the alert decision; leaders feared Moscow might mistakenly assume that the U.S. executive would be paralyzed.

As a result, few took the alert as a genuine sign of intent to fight. Indeed, if combat with Soviet forces had really been imminent, the strictly logical move in principle would have been to go to DEFCON-2—the level closer to wartime operating readiness. Given the timing of events surrounding the Brezhnev note, the prospect of military engagement should have seemed either imminent or remote, but not in between. Thus SAC did not undertake

134. Ibid., pp. 153–54.
135. Ibid., p. 140; Hart, "Soviet Approaches to Crisis Management," p. 216.
136. Kissinger, *Years of Upheaval*, p. 591.

more of the preparations that would have been a real preface to wartime operation; the organization went through the motions in responding to the alert order, but did not take it very seriously.[137]

Nevertheless, in their statements on the twenty-fifth, Kissinger and the president, who had not been involved in the WSAG decision and may not even have known about it until the following day, exploited the signal.[138] Nixon, rejecting the Soviet demands, said that unilateral action would violate Article 2 of the Agreement on Prevention of Nuclear War, and that "we could in no event accept unilateral action. . . . such action would produce incalculable consequences which would be in the interest of neither of our countries."[139] In his press conference on the twenty-fifth Kissinger more than once stressed nuclear risks, for example warning, "We possess, each of us, nuclear arsenals capable of annihilating humanity."[140] There are disagreements as to whether the crisis had been resolved by then anyway, but it was not until late on the twenty-fifth that the Soviets desisted in their United Nations effort for a joint superpower peacekeeping force.[141] The U.S. alert was rescinded the following day.

Reactions

Brezhnev replied to the American note on the twenty-fifth, not mentioning the U.S. alert, but accepting Nixon's alternative of sending Soviet observers to monitor reestablishment of the cease-fire. After termination of the alert, on the twenty-sixth, another Brezhnev message asking Washington to rein in the Israeli advance and allow supplies to Egypt's surrounded Third Army Corps referred to the alert. Brezhnev said that he had been surprised by the alert, and made a point that Moscow had not responded to it, even though the U.S. action was not conducive to relaxing tension.[142]

---

137. Steinbruner, "Assessment of Nuclear Crises," p. 43n. Steinbruner reports a personal communication that SAC's commander, on the golf course when informed by aides of preparations getting under way, nonchalantly continued his game. And, according to interviews, "After the Joint Chiefs issued DEFCON 3 orders . . . they immediately began rescinding items on that checklist." Bruce G. Blair, "Alerting in Crisis and Conventional War," in Ashton B. Carter, John D. Steinbruner, and Charles A. Zraket, eds., *Managing Nuclear Operations* (Brookings, 1987), p. 115.

138. Garthoff, *Détente and Confrontation*, pp. 378–79, 379n.

139. Richard Nixon, *RN: The Memoirs of Richard Nixon* (Grosset and Dunlap, 1978), p. 940; see also Kissinger, *Years of Upheaval*, p. 591.

140. Quoted in Blechman and Hart, "Political Utility of Nuclear Weapons," p. 143.

141. Ibid., pp. 143–44.

142. Garthoff, *Détente and Confrontation*, pp. 380–81. Quotation on p. 381.

One incident sometimes cited as an indication of a *Soviet* nuclear threat in the crisis—though it could not have been a reaction to DEFCON-3, given the timing—was the U.S. detection of neutron emissions from a Russian freighter that transited the Bosporus on October 22 and docked at Alexandria three days later. The emissions suggested the possibility of nuclear weapons on board, and some sources have made the unlikely claim that U.S. surveillance also found nuclear warheads near SCUD missiles in Egypt. The freighter may have been supplying the Soviet fleet, which stocks nuclear weapons, on the same trip. William Quandt, who served on the NSC staff during the war, noted these speculations and emphasized that "there is no reliable evidence that nuclear weapons ever entered Egypt."[143]

The American alert did not resolve the issue in dispute—stopping the Israeli advance—though it may have prevented Moscow from sending troop units—which was the purpose of the decision of October 24.[144] Other than the timing of Brezhnev's shift from the threat to send forces to the plan to send observers, there is scant reason to impute coercive success to the U.S. alert. The Soviets quickly got what they wanted: a firm cease-fire.

Nasser's confidant Mohamed Heikal diagnosed the U.S. alert as a move by Washington "which astonished rather than frightened its enemies," and reported that Brezhnev characterized the alert to Algerian and Syrian leaders Houari Boumedienne and Hafiz al-Asad as "all a false alarm resulting from an American desire to overdramatize the crisis. If, he said, it was meant as a warning to the Soviet Union, the message had the wrong address on it."[145] It is interesting to compare this facile dismissal by Brezhnev, however, with Heikal's report of what he had said about the Six Day War, in which the USSR had not achieved its minimal objective. When Boumedienne had visited Moscow in 1967 and complained about Soviet caution in that war, the Soviet leader responded, "What is your opinion of nuclear war?"[146]

A Kissinger staff source cited by Blechman and Hart argued that while Brezhnev spoke publicly about the "absurd" response by "some NATO

143. William B. Quandt, "Soviet Policy in the October Middle East War—II," *International Affairs* (London), vol. 53 (October 1977), pp. 596, 597. Quandt made the point again on p. 597n.

144. Garthoff, *Détente and Confrontation*, p. 380.

145. Mohamed Heikal, *The Road to Ramadan* (Quadrangle, 1975), pp. 243, 255.

146. Quoted by Heikal in *Al-Ahram*, August 25, 1967, cited in William B. Quandt, *Soviet Policy in the October 1973 War*, R-1864-ISA (Santa Monica, Calif.: Rand Corporation, 1976), p. 24.

countries" in 1973, Soviet representatives in private conversations never protested that Washington had misinterpreted Moscow's position or overreacted. The Soviets, in his view, were clearly contemplating intervention and "understood the seriousness of the American signals sent by the nuclear threat."[147] Yet more than in most cases, the circumstantial evidence for inferring efficacy in the U.S. nuclear threat is weak, and much points in the direction of concluding that it was beside the point. If the alert was influential, it is also hard to argue against the proposition that the conventional force elements in it were sufficient, the nuclear component superfluous.

One could make an indirect case that the alert had some significance by citing the correlation between U.S. objectives at the time and the ultimate results of the crisis. Kissinger wanted the alert to show American toughness against Moscow and also to freeze the Soviets out of the resolution of the crisis.[148] The latter aim was achieved in spades. Sadat had wanted Moscow to intervene, but he was left in the lurch and saved instead by U.S. pressure on Israel. Within a short time, Sadat's policy shifted to cooperation with the United States, and the Soviets were ejected from their role in Egypt. That SAC could take any credit for this is doubtful yet impossible to disprove.

The Carter Doctrine, 1980

Following the Soviet invasion of Afghanistan at the end of 1979 the Carter administration solidified and accelerated a U.S. military commitment, which had been nascent since the issuance of Presidential Directive 18 in 1977, to defend the Persian Gulf region.[149] The veiled nuclear signals involved were not aimed at blocking a specific action that the adversary had threatened to take, as in most of the other cases discussed, but were part of a general plan for deterring potential moves; hence the appellation of "doctrine" to the Carter initiative. The case is mentioned briefly here, however, because even more clearly than the 1973 war, it illustrates the limits of the view that parity prevents manipulation of nuclear risk.

147. Blechman and Hart, "Political Utility of Nuclear Weapons," p. 149.
148. Garthoff, *Détente and Confrontation*, pp. 383–84.
149. The United States had long recognized a strategic interest in the Middle East, but had ceded the principal policing function for Gulf security to the British until they withdrew from East of Suez in the late 1960s and then to Iran until the revolution.

Less than a month after the Afghanistan invasion, unofficial "back-grounders" from administration sources led to press reports about the possibility of nuclear war if the USSR invaded Iran.[150] President Carter's State of the Union message on January 23, 1980, did not mention that specific possibility when he declared that U.S. military force would meet a Soviet assault in the Persian Gulf, but the nuclear element entered commentators' speculations. Carter later asserted that the response he threatened would be one "not necessarily confined to any small invaded area or to tactics or terrain of the Soviets' choosing."[151]

Shortly after the president's speech an anonymous high official giving a background briefing remarked, "We are thinking about theater nuclear options in other areas than NATO." At the beginning of February a year-old Defense Department study mentioning the need to "threaten or make use of tactical nuclear weapons" against a Soviet move into Iran was resurrected and leaked.[152] The next day, the assistant secretary of defense for public information, William Dyess, answered "No Sir," when asked on NBC television if the United States was "committed not to make the first strike" in nuclear conflict. He continued, "The Soviets know that this terrible weapon has been dropped on human beings twice in history and it was an American president who dropped it both times. Therefore, they have to take this into consideration in their calculus."[153]

The question of nuclear threats did not dominate public attention to the Carter Doctrine, and administration planning focused on developing conventional military options. In open signaling, however, nuclear elements were interlarded with conventional ones, and Moscow took notice. In late February an authoritative *Pravda* article noted U.S. nuclear contingency planning. In the first six months of 1980 U.S. B-52 bombers flew reconnaissance missions in the Arabian Sea. No pretense was made that they had a nuclear mission, but in a manner similar to the sending of B-29s to Europe in 1948, the use of craft that were identified principally as strategic nuclear delivery systems carried some symbolism.[154] In a speech

150. For example, see the January 18, 1980, *Los Angeles Times* story cited by Daniel Ellsberg in "Introduction: Call to Mutiny," in E. P. Thompson and Dan Smith, eds., *Protest and Survive* (Monthly Review Press, 1981), pp. ii–iii.

151. Jimmy Carter, *Keeping Faith: Memoirs of a President* (Bantam Books, 1982), p. 483.

152. Both the anonymous official and Dyess are quoted in Barry Blechman and Douglas Hart, "Dangerous Shortcuts," *New Republic* (July 26, 1980), p. 14.

153. Quoted in Ellsberg, "Introduction," p. iv.

154. Blechman and Hart, "Dangerous Shortcuts," pp. 14–15.

in early March Secretary of Defense Harold Brown emphasized the push for conventional military options. He did so, however, after referring to reports of plans for use of nuclear weapons, saying that any U.S.-Soviet war risked escalation, and that "we cannot concede to the Soviet full choice of the arena or the actions."[155]

Later that year, in August, a scare over Soviet mobilization and exercises in the Transcaucasus region near Iran prompted renewed discussion within the Pentagon of nuclear options for the Gulf. There were no firm recommendations or decisions, however, and no attempts to signal Moscow. Indeed, word of these events did not leak into the press until years later.[156]

Although minor in overall significance for the Gulf crisis, the muted invocation of nuclear first-use threats in the earlier part of 1980 is instructive. After the 1960s many American observers assumed that the credibility of extended deterrence in Europe was at best eroded or at worst a hollow shell. But maintenance of the formal doctrinal commitment to NATO could be easily explained by the force of inertia and tradition, the diplomatic costs for alliance solidarity of an initiative to change it, and the lack of danger that it could be called to the test after détente and stabilization of the Berlin issue.

None of these explanations, however, applies to the Carter Doctrine. It was an active innovation rather than continued acceptance of an old commitment; it was undertaken unilaterally rather than at any clients' behest; and the volatility of the situation in the Near East made the possibility of conflict, miscalculation, or unintended engagement greater than it ever had been in Europe. Yet faced with the development of an interest deemed vital, and with conventional options for deterrence or defense even weaker than NATO's, the American government again reached gingerly for the nuclear crutch—despite a nuclear equation characterized by optimists as parity and by pessimists as emergent inferiority.

155. Quoted in "U.S. Retains Nuke Option in Persian Gulf: Brown," *New York News,* March 7, 1980.

156. A rather breathless article portrays the anxiety over Soviet mobilization and the U.S. nuclear contingency planning as extremely serious. Benjamin F. Schemmer, "Was the U.S. Ready to Resort to Nuclear Weapons for the Persian Gulf in 1980?" *Armed Forces Journal International,* vol. 124 (September 1986), pp. 92–96. Top officials, however, including Harold Brown, had more moderate recollections. Ibid., pp. 100, 102.

CHAPTER FOUR

Brinks and Balances:
Interests, Vulnerability, Resolve

Two additional characteristics of present American policy increase the significance of the current commitment to immediate and massive retaliatory action. First is the fact that . . . . this is not simply one way of dealing with the Soviet Union in the event of war; it appears to be the only way now seriously considered. . . . Second, this intensive preoccu- pation with the development of a massive capacity for atomic attack is not matched by any corresponding concern for the defense of the US in case of a similar attack on the part of the Soviet Union. Indeed both the public and the responsible military authorities appear to be persuaded that the important characteristic of the atomic bomb is that it can be used against the Soviet Union; much less attention has been given to the equally important fact that atomic bombs can be used by the Soviet Union against the United States. This situation results partly from . . . an apparent reluctance to face the simple but unpleasant fact that the atomic bomb works both ways.

Report by the Panel of Consultants
of the Department of State, January 1953

EXCEPT OVER Cuba, the cold war crises never really brought the super- powers close to war. The nature of the evidence precludes conclusions about whether peace was maintained because of nuclear threats or in spite of them—or about how much impact the hints of blackmail had either way. Yet the incidence of such signals shows that decisionmakers believed they had something to gain from manipulating nuclear risks. Rather than raise the political risk that they would have to accept territorial losses, they preferred to raise military risks and edge a bit closer to war.

American threats were amply hedged, but often more concrete and less cautious than those of the Soviets. Unlike Washington, Moscow never went beyond rhetoric to alerts of nuclear forces. The record of results was also mixed, with few unambiguous or lopsided "wins" for either side. Yet overall, in terms of stated objectives at the outset of confrontations, U.S. presidents suffered less embarrassment in the outcomes than did leaders in Moscow. For reasons of evidence as well as relevance to American policy, this chapter concentrates on the rationales for U.S. behavior.

Two general arguments have been offered to make the case that it was not crazy for U.S. leaders to exploit the danger of nuclear conflict as a bargaining tactic. Why should they have believed that the implicit risks were lower than the dangers of weakening their hand by keeping the nuclear crutch in the closet? One argument is that the political balance of interests assured that American resolve would be more credible than U.S. adversaries'; the stakes in dispute being more important to the West than to Moscow or Beijing, Washington had an inherent edge in the competition of risk taking. Nuclear blackmail could work because it was in a good cause. The other argument is that the U.S. advantage in nuclear capability offered the capacity to follow through with threats if necessary, at a price that could be lower than bowing to the opponent's advance; the imbalance of vulnerability to nuclear attack made first-use threats reasonably safe because the USSR had too weak a deterrent to stand up to them. Nuclear blackmail could work because nuclear war would be unthinkable for the Russians but not for the United States.

The analysis that follows finds both general explanations for behavior partially valid, but neither one sufficient to account simultaneously for the thinking of both sides as they moved around the brink. The balance of interests is more significant in accounting for American willingness to threaten escalation, while the balance of power seems a more plausible explanation for Soviet decisions against contesting the threats. To the extent that this combination of the explanations is true, as the last two chapters will elaborate, the implications for the future are unsettling.

Right Makes Might? The Balance of Interests and Resolve

Crises between the United States and the Soviet Union have been over territories in third areas, not territorial demands against their respective homelands. The breadth of the superpowers' commitments is what distinguishes them from minor powers who can rarely spare much effort beyond guarding their basic national integrity. That same breadth makes it difficult to evaluate the relative intensity of U.S. and Soviet interests engaged in crises, and therefore the strength of political motives that competed with military prudence.

Deterrence is a psychological phenomenon that depends on the beliefs of the deterree. Therefore no necessary consistency exists between an explanation that illuminates the thinking of the deterrer and one that accounts for the *results* of the action he takes. The deterree may accede to threats for those reasons or for different ones. Both can sincerely perceive each other as the blackmailers and themselves as the victims.

The balance of interests explanation implicitly and dubiously assumes that both U.S. and Soviet leaders agreed that U.S. interests in the crises were paramount. But while there is no solid evidence on how Soviet leaders privately assessed the balance of interests or American resolve, their public statements and writings indicate their conviction that the disputed issues were important to Soviet security, that Soviet positions were morally and legally justifiable, and that the United States, being imperialist by nature, was the aggressor. Since Americans believe none of this, they tend to dismiss Soviet rhetoric as completely disingenuous. But there are reasons implicit in geography, history, and ideology to doubt that Soviet leaders disbelieve their own statements and to question the assumption that the Soviets usually recognized U.S. interests as greater than their own. Thus it is quite possible that while the U.S. perception of the balance of interests determined U.S. leaders' resolve to run the military risks of a nuclear threat, the Soviet perception of that balance, in itself, gave Moscow's leaders no obvious reason to cave in.

One dimension of the balance of interests is relative magnitude. Is the territory in dispute intrinsically more important—in size, population, economic value, strategic proximity, or political affinity—to one side than to the other? Presumably the side with the greater stake will be proportionally more willing to take risks for it. Another aspect is relative legitimacy. Does one side have a clearer claim to rights on the matter than the other does? If material interests and power are equal, the side whose leaders believe most intensely that its claim is just is likely to fight harder for it.

Characterizations in either dimension were especially subjective during cold war crises. The magnitude of particular interests, at least from the American point of view, was usually inflated because of the Munich analogy or domino theory. Few of the crises in which nuclear threats occurred involved direct threats to major interests—the sovereignty of Western European countries, Japan, or even the Israeli homeland. To the extent that a Chinese attack on the offshore islands would have been linked to invasion of Taiwan, those Asian confrontations are exceptions. Most of the crises were over small territories whose significance to U.S. leaders was determined symbolically, by how their loss would whet communist appetites, demoralize allies, or contribute to gradual erosion of containment if they were tolerated piecemeal.

Should Moscow and Beijing have seen the size of their material stakes in the same terms as Washington did? Was the freedom of fewer than 3 million people in West Berlin in itself more valuable to the West than the elimination of what appeared to be an anomalous cancer threatening the viability of the far larger and more populous German Democratic Republic was to the Soviet Union? Were Quemoy and Matsu of more intrinsic interest to Beijing or to Washington? Missiles in Cuba would have changed the superpower military equation by making it less imbalanced; was the danger of reduced superiority more important to Washington than the relief of reduced inferiority would have been to Moscow? However a disinterested observer might weigh such interests, it is hard to believe that Soviet, Chinese, and American leaders would agree on their relative importance. Indeed, the fact that national leaders so often referred to each other's tactics as nuclear blackmail, while never admitting to indulging in blackmail themselves, reflects the emotionally charged quality of the disagreements as well as the difference in views of legitimacy.

Because so many of the crises concerned stakes of symbolic significance, and because the camps in the cold war conflict were defined so much by ideology, the nature and extent of interests are hard to disentangle from notions of legitimacy. Could both sides in the various crises see the most "rightful" claim to interests in the same way?

Ideology, Perception, and Aggression

The balance of interests thesis assumes that the natural advantage in a competition in risk taking accrues to the side resisting aggression. The assumption may often be true, but not always. German and Japanese leaders in 1938–41 proved to have more alacrity in risk taking than French, British, Russian, or American leaders did. One might argue that if both sides had possessed nuclear weapons in 1939, even Adolf Hitler would not have risked Berlin for Paris. But would he have been equally fearful of testing French resolve to risk Paris for Prague or Warsaw—the closer analogues to territorial crises in the cold war? It is hard, in hindsight, to impute credibility to a hypothetical French nuclear threat, considering the moral collapse in 1940. The French chose to surrender rather than to evacuate the government and carry on the war from the empire, an alternative far less appalling than nuclear incineration. Japanese leaders were adventurous enough in 1941 to launch a war against a power they knew they could not defeat in an unlimited war. Was that risk so much less unthinkable than using a nuclear deterrent force to shield their conventional attack in the Pacific against American escalation?

One can argue that the USSR and PRC were less fanatical and less motivated to expand during the cold war than were the fascist regimes during World War II. The argument is probably true, but it causes another problem. Since deterrence is in the eye of the beholder, the balance of interests thesis requires that the aggressor himself recognize that he is engaged in aggression. The question of self-image poses the most trouble for the theory. That the USSR was the aggressive party in cold war conflicts has been the conventional wisdom in the West, except among critics on the radical fringe. The lessons of Nazi advances in the 1930s, especially the Rhineland and Munich crises, loomed large as U.S. policymakers contemplated Soviet behavior. But Moscow is unlikely to have viewed its own initiatives as being like Hitler's, or Washington's actions as purely defensive. Indeed, separating defensive motives from aggressive action is often impossible, and assuming identical perceptions of rights and responsibilities between antagonists in international conflict is usually unwarranted.[1]

Raising that point does not imply that Soviet propaganda about aggressive U.S. imperialism should be viewed sympathetically, only that such assertions not be assumed to be disingenuous; incompatible interests can be equally intense. Nor does the point imply a charitable explanation of Soviet behavior or any notion of "moral equivalence" between the superpowers. It holds as long as ideology is considered an influence on Soviet perceptions and self-image. Indeed, in this respect it is the moral *non*-equivalence of the two sides that is most relevant. Marxism-Leninism is an empirical ideology as well as a normative one. It claims not only to prescribe how the world *should* be, but to describe how the world is. Marxism sees the interests of capitalism and socialism as opposed; Leninism sees capitalism as driven by its natural dynamics toward imperialism. If they have any role, the descriptive aspects of ideology make the lenses through which cold war crises were refracted in Soviet eyes quite different from those of democratic leaders in the West.[2]

---

1. See Marc Trachtenberg, "Strategists, Philosophers, and the Nuclear Question," *Ethics*, vol. 95 (April 1985), p. 735; and Richard K. Betts, *Surprise Attack: Lessons for Defense Planning* (Brookings, 1982), pp. 141–44.

2. There are reasons apart from ideology that someone living in the Soviet Union—

Two arguments could be used to dispute the importance of Marxism or Leninism in shaping the Soviet self-image. One is that Soviet leaders, for whom ideology long ago became a hollow shell, do not take it seriously themselves; another is that they realize that its original formulations have been modified by the modern military reality that makes coexistence necessary and therefore possible. Both are valid to a point, but neither salvages the balance of interests explanation for the logic of U.S. threats.

The first argument fails to see that ideologies can be malleable or debased without losing their influence. There is a middle ground between being a crude ideologue or a rudderless cynic. Ideology does not preclude pragmatism, except for fanatics; it may still shape the aims that pragmatic tactics pursue. The fact that individuals act in ways that seem to others glaringly inconsistent with declared values does not make the values irrelevant to their perceptions. Many professed Christians who do not practice the charity, humility, or pacifism preached in the Sermon on the Mount may nevertheless view the world in many respects through norms of the Christian tradition. Top Soviet leaders have had negligible personal experience of Western life and were acculturated to Marxist-Leninist outlooks in the crucible of revolution, civil war, and Western intervention, or were indoctrinated in Marxism-Leninism at least as thoroughly as Americans are in the different canons of liberal democracy. Their view of the world could hardly be free of the precepts of class struggle. The same was true in China. Mao Tse-tung downplayed the danger of nuclear war to China by arguing how counterproductive it would be for the imperialists' aims:

Exploitation means exploiting people; one has to exploit people before one can exploit the earth. There's no land without people, no wealth without land. If you kill all the people and seize the land, what can you do with it? I don't see any reason for using nuclear weapons, conventional weapons are better.[3]

---

even someone utterly skeptical of communist dogma—might view the United States as an aggressive, revisionist power, but this section focuses on the narrow factor of ideology to make the minimum case.

3. Quoted in Michael B. Yahuda, *China's Role in World Affairs* (St. Martin's Press, 1978), p. 109. A more breathtaking example of the impact of ideology on Mao's view of nuclear war was his statement that if it nevertheless occurred because of imperialist irrationality, even the death of two-thirds of world population meant that "several Five Year Plans can be developed for the total elimination of capitalism and for permanent peace. It is not a bad thing." Ibid.

The second argument, that Soviet leaders accepted the limitations that nuclear weapons place on the international class struggle,[4] reflects the logic of the balance of power. It does not automatically bear on the Soviet view of the relative import or legitimacy of interests of the two sides, or which was more aggressive, in the disputes that elicited American nuclear threats. And it is the clarity of aggressive and defensive status that lies at the heart of the balance of interests thesis.

Understanding the issue of Soviet motivation is sometimes complicated by a tendency to identify motives with morality. There are three ways of characterizing Soviet motives as they would bear on the role of perceived legitimacy of interests in a competition in risk taking: immoral (unprovoked aggression—the official Western view); moral (defense of the revolution and socialist allies—the official Soviet view); or amoral (prudent opportunism—a realpolitik view). The first two, discussed in the preceding paragraphs, bear most on how leaders in the opposing capitals viewed their own rights and incentives and suggest the asymmetry of views that complicates the balance of interests explanation for resolve. The third, however, might be expected to avoid the perceptual pitfalls of the first two because it bears on how more ideologically neutral standards for evaluating the balance of interest might be expected to affect the competition of resolve. But even this alternative does not rescue the general explanation.

Defense of the Status Quo

Given disagreements about the legitimacy of opposed interests, there is a strong practical presumption in favor of the status quo in international conflicts. The party seeking to change it has a heavier burden of proof, and inertia should give the advantage to the status quo power in the contest of resolve. Territorial interests can be separated from ideological legitimacy, and ambiguities can be ironed out by defining the side that challenges the existing situation as the party at fault. Since deterrence is assumed to be easier than compellence, the status quo party has the advantage.[5] It is generally assumed that U.S. nuclear threats were made to shore up the status quo against Soviet or Chinese attempts to revise it. For the most part

4. This was a prime source of the Sino-Soviet split. The Russians proclaimed to the Chinese in 1963, "The atomic bomb does not observe the class principle." Quotation in William Zimmerman, *Soviet Perspectives on International Relations, 1956–1967* (Princeton University Press, 1969), p. 5.

5. Robert Jervis, *The Illogic of American Nuclear Strategy* (Cornell University Press, 1984), pp. 134, 153–54.

the assumption is true, and since American leaders certainly thought so, it helps explain why *they* did not blink first at the brink. It does not, however, explain why Russian or Chinese leaders did blink. The problem lies in simplistic assumptions about the concept and nature of the status quo.

First, the status quo is not all of a piece. The same side can be defending one aspect of it while challenging another. Thus the assumption that deterrence is easier than compellence may not clarify which side has the logical advantage, since either one may be attempting *both* types of coercion at the same time—and what one side sees as defensive deterrence, the other may consider as offensive compellence.

Second, conflicting views of legitimacy and legality can combine with concerns about larger issues to override the significance of the immediate status quo. In the Taiwan Straits crises, for example, Beijing saw the issue as the final mopping up phase of the Chinese Civil War. What Washington saw as support of the status quo, the PRC saw as illegal intervention and aid to domestic outlaws. West Berlin's independence of the East German regime, in turn, struck the Soviets as legally anachronistic, inherently unstable, and a threatening challenge to the postwar division of Europe. To the Soviets and Chinese, therefore, actions to tidy up these problems may well have seemed less provocative than U.S. interference to buttress the illegitimate and dangerous status quo.

Third, crisis by definition involves flux, rapid change in a situation, in the course of which status can shift day by day. One side may be trying to restore yesterday's situation while the other is trying to preserve today's. Either one may be trying to deter at one moment and to compel at the next. Which then is clearly the status quo power? Esoteric as such confusions may be, they impair clarity about the logical distribution of interests and resolve. The confusions occur in some form or degree in most of the cases.

In the Berlin crises, Stalin and Khrushchev attacked the status quo of the city itself. In the first case, the blockade, the Soviets' action was clearly aggressive in this respect, but it was also a reaction to the "provocation" of currency reform and moves toward reconstitution of a German state in the western zones of occupation—an anti-Soviet change in the larger national status quo. In the second and third crises, Khrushchev took his initiative in the name of the higher territorial and political status quo—the division of Germany into two separate national states, a condition that the West recognized as a temporary fact but refused to accept as permanent. In this light the Soviets portrayed the independence of West Berlin as a vestige of the temporary postwar occupation that challenged the sovereignty of the German Democratic Republic. Soviet démarches in 1958 and 1961 emphasized the need to stabilize the larger regional status quo by legally ending the state of war with Germany through a peace treaty. The aim was linked to squelching Western ambitions to reunify Germany and revise the postwar borders by regaining territory annexed in 1945 by Poland and the USSR. West Berlin was cited as a base used by West German "revanchist circles" to "continually maintain extreme tension and organize all kinds of provocations very dangerous to the cause of peace," and as "a dangerous hotbed of tension."[6] In short, the particular status quo in Berlin was threatening the general status quo in central Europe.

In the 1961 crisis, Moscow was also trying to preserve the economic viability of East Germany, which was threatened by the exodus of population through the West Berlin escape hatch: at the most delicate point of confrontation, the Russians were acting to preserve the status quo.[7] These points were not completely lost on Washington. As McGeorge Bundy's right-hand man, Carl Kaysen, wrote in a secret memo at the peak of the crisis, "What the Russians want above all is a stabilization of the situation in Eastern Europe. This means recognition of the Oder-Neisse boundary . . . legitimacy of the GDR, and stability in East Germany." Kaysen continued, "It is a fair question to what extent political stability in East Germany is compatible with the existence of a free West Berlin."[8] Other analysts argue that the prime Soviet motive in the second and third crises was to prevent Bonn from obtaining nuclear weapons.[9] If they are right, it would make an even stronger case for characterizing Moscow as a status quo party in the conflict.

In the Taiwan Straits, the Chinese communists cited U.S. threats as interference in China's internal affairs, initiatives to intervene forcibly in the ongoing Chinese Civil War.[10] Although the PRC was indeed challenging the status quo more than was the United States, the definition of the issue in these terms makes it unlikely that leaders in either Beijing or Moscow

6. "Aide-Mémoire From the Soviet Union to the United States on the German Question, Handed by Chairman Khrushchev to President Kennedy at Vienna, June 4, 1961," in United States Department of State, *Documents on Germany, 1944–1985* (Government Printing Office, 1985), pp. 730–31.

7. Hannes Adomeit, *Soviet Risk-Taking and Crisis Behavior: A Theoretical and Empirical Analysis* (London: George Allen and Unwin, 1982), p. 335.

8. Carl Kaysen, "Thoughts on Berlin," August 22, 1961, p. 2, in John F. Kennedy Library (JFKL)/National Security Files (NSF), Meetings and Memoranda Series, Box 320.

9. Trachtenberg, "Strategists, Philosophers, and the Nuclear Question," p. 735.

10. John R. Thomas, "Soviet Behavior in the Quemoy Crises of 1958," *Orbis,* vol. 6 (Spring 1962), p. 46n.

saw communist interests in completing the extension of control over Chinese territory as less vital than Washington's interest in opposing it.

In the 1962 Cuban crisis, installation of Soviet missiles challenged the military status quo—the nuclear balance of power and U.S. immunity from weapons based in its hemisphere—but supported the political status quo— consolidation of the Cuban revolution in the face of U.S. hostility and potential inclination to invade. By the time the missiles were discovered, Washington's demand that they be removed was a demand for change in the newborn military status quo. Kennedy's earlier warnings against emplacement of offensive weapons had been aimed at deterrence; his threats in October were aimed at compellence.

In the 1973 Middle East War, the U.S. global alert was intended to deter Soviet intervention, but Moscow's intervention threat had been aimed against the unfolding Israeli attempt to overturn the immediate status quo, truce in the war, as well as the prewar situation—the Israeli army was advancing deep to the west of the Suez Canal. Of course the Egyptians had initiated the challenge to the status quo by attacking eastward in the first place, although they stopped their advance well inside the Sinai, their own territory conquered six years earlier in a preemptive attack by Israel. Every initiative creates a new status quo, making restoration of the status quo ante a revisionist action.

Status, Stance, and Resolve

In short, differences between contestants' views of stakes and views of which side is being more provocative make it difficult to say which side has most reason to view its interests as more vital and its actions as more defensive. American presidents appear to have been equally bent on demonstrating superior resolve when they were trying to deter enemy aggression against allied territory, as in Berlin or Quemoy and Matsu, and when they were trying to deter Soviet defense of allies whose territory was under attack, as in Egypt in 1956 and 1973.[11]

The two cases that show most clearly the weaknesses of the balance of interests theory are the Berlin and Cuban crises, in which U.S. and Soviet strategic and legal positions were nearly inverted, while their relative resolve and the outcomes of the confrontations were not. There are of

11. An important difference in the Suez case, however, was that the United States was virtually supporting Egypt against U.S. allies; the U.S. nuclear counter-threat was to prevent Soviet action. The United States also pressured Israel in 1973, but not as dramatically as it had pressured Britain and France in 1956.

course important limits to an analogy between U.S. interests and behavior in one case with Moscow's in the other. For example, the Soviets bore responsibility for precipitating both confrontations and aggravated the circumstances of the second by lying about their intention to install missiles. But the similarities are sufficient to shake the theory.

Both Berlin and Cuba were isolated from their superpower protectors, enveloped in the opponent's core security zone and recognized territorial sphere of interest. Neither was militarily defensible by its patron's conventional forces. Both were small territories of more symbolic than substantive importance to their allies. Both were seen by the opposing powers as serious irritants, undermining stability in their surrounding areas, yet both were nonetheless legitimate entities under international law.

Both superpowers deployed intermediate-range nuclear missiles to buttress the political status quo in the respective regions and, as a stopgap measure, to cope with apparent dangers in the overall nuclear balance of power. Washington acted during the late 1950s, at the time of the missile gap scare, and during the early 1960s, installing Thor and Jupiter ballistic missiles in Britain, Italy, and Turkey, and Mace cruise missiles in Germany; Moscow acted in Cuba in 1962, after it had been demonstrated that there was indeed a missile gap but that it was grossly in U.S. favor. Yet the American missiles went into place without a dangerous confrontation, while the Soviet installations provoked the United States to threaten an attack on Cuba unless they were removed.

Despite the inverse nature of U.S. and Soviet positions in the two cases, outcomes were similar. Washington conceded less from its opening demands than Moscow did in both instances. That the United States made some concessions—for example, accepting the construction of the Berlin Wall, offering a pledge not to invade Cuba, and tacitly trading the Jupiters in Turkey for the missiles in Cuba—does not discredit the notion of net U.S. advantage in the outcomes. The wall imprisoning East Germans was not the principal subject of the Berlin crisis; the challenge Washington resisted was the prospect that West Berlin would be absorbed by the East German regime. The no-invasion pledge for Cuba was a declaration of intent of the sort that never provides real confidence to a suspicious enemy. After all, Moscow had offered verbal softeners about "free city" status for Berlin. The missiles withdrawn from Cuba, on the other hand, were a concrete deterrent capability. Moreover, the no-invasion pledge was immediately aborted because Castro refused to allow the on-site verification of the missiles' withdrawal that had been the U.S. condition for the reassurance.[12]

The tacit trade of the Jupiters is the most substantial qualification to the American victory, but its significance is severely compromised by the lengths to which U.S. leaders went to make sure that no exchange could be claimed. When Khrushchev demanded a trade in his letter of October 27, 1962, the U.S. government refused, and Robert Kennedy informed the Soviet ambassador that unless the Soviets promised by the following day to remove the missiles in Cuba, the United States would remove them. The attorney general made clear to Soviet Ambassador Anatoly Dobrynin that the Jupiters would be gone from Turkey within five months, but that there was no quid pro quo and that if Moscow asserted that there was, the U.S. intention would no longer hold.[13] Moreover, Mace B missiles (with a range 500 miles beyond Moscow) remained deployed in Germany for another seven years,[14] and Pershing II and ground-launched cruise missiles were deployed in Europe in the early 1980s with scarcely any discussion that they could contravene understandings over the old Cuban crisis.

The difference in American and Soviet resolve to back their commitments in Berlin and Cuba proved greater than the difference in their respective interests. Other explanations for respective resolve are possible—a few are discussed at the end of the chapter. Yet while it is easy to believe that American officials considered their stakes more vital than the Soviets', it remains hard to assume that Moscow's leaders agreed. On the question of the balance of nuclear power, in contrast, the two sides may have had a similar assessment of what it was, but apparently entered the crises with different views of how it should affect commitment. Khrushchev and his cohorts appeared puzzled at the prospect that any but "madmen" would court nuclear war over something like the small enclave of West Berlin. To the extent that the Soviets exited crises having made accommodations more prejudicial to their objectives than to those of the Americans, perceived power may offer a less unsatisfactory accounting for Soviet

12. Raymond L. Garthoff, *Soviet Military Policy: A Historical Analysis* (Praeger, 1966), p. 122.

13. Robert F. Kennedy, *Thirteen Days: A Memoir of the Cuban Missile Crisis* (W. W. Norton, 1969), pp. 108–09; Robert Kennedy's personal notes, cited in Arthur M. Schlesinger, Jr., *Robert Kennedy and His Times* (Houghton Mifflin, 1978), p. 523.

14. George H. Quester, "Arms Control: Toward Informal Solutions," in Richard K. Betts, ed., *Cruise Missiles: Technology, Strategy, Politics* (Brookings, 1981), pp. 277–78.

adjustment than do perceived interests. But did the Americans have the confidence in that power that this hypothesis implies?

The Nuclear Balance before Parity: Myth of a Golden Age

Most ordinary Americans in the 1950s assumed that nuclear war would be unimaginably devastating to the United States. Many specialists at times have thought they knew better. The significance of U.S. superiority in the first two decades after 1945 is accepted by many on both sides of the more recent strategic debate among experts. Some doves admit that superiority may have accorded the United States an advantage in the early years, but they focus on the point that its passing is irrevocable and invalidates any relevance of the past to the future. Some hawks, on the other hand, lament the passing of a golden age when little stood in the path of American sway, a time like that portrayed satirically in *Dr. Strangelove,* when General Buck Turgidson advises the president to mount an all-out attack on the USSR with the breezy qualification, "I'm not saying we wouldn't get our hair mussed." It is common to hear analysts refer to the period before 1957, when Moscow deployed long-range bombers and demonstrated ICBM capability, as one of American invulnerability and the period up to the mid-1960s as one of only middling vulnerability. What denizen of the Washington strategic dinner seminar circuit has not at some time beheld a one-time or would-be insider with a wistful glint in his eye, recalling with a shake of the head the good old days when the United States could have "cleaned the Russians' clock"? As Colin Gray writes, SAC probably "could have won a World War III at any time from the early 1950s until the mid-1960s, at very little cost in direct nuclear damage to U.S. society."[15]

In reality, the situation in the two decades after 1945 was never as rosy as those nostalgic for it seem to think, because there was never a time when leaders were *confident* that the United States could wage nuclear war successfully—that is, parry and repel a Soviet attack in Europe while restricting damage of the West to "acceptable" levels. During the brief period of effective nuclear monopoly, U.S. forces lacked what would now

15. Colin S. Gray, *Nuclear Strategy and National Style* (Hamilton Press/Abt Books, 1986), p. 103. See also, for example, Henry A. Kissinger, "NATO: The Next Thirty Years," *Survival,* vol. 21 (November–December 1979), p. 266, and his *White House Years* (Little, Brown, 1979), p. 198, where he implies that "tens of millions" of U.S. casualties in a nuclear war were only becoming a possibility at the time he came into office.

be called "assured destruction" capability. Fission weapons were too few and too low in explosive power. SAC could have inflicted great destruction on the USSR, but there was grave doubt that U.S. atomic attacks could prevent the Soviet army from rolling to the English Channel and the Pyrenees.

As that doubt passed by the early 1950s, so did the West's nuclear immunity. Even though Soviet nuclear capability against the continental United States was minimal, it was appreciable against the prospective bone of contention: Western Europe. With even a few weapons, the USSR could have devastated Britain, preventing use of the island as a base from which U.S. forces could move back to the continent as in 1944.[16] With more weapons, the Soviets could have gravely damaged France, West Germany, and other countries. In terms of cold logic, and as Soviet strategists might well have seen the problem, it would avail little for the Americans to fight over a prize that would have been rendered radioactive rubble. Although that point seems to have appeared remarkably incidental to American strategists, it did not to allies in Europe, and it is hard to believe that if the real moment of truth had ever arrived—if a Berlin crisis had progressed from the stage of political warning to the point of strategic warning of Soviet mobilization for conventional war—NATO would not have been internally convulsed by the notion of following through with its first-use plans for self-defense. And the "Hostage Europe" problem was not the only one. Contrary to the mythology that has grown over time, U.S. leaders also had no confidence, even in the early period, that they could prevent significant Soviet nuclear retaliation against the American homeland. That is the point elaborated in the rest of the chapter.

If what follows discredits hawkish nostalgia to some degree, it also shakes some doves' categorical inferences about the irrelevance of earlier cases to the future. In earlier crises, Washington leaned on the crutch of nuclear threats despite belief in significant American vulnerability to nuclear attack. That inclination diminished as the vulnerability grew, but it did not disappear, even after full parity arrived.

Perhaps because estimates of U.S. vulnerability in the alleged golden age never reached the point of what specialists have come to see as assured destruction, some have assumed, looking back, that they were not very inhibiting. But it is important to remember a few points about the concept

16. Mark Edward Matthews, "The Bomb and Korea: A Reexamination of the United States' Nuclear Restraint in the Korean War 1950–1953" (senior honors thesis, Harvard College, March 1981), p. 36.

of assured destruction embedded in the currency of strategic discourse by Robert McNamara's stipulated criteria: 20–25 percent of population and 50 percent of industry.[17] First, the numbers were arbitrary, selected in part because they corresponded with the point of diminishing returns from increases in U.S. capabilities. Second, they were *conservative* estimates of what would deter the *Soviets*, not necessarily what should frighten American leaders who were assumed to be less adventurous or ruthlessly insensitive to domestic losses. And, finally, no one ever assumed that a level of destruction of the United States that was substantially lower would be an acceptable price to pay in war. Unacceptable damage is a subjective judgment, but it could be measured either relative to the stakes, as anything grossly disproportionate to the value of the territories disputed in the crises, or absolutely, as, say, tens of millions of fatalities. Because the domino theory inflated the significance of conflicts over small territories, American leaders might conceivably not have felt that they faced unacceptable damage in the former sense, but they did in the latter terms by the mid-1950s.

The examples of contemporary damage estimates discussed below are not comprehensive, and they vary in their terms of evaluation, specificity, and conclusions.[18] To understand the point of the survey that follows, two distinctions should be borne in mind, because arguments on this subject are often muddled by shifting frames of reference. One distinction is between what was known or believed at the time and what became known, or believed with greater certainty, later. Many of the early damage estimates were probably excessive because, with the partial exception of some CIA contributions, they tended to give insufficient allowance for the severe operational deficiencies and underdeveloped character of Soviet intercontinental bombing capabilities. Thus while the 1950s might conceivably have been a golden age of only modest vulnerability, few of the most important leaders at the time believed that it was. The other distinction is

17. Alain C. Enthoven and K. Wayne Smith, *How Much Is Enough? Shaping the Defense Program, 1961–1969* (Harper and Row, 1971), p. 175.

18. Some of the most relevant estimates are those of the Net Evaluation Subcommittee of the National Security Council, an interagency body commissioned by Eisenhower to provide annual assessments of the damage the United States and Soviet Union could inflict on each other under various conditions of attack. See, for example, NSC 5605, "A Net Evaluation Subcommittee," May 24, 1956, pp. 1–5, in Dwight D. Eisenhower Library (DDEL)/White House Office (WHO), Office of the Special Assistant for National Security Affairs, NSC Series, Policy Papers Subseries, Box 17. Almost all of the substantive records of the net assessments remain classified, although fragments of information about them are revealed in other sources cited below.

between judgments about first-strike counterforce and second-strike countervalue capacity. Some of the estimates do not give a clear indication of
the assumed scenario behind them—whether the first strike was Soviet or
American, with or without warning. American debates about nuclear
strategy have usually focused on Soviet capacity to destroy U.S. retaliatory
forces. For judging the logic of U.S. first-use threats, however, Soviet
second-strike capability is what matters. Later in the chapter I will
demonstrate why a U.S. first-strike plan *under plausible circumstances*
would not have pushed the estimates down to an acceptable level.

From Monopoly to Superiority

By any reasonable "best" estimate, the Soviet Union would have been
unable to do devastating damage to the United States before at least the
mid-1950s, even by striking first. Leaders contemplating war, however,
ought to be reluctant to rely on best estimates. In terms of cautious
estimates, Moscow had a finite deterrent even before the end of the Korean
War.

The common assumption that the Soviets could not deliver a bomb even
after they developed one was not accepted by many inside the government.
The Soviets' TU-4 bomber, a copy of the American B-29, was revealed in
1947. In September of that year a U.S. Air Policy Board briefing noted that
many U.S. fuel storage, aircraft and plutonium production, and iron ore
transshipment facilities were sited near borders, and hence, allegedly, were
vulnerable to Soviet attack, while "critical targets" in the USSR lay further
inland, harder to reach. In 1948 the military's Joint Intelligence Committee
estimated that the Soviets had 200 TU-4s.[19] The following year the Joint
Chiefs of Staff predicted the number could be 415 by mid-1950 and 1,200
by mid-1952. Without refueling, assessment claimed, those bombers could
reach only the northwestern United States if they were to return to the
USSR, but could "reach every important industrial, urban and governmental control center in the United States on a one-way mission basis."[20] One-
way missions could hardly have been excluded for anything as epochal as

19. Harry R. Borowski, *A Hollow Threat: Strategic Air Power and Containment
Before Korea* (Greenwood Press, 1982), pp. 99–100; JIC 380/2, "Estimates of the Intentions
and Capabilities of the USSR Against the Continental United States and the Approaches
Thereunto, 1948–57," February 16, 1948, cited in Joseph T. Jockel, "The United States
and Canadian Efforts at Continental Air Defense, 1945–1957" (Ph.D. dissertation, Johns
Hopkins University, 1978), p. 18.

20. JCS 2801/1, quoted in Jack H. Nunn, *The Soviet First Strike Threat: The U.S.
Perspective* (Praeger, 1982), p. 95.

nuclear war or for a Soviet military establishment as ruthless as Americans believed the Soviets' to be. Even through the 1950s it was widely assumed that many U.S. bombers would not be able to return in event of war.

These judgments did not imply impressive Soviet first-strike capability. The TU-4 force was rickety. Such Soviet operational inhibitions as lack of crew training and proper equipment and vulnerability to interceptors were recognized as severe constraints on Soviet options. But, at the same time, the United States had virtually no air defense and negligible early warning capability.[21] In the year following the first Soviet nuclear test, nevertheless, NSC 68 stated, "The Soviet Union now has aircraft able to deliver the atomic bomb," and reported intelligence estimates that the Soviets would have 10–20 bombs by mid-1950, with the stockpile increasing to 200 by mid-1954, and with "40–60 percent of bombs sortied" having accuracy on target comparable to that of the United States. On the basis of those judgments NSC-68 identified 1954 as the year of maximum danger, "for the delivery of 100 atomic bombs on targets in the United States would seriously damage this country."[22]

The report qualified the estimate by stipulating Soviet surprise attack against "no more effective opposition than we now have programmed."[23] By late 1950 an assessment by the Weapons System Evaluation Group warned that deficiencies in the hastily inaugurated "Lashup" air defense system made it possible that *all* Soviet bombers might penetrate to targets.[24] With constraints on defense programming stripped away by the Korean War, air defense did improve, but did not outpace Soviet offensive capability. Truman did not even authorize building a radar net that would provide from three to six hours tactical warning until he was about to leave office in December 1952.[25] Soviet detonation of a hydrogen bomb in August 1953 also gave the USSR potential destructive capability beyond

21. Ibid., p. 96.
22. "A Report to the President Pursuant to the President's Directive of January 31, 1950," April 7, 1950 (NSC 68), in *Foreign Relations of the United States, 1950,* vol. 1: *National Security Affairs; Foreign Economic Policy* (GPO, 1977), p. 251.
23. Ibid., p. 266. Judging from similar language, NSC 68 apparently drew on the CIA's "Estimate of the Effects of the Soviet Possession of the Atomic bomb Upon the Security of the United States and Upon the Probabilities of Direct Soviet Military Action," ORE 91-49, April 6, 1950 (declassified July 1978), pp. 1, 3, 6 (Carrollton Press collection). The State, Army, Navy, and Air Force representatives dissented vigorously from the paper's benign estimate of Soviet intent, but did not challenge the estimate of capabilities.
24. Jockel, "United States and Canadian Efforts," p. 114.
25. David Alan Rosenberg, "The Origins of Overkill: Nuclear Weapons and American Strategy, 1945–1960," *International Security,* vol. 7 (Spring 1983), p. 31.

the "serious" damage level envisioned by the NSC estimate as one hundred fission bombs on target.

Other estimates in 1949 saw major danger in even small numbers of bombs.[26] An Army Intelligence briefing delivered to the NSC at the beginning of February indicated that just eighteen weapons on nine critical targets would "wipe out one-third of U.S. steel and iron production, cripple governmental operations in Washington, and hamper and delay mobilization and retaliatory efforts."[27] In March the air force argued that delivery of fifty bombs could prevent effective mobilization for the defense of Europe.[28]

The 1951 MacArthur hearings included secret testimony deleted from the public record that indicated that the Soviets already had the nuclear capability to inflict substantial damage on U.S. cities.[29] In 1952 although national intelligence estimates cited only 50 bombs and 800 TU-4s in the Soviet inventory at the time, CIA reports were saying that Soviet technology had advanced to the point that "military requirements rather than technical limitations" would determine the stockpile.[30]

In January 1953, as Eisenhower was about to take the reins, several studies pointed to the mounting vulnerability of the continental United States. The secretaries of state and defense reported that since mid-1952, "probably 65–85% of the atomic bombs launched by the USSR could be delivered on target in the United States"; that U.S. civil defense "is only 10% to 15% effective at the present time"; and that current programs would "no more than double this effectiveness by the end of 1954."[31] NSC 141 estimated that Moscow would have 300 bombs, but possibly as many

26. If taken in isolation, such estimates would seem more alarming than if one assumed realistically that a countervalue first strike by the Soviets would be nonsensical.

27. Steven L. Rearden, *History of the Office of the Secretary of Defense*, vol. 1: *The Formative Years, 1947–1950* (Washington, D.C.: Historical Office, Office of the Secretary of Defense, 1984), p. 525.

28. Jockel, "United States and Canadian Efforts," p. 95.

29. John Edward Wiltz, "The MacArthur Inquiry, 1951," in Arthur M. Schlesinger, Jr., and Roger Bruns, eds., *Congress Investigates: A Documented History, 1792–1974*, vol. 5 (Chelsea House/R. R. Bowker, 1975), p. 3633.

30. NSC 135/1 Annex, "NSC Staff Study on Reappraisal of United States Objectives and Strategy for National Security," August 22, 1952, in *FRUS, 1952–54*, vol. 2: *National Security Affairs* (GPO, 1984), pt. 1, p. 105; JCS 2101/75, NIE 64, and NIE 64-66, cited in Rosenberg, "Origins of Overkill," p. 23; CIA reports quoted in Nunn, *Soviet First Strike Threat*, p. 93.

31. "Report by the Secretaries of State and Defense and the Director for Mutual Security on Reexamination of United States Programs for National Security," January 16, 1953, in *FRUS, 1952–54*, vol. 2: *National Security Affairs*, pt. 1, p. 214.

as 600, by 1955, and Secretary of State Acheson's Policy Planning Staff director, Paul Nitze, told him that the study "makes clear . . . that the net capability of the Soviet Union to injure the United States must *already* be measured in terms of many millions of casualties."[32] As noted in the epigraph to this chapter, a prestigious panel of consultants to the State Department criticized U.S. preoccupation with building up American nuclear offensive capacity and emphasized "the simple but unpleasant fact that the atomic bomb works both ways."[33]

Undeterred, Eisenhower moved to implement the New Look.

From Overweening Superiority to Superior Sufficiency

One reason for optimism could have been that improved defenses were expected to negate the nascent Soviet offensive capability. Defensive improvements, however, lagged behind Soviet offensive gains. The State Department consultants' panel reporting in January 1953 argued that under current conditions "we should be lucky to get one in five" of attacking bombers. As subsequent studies and exercises demonstrated, that guess was optimistic. Just days before the May 20 NSC decision to escalate in Korea if negotiations did not conclude, the NSC's Special Evaluation Subcommittee said that by mid-1953 U.S. air defenses could " 'kill,' before bomb-release line, about 7 percent of the attacking bomber force"; in two years that figure would rise to 27 percent, though the attacking force would also be larger by then.[34] That estimate was similar to, though slightly less optimistic than, that produced by Air Defense Command war games the year before, which predicted potential attrition of 23–37 percent by 1955.[35]

On July 11, 1953, SAC instituted Operation Tailwind, simulating Soviet

32. "Memorandum by the Director of the Policy Planning Staff (Nitze) to the Secretary of State," January 12, 1953, in *FRUS, 1952–54*, vol. 2: *National Security Affairs*, pt. 1, p. 203 (emphasis added); Jockel, "United States and Canadian Efforts," pp. 159–60.

33. "Armaments and American Policy," Report by the Panel of Consultants of the Department of State, to the Secretary of State, January 1953, in *FRUS, 1952–54*, vol. 2: *National Security Affairs*, pt. 2, p. 1071.

34. Ibid., p. 1067; "Report of the Special Evaluation Subcommittee of the National Security Council," in *FRUS, 1952–54*, vol. 2: *National Security Affairs*, pt. 1, pp. 337–38; See also DCI Allen Dulles's comments on the study (pp. 356–57), increasing the estimate of Soviet TU-4s in 1953 from 1,000 to 1,600, with production continuing at 35 per month. The size of the Soviet force was cited as allowing "the Soviet Long-Range Air Force to expend planes relatively plentifully on one-way missions."

35. Jockel, "United States and Canadian Efforts," p. 160.

strikes on U.S. cities, to test the Air Defense Command. By SAC's account the drill was a disaster; defenses "only scored one-half of a 'kill' before bomb release and only 1 'kill' after bomb release."[36] Later that month NSC 159 concluded:

> The present continental defense programs are not now adequate either to prevent, neutralize or seriously deter the military or covert attacks which the USSR is capable of launching, nor are they adequate to ensure the continuity of government, the continuity of production, or the protection of the industrial mobilization base and millions of citizens in our great and exposed metropolitan centers.[37]

In August 1953 the Soviets detonated a hydrogen bomb. On October 7 the NSC met to discuss the draft of NSC 162, which established the New Look and massive retaliation doctrine. Three nuances of alternate wording bearing on the degree of damage a Soviet nuclear attack could exact were discussed. One was whether the adverb "very" should precede "serious damage"; another was whether the phrase "shortly will have" should be deleted from the sentence stating that "the USSR has or shortly will have sufficient bombs and aircraft" to inflict such damage; and the third was whether the degree of damage should be characterized as "possibly crippling." In all cases the more severe wording was selected.[38] Although these may seem trivial distinctions today, it is notable that U.S. leaders' reliance on nuclear forces did not rest on an optimistic premise of U.S. immunity even in the short term.

What did "very serious damage" mean? Nothing, of course, like the level of destruction taken for granted in recent years. Depending on plausible variations in the scenario, however, it was still extensive. In January 1953 NSC 141 posited an attack with one hundred bombs of fifty kilotons—not the highest-yield bombs that it was believed the Soviets could produce—and calculated total casualties of 22 million.[39] The May 1953 NSC estimate assumed a Soviet surprise attack against U.S. bomber

36. "Memorandum Op-36C/jm, 18 March 1954," reprinted in *International Security*, vol. 6 (Winter 1981–82), p. 24.

37. Cited in "Continental Defense," Draft Statement of Policy Proposed by the National Security Council, February 11, 1954, in *FRUS, 1952–54*,vol. 2: *National Security Affairs*, pt. 1, p. 613.

38. "Memorandum of Discussion at the 165th Meeting of the National Security Council, Wednesday, October 7, 1953," *FRUS, 1952–54*, vol. 2: *National Security Affairs*, pt. 1, p. 531; the draft discussed is on pp. 491–514.

39. Cited in Jockel, "United States and Canadian Efforts," p. 159.

bases, with leftover assets targeted against population. Such an attack would destroy 24 percent of U.S. nuclear delivery capability in 1953, and about 30 percent in 1955; would cause "initial paralysis" of one-third of total industrial production in 1953 and two-thirds two years later; and could "produce a maximum of 9 million casualties in 1953, and 12.5 million in 1955, one-half of which might result in deaths." The report suggested that casualties might be as low as half the figures cited and noted that failure of strategic surprise or improvement in tactical warning "would greatly reduce the damage indicated."[40] Had the fate of Europe been at stake, such "very serious damage" might have been seen as acceptable. But there were two reasons for fearing that damage could be greater.

First, the NSC estimate assumed that almost half of Soviet bombs were expended against airbases. One of the principal scenarios that has concerned strategists and posed the most vexing dilemmas for extended deterrence is that the Soviets could launch a conventional invasion while holding their nuclear force in reserve as a shield to deter U.S. escalation. With Soviet nuclear weapons programmed for retaliation rather than a counterforce first strike, a much larger fraction of them might have been aimed at cities. When the May 15 NSC estimate considered that possibility, it calculated casualties up to 24 million in 1953 and 31 million in 1955.[41] Second, the May estimate assumed 300 Soviet bombs of about eighty kilotons by mid-1955. The hydrogen bomb that arrived on the scene just a few months later represented a markedly different threat. A year later, in 1954, national intelligence estimates cited more than a fourfold increase in total Soviet explosive power from the previous year's judgment, from six to twenty-five megatons.[42]

Even including planned improvements in air defense and assuming that some bombers failed to reach targets for other reasons, estimates for a scenario in which most Soviet weapons were targeted on cities suggest that thoughtful leaders should have considered the possibility that war could bring down at least five to ten megatons—in simplistic terms, 400–800 times the explosive power of the Hiroshima bomb—on U.S. population centers in the course of 1954 or 1955.[43] Indeed, in February 1953 an

40. "Report of the Special Evaluation Subcommittee," pp. 332–34 (cited in note 34).
41. Ibid., p. 343.
42. Ibid., p. 334. For NIE 11-5-54 and NIE 13-54, see *FRUS, 1952–54*, vol. 2: *National Security Affairs*, pt. 1, p. 725.
43. Analysis later made clearer that destructive power of gross megatonnage in an arsenal of high-yield weapons cannot be equated with the sum of explosive power of a

independent Lincoln Laboratory group calculated hypothetical results of a Soviet attack on one hundred urban targets with just one hundred bombs including eleven of one megaton, and concluded that there would be 19 million fatalities.[44]

Given the number of variables and uncertainties, as well as of the government organizations making calculations, judgments varied. In early 1954 a special national intelligence estimate put more weight on Soviet operational inhibitions due to reliance on the TU-4 and undeveloped forward basing and calculated that at the time no more than 250 Soviet bombers, some of which might not be bomb-carriers, could then reach targets—and the number would probably be fewer.[45] In that year and the next, however, the Soviets revealed two new bombers, including the turbojet MYA-4 Bison. Deployed American air defense interceptors, the F-86, F-89, and F-94, were not judged capable of dealing with jet bombers. Although Khrushchev's memoirs reveal his lack of confidence in the Bison due to test and range problems, his doubts were not well recognized in the United States, as reflected in the "bomber gap" controversy that ensued in the intelligence community.[46]

Concern about new bombers was still directed toward the future, but vulnerability in 1955 was nonetheless great enough to worry decision-makers when they confronted it. In June Operation Alert, an exercise complete with a cabinet meeting at an alternate national command post, simulated decision problems under nuclear attack. Fifty-three cities were assumed bombed, with 8.5 million *immediate* fatalities, 8 million injured, unknown numbers of fallout casualties, and 25 million homeless people in need of food and shelter. The cabinet secretary's minutes recount, "The president's one comment was: staggering." Eisenhower discussed the

larger number of low-yield weapons, because effects are attenuated as yield increases. To account for the difference, the concept of "Equivalent" Megatonnage (EMT) was invented and a semi-arbitrary formula came to be accepted: equivalent megatonnage equals yield to the power of two-thirds. In the early period, however, most observers still thought in terms of gross megatonnage, and the Soviet stockpile would have been fractionated anyway.

44. MIT Lincoln Laboratory, "Final Report of Summer Study Group," February 10, 1953, vol. 1, cited in Jockel, "United States and Canadian Efforts," p. 157.

45. SNIE 11-2-54, "Soviet Capabilities for Attack on the U.S. Through 1957," February 24, 1954 (declassified June 1978), p. 8. For 1957, the estimate was 700 (pp. 8–9).

46. Jockel, "United States and Canadian Efforts," p. 163; Strobe Talbott, ed. and trans., *Khrushchev Remembers: The Last Testament* (Little, Brown, 1974), p. 39. On the bomber gap dispute see Lawrence Freedman, *U.S. Intelligence and the Soviet Strategic Threat*, 2d ed. (Princeton University Press, 1986), pp. 65–67; and John Prados, *The Soviet Estimate: U.S. Intelligence Analysis and Soviet Strategic Forces*, 2d ed. (Princeton University Press, 1986), chap. 4.

results of the exercise at a news conference the following month.[47] Confidence continued to rest more on high deterrence than on low vulnerability. The official 1955 net evaluation projected that "as of 1958, the estimated Soviet nuclear stockpile and delivery capability will be inadequate to 'knock out' the United States." The judgment, however, was couched not so much in terms of acceptable damage to the United States as in terms of the greater American capacity for a counterblow: "Although the USSR could damage the United States on a scale unprecedented in human experience, it could not prevent the delivery of an even more devastating retaliatory attack."[48]

Of course even the enthusiasts for the New Look had recognized from the beginning that U.S. nuclear superiority was a wasting asset. An Eisenhower memo to Dulles in August 1953 noted that the hydrogen bomb might enable Moscow to cripple the United States, whereupon American deterrence would have to rest on the ability "to inflict greater loss against the enemy than he could reasonably hope to inflict upon us."[49] So it is not surprising that between 1955 and 1956 the administration shifted to a policy emphasizing "sufficiency" rather than the air force's version of superiority.[50] Although sufficiency bowed to Soviet capacity to inflict serious damage, it was not generally assumed to be an acceptance of *equal* damage.

But would there be a point at which absolute U.S. vulnerability made the relative difference in Soviet vulnerability insufficient comfort for deterrence? That remained a matter for theoretical debate until near the end of the decade and did not impinge much on nuclear threats until then because they involved the Soviets only indirectly or tentatively, as in Korea and the Taiwan Straits, or because there was little reason to worry that the crisis might escalate, as in Suez and Lebanon. Yet the record of the later 1950s showed that while the president did not change his reliance on the

47. Maxwell M. Rabb, "Minutes of the Second Plenary Meeting of the Interim Assembly Ravenrock Conference Room, 11:00–12:15 A.M., Friday, June 15, 1955," pp. 5, 7, in DDEL/Ann Whitman File (AWF), Cabinet Series, Box 5; *Public Papers of the Presidents of the United States: Dwight D. Eisenhower, 1955* (GPO, 1959), pp. 671–72.

48. Quoted in Arthur Radford, Memorandum for the Special Assistant to the President, National Security Affairs, "Implications of the Revised Estimate of Soviet Nuclear Capabilities with Respect to the Conclusions of the 1955 Net Evaluation," May 31, 1956, p. 1, in DDEL/WHO, Office of the Special Assistant for National Security Affairs, NSC Series, Policy Papers Subseries, Box 17.

49. Quoted in Rosenberg, "Origins of Overkill," p. 33.

50. Jerome H. Kahan, *Security in the Nuclear Age: Developing U.S. Strategic Arms Policy* (Brookings, 1975), pp. 31–34.

nuclear threat to deter Soviet action, his grounds for seeing nuclear war as at all manageable worsened still further.

From Sufficiency to High Vulnerability

Eisenhower kept a personal diary. Given the various inconsistencies in what he told colleagues or the public and given the Machiavellian interpretations by revisionist scholars of the reasons for such contradictions, that source—written at the time and not aimed at anyone then involved in policy—should be at least as indicative as any other of his "real" thinking. A January 23, 1956, diary entry goes on at a length quite remarkable for a busy chief executive about an air force briefing on net evaluation of nuclear damage projected for two war scenarios occurring in midyear. Of one scenario, a surprise attack, Eisenhower wrote:

> The United States experienced practically total economic collapse. . . . a new government had to be improvised by the states. Casualties were enormous . . . something on the order of 65% of the population would require some kind of medical care, and in most instances, no opportunity whatsoever to get it. . . . While these things were going on, the damage inflicted by us against the Soviets was roughly three times greater.[51]

The second scenario assumed that the Soviets attacked after a month of strategic warning and concentrated against U.S. air bases rather than the continental United States alone. "Nevertheless," Eisenhower wrote, "there was *no significant difference* in the losses we would take." The president went on to speculate about the desirability of a U.S. first strike in this situation, but rejected the option.[52] The diary entry was written three years before the second Berlin crisis.

Not all assessments were so bad, but the lower ones were hardly reassuring. Wording in the immediate threat estimate in June in NSC 5606, a Planning Board report, was not quite as apocalyptic as Eisenhower's musings, perhaps because it was not solely an air force product, as the briefing discussed in the diary was. NSC 5606 cited "some time in 1958" or "possibly as early as 1957" as the date at which the USSR would develop the capability for "a crippling blow."[53] A special panel reporting in

51. "Jan '56 Diary," pp. 1–2, in DDEL/AWF, DDE Diaries, Box 12.
52. Ibid., p. 2 (emphasis added).
53. NSC 5606, "Continental Defense," Report by the NSC Planning Board to the NSC, June 5, 1956, Annex A, "Estimate of the Threat," p. 22, in DDEL/WHO, NSC Series, Policy Papers Subseries, Box 17. The estimate noted that "over 71 percent of the

November also projected immediate fatalities of 30–35 million and total casualties of 50 million in a scenario of Soviet attack three years later.[54] And there are indications that the president, concerned with uncertainties about the precise extent and forms of damage the United States would suffer in nuclear war, continued to consider the question of whether the country could somehow stand it. At the end of 1956 he told the NSC that given "the picture of terrific destruction," analysis should be done to see how much the United States could "absorb and still survive."[55] As late as mid-1959, after the Berlin Deadline crisis, he was asking for studies "to see what this country would look like five days or so following a nuclear attack . . . just what the situation would be."[56]

Defensive improvements, the hope for retarding Soviet striking capability, were also languishing. Technological breakthroughs in radar and data handling were not being exploited expeditiously, and administration economies slowed innovation. In February 1955 a specially constituted Technological Capabilities Panel reported continuing deficiencies in the number and quality of air defense systems, including serious gaps in radar coverage at high and low altitudes, and major inadequacies in interceptors and other weapons.[57] In midyear another panel produced a pessimistic analysis predicting that Soviet gains in technology could soon surpass those of the United States.[58] That dire judgment predated by more than

---

Defense-supporting industry (59 percent of all manufacturing industry) and 54 percent of the workers engaged in manufacturing are located in 59 large metropolitan centers." Annex B, "Summary of U.S. Capabilities As To The Elements of Continental Defense," pp. 28–29.

54. "The Human Effects of Nuclear Weapons Development," November 1956, cited in Wm. F. Vandercook, "Making the Very Best of the Very Worst," *International Security,* vol. 11 (Summer 1986), p. 190.

55. J. Patrick Coyne, Memorandum, "Discussion at the 306th Meeting of the National Security Council, Thursday, December 20, 1956," December 21, 1956, pp. 3–4, in DDEL/ AWF, NSC Series, Box 8.

56. Gordon Gray, "Memorandum of Meeting with the President," May 7, 1959, in DDEL/WHO, Office of the Special Assistant for National Security Affairs, Special Assistant Series, Presidential Subseries, Box 4; quotation from A. J. Goodpaster, "Memorandum of Conference With the President," July 27, 1959, p. 2, in DDEL/WHO, Office of the Staff Secretary, Subject Series, DoD Subseries, Box 4.

57. Technological Capabilities Panel of the Science Advisory Committee, "Meeting the Threat of Surprise Attack," February 14, 1955, vol. 2, pt. 4, p. 75, in DDEL/WHO, Office of the Special Assistant for National Security Affairs, NSC Series, Subject Subseries, Box 11; Jockel, "United States and Canadian Efforts," pp. 173–77.

58. Ellis Johnson, "The Comparative Military Technology of the U.S. and USSR," Annex A, Tab 2, Report of the Quantico Vulnerabilities Panel, reprinted as Appendix F in W. W. Rostow, *Open Skies: Eisenhower's Proposal of July 21, 1955* (University of Texas Press, 1982), pp. 147–54.

two years the alarm surrounding Sputnik and the Gaither Committee.[59] By the following year Air Force Secretary Donald Quarles admitted that in coping with vulnerability, "we lost ground."[60] NSC 5606 reaffirmed the air defense deficiencies outlined by the Technological Capabilities Panel and noted that improvements in continental defense were consistently negated by increases in the Soviet nuclear stockpile and delivery capability.[61]

There was no significant improvement during the remainder of the administration's term. Assessments in 1957 by the Continental Air Defense Command, based on optimistic assumptions, still estimated defenses as capable only of preventing the Soviets from bombing 40 percent of their targets at the time. The assessment projected improvements to 60 and 80 percent for 1960 and 1963, but considered only bombers, ignored degradation of defenses by electronic countermeasures, and assumed substantial improvements in the air defense system.[62] By the end of the 1950s the president's Science Advisory Committee cited the SAGE air defense system as only "far better than nothing," and noted "that perfectly feasible plans of air attack could be devised which would make it inoperable."[63] And by that time the ICBM threat was in sight. An NSC briefing in late 1960 summed up the record of the race between offense and defense: "As the enemy capability increased, it became necessary to build [air defense] weapons of increasing capability. The modern interceptor. . . . is no more effective in coping with this [current] kind of a threat than the early fighters were in coping with an earlier threat." The briefing also addressed early hopes for missile defense, especially for the Nike-Zeus interceptor. The briefing assumed what became the conventional wisdom leading to the 1972 Antiballistic Missile (ABM) treaty—there were no good prospects. Interceptors could raise the price of penetration, but exchange ratios would always favor enemy missiles.[64]

59. The Gaither Committee—officially the Security Resources Panel, commissioned by the president and chaired by H. Rowan Gaither—submitted an alarming report in late 1957 warning that Soviet nuclear superiority could be imminent.

60. See Nunn, *Soviet First Strike Threat*, pp. 116–21; quotation on p. 121.

61. NSC 5606, Annex B, pp. 25–26 (cited in note 53).

62. JCS 1899/339, cited in Jockel, "United States and Canadian Efforts," pp. 165, 166n.

63. July 28, 1959, meeting, reported in George B. Kistiakowsky, *A Scientist at the White House: The Private Diary of President Eisenhower's Special Assistant for Science and Technology* (Harvard University Press, 1976), p. 24. "SAGE" is the acronym for Semi-automatic Ground Environment.

64. "Continental Defense," Minutes of Briefing to NSC by John H. Rubel, September

Damage estimates continued to creep upward, even before Sputnik was launched and the missile gap controversy heated up. In May 1957 Eisenhower referred in conversation with Senator Styles Bridges to a net evaluation study citing 25 million dead and 60 million other casualties. A month later a JCS study that included fallout effects estimated between 46 million and 117 million fatalities, although it assumed that all bombs were aimed at population targets. A Federal Civil Defense Administration estimate assuming a third of the targets would be military installations nevertheless cited 82 million Americans dead as the result.[65] The national intelligence estimate in November 1957, however, emphasized continuing restrictions on efficacy of Soviet forces, such as "the relatively small numbers of operational heavy bombers, the status of support facilities at Arctic bases, and the lack as yet of a substantial in-flight refueling capability," though it also mentioned Soviet ability to employ "small numbers of both bomber-launched air-to-surface missiles and submarine-launched surface-to-surface missiles against targets in the continental U.S."[66]

Although the post-Sputnik ICBM scare remained a political football through the 1960 election, the controversy within the executive branch was being resolved in favor of more relaxed near-term estimates by the end of 1958—and the president had never taken the missile gap seriously anyway. In secret testimony in January 1959 military representatives reported revised estimates of Soviet capabilities that pushed possible deployment of 100 ICBMs back to 1960 or 1961; lowered the number, quality, and range of cruise missiles that could be launched from submarines; and cited no more than 125 heavy Bear and Bison bombers.[67]

The Russians' absolute countervalue capability aside, U.S. nuclear superiority in the relative balance of forces was clearly still overwhelming, and Moscow certainly had no meaningful first-strike option against U.S. nuclear forces. Many then, and today, have seen that U.S. edge as ample grounds for the credibility of U.S. nuclear threats. That view might be

15, 1960, p. 3, in DDEL/WHO, Office of the Staff Secretary, Subject Series, Alphabetical Subseries, Box 19.

65. Eisenhower quoted in Fred I. Greenstein, *The Hidden-Hand Presidency: Eisenhower as Leader* (Basic Books, 1982), pp. 47–48; JCS 1899/339 and FCDA study cited in Jockel, "United States and Canadian Efforts," pp. 163–65.

66. NIE 11-4-57, "Main Trends in Soviet Capabilities and Policies 1957–1962," November 12, 1957, p. 37 (Carrollton Press Collection).

67. *Executive Sessions of the Senate Foreign Relations Committee (Historical Series)*, vol. 11, 86 Cong. 1 sess., 1959 (GPO, 1982), pp. 20–23.

defensible for a case such as the 1958 Taiwan Straits crisis, in which the Soviet Union would not have been the target of U.S. nuclear first use and would have had to strike the first nuclear blow against the United States if it had supported the PRC in war, or the Caribbean half of the 1962 missile crisis, where U.S. strategy did not rely on first use but on deterrence of Soviet escalation. But if the issue had ever come to actually implementing the military strategy backing the U.S. position in the second Berlin crisis, population vulnerability to Soviet second-strike retaliation—not the disproportion in force levels—would have been the crucial factor. Even with advance warning of attack, U.S. vulnerability to countervalue strikes was judged to be extremely high by the late 1950s.

Apex of the Golden Age?

The ratio of American to Soviet vulnerability may have improved briefly in the late 1950s and early 1960s because the Soviets continued to dawdle in development of modern delivery systems, while U.S. offensive forces grew quickly. The implications of the ratio, however, depended on the issue considered. The principal U.S. advantage that accrued from the Kennedy buildup was in counterforce capability against unready Soviet forces. Depending on the scenario, U.S. population vulnerability remained quite high.

A 1960 air force study that projected war in 1963 reportedly came up with the assessment that an indiscriminate Soviet first strike would kill 150 million Americans, or 77 percent of the total population, and that even Soviet *retaliation* after an indiscriminate U.S. first strike would kill 110 million, or 56 percent.[68] The horrifying estimates may have been due to air force inflation of projected Soviet forces, but the figure of 150 million dead on both sides has been cited as what President Kennedy took away from his first briefing by the JCS.[69]

At the height of the Berlin crisis in 1961 the air force advised that a U.S. first strike might keep losses below 10 million. Although the figure was glaringly inconsistent with SAC's position in other forums that the Soviets might have hundreds of missiles that were undetected, and therefore, necessarily, untargeted,[70] it tallied with that supplied by the civilian staff

68. Richard Fryklund, *100 Million Lives: Maximum Survival in a Nuclear War* (Macmillan, 1962), pp. 3–4, 21–22. The study helped point the way to the counterforce doctrine; it projected U.S. and Soviet fatalities as 3 million and 5 million respectively in a "no cities" exchange (pp. 13–14).
69. Gregg Herken, *Counsels of War* (Alfred A. Knopf, 1985), p. 161.
70. Ibid., p. 145.

planners working separately under Paul Nitze. In July, however, Carl Kaysen informed McGeorge Bundy that without an effective first strike, even the full planned civil defense shelter program would not reduce U.S. fatalities below 39–56 million if a fair number of high-yield Soviet weapons were aimed at cities, with fatalities rising to 62–100 million without shelters. According to Kaysen, "As few as 15 missiles diverted to the attack of cities will cause between 10 and 20 million fatalities" with full civil defense. These estimates, from studies by several analytical organizations in and outside government, assumed a 350-megaton attack, but with most weapons aimed at military targets. A smaller retaliatory attack aimed primarily at cities would probably have produced similar casualty levels. And even a counterforce version of the 350-megaton strike was predicted to yield 11–40 million dead without the shelter program in place.[71]

A major intelligence assessment produced shortly before the 1962 missile crisis said that for the next five years, "even in the most favorable case with restraints in targeting on both sides, civil casualties in the United States and Western Europe could be on the order of ten million each," and up to 100 million or more each without restraints.[72] In neither of the confrontations over Berlin or Cuba, however, were there sound reasons for assuming favorable conditions. The planned shelter program never got very far, and only game theory—not any evidence about Soviet views or plans—supported the notion that Moscow might restrain targeting of civilian assets. Later recollections of participants also suggest widely divergent vulnerability assessments at the time. For example, in 1979 Admiral Elmo Zumwalt claimed that during the missile crisis, he and his boss, Paul Nitze, told Kennedy that the ratio of fatalities in a nuclear exchange would be ten to one in U.S. favor. Robert McNamara, on the other hand, asserted in 1982 that less than a month after the Cuban crisis he told the president that even a U.S. first strike would leave surviving Soviet forces that could kill 50 million Americans *directly*.[73] Although

71. Carl Kaysen, Memorandum for Mr. Bundy, "Berlin Crisis and Civil Defense," July 7, 1961, Appendix, pp. 2–3, in JFKL/NSF, Countries Series, Box 81.

72. "Report of the Special Inter-Departmental Committee on Implications of NIE 11-8-62 and Related Intelligence," reprinted in Raymond L. Garthoff, *Intelligence Assessment and Policymaking: A Decision Point in the Kennedy Administration* (Brookings, 1984), p. 44.

73. Zumwalt quoted in Symposium, "Is War Inevitable in the Eighties?" (Washington, D.C.: Center for International Security, June 7, 1979), p. 4F (DoD Current News edition, July 24, 1979); McNamara cited in Robert Scheer, "Interview With McNamara: Fear of a U.S. First Strike Seen as Cause of Arms Race," *Los Angeles Times*, April 8, 1982.

McNamara's recollection may be faulty, such differences suggest at least that there was no high-level consensus about U.S. vulnerability that was clear enough to have burned itself into leaders' minds. They also reflect how confused recollections have helped various myths to creep into strategic debate.

Limits of the U.S. First-Strike Option

Some would debunk the relevance of the vulnerability estimates discussed so far by arguing that they were excessively pessimistic because they avoided factoring in the full meaning of U.S. counterforce capability. It is no secret that a first-strike option was a serious element of U.S. policy through much of the postwar period. Indeed, it was the essence of massive retaliation, and in more ambiguous or limited forms remained part of the logic of flexible response. But U.S. first-strike capacity does not prove to mitigate the significance of the previous estimates much when practical limitations of both U.S. intentions and capabilities are considered.

A first strike can take three forms. A preemptive attack is one made in immediate anticipation of enemy attack. A surprise strike against an enemy who is not yet preparing his own attack is either simply aggressive, or if undertaken from fear of an *eventual* threat posed by the enemy, preventive.[74] No responsible Americans have ever contemplated an aggressive first strike, but the difference between the preemptive and preventive variants has often been confused, even by professional strategists. The confusion is symptomatic of the mistakes in overestimating first-strike capability. Politically, it is much easier to rationalize preemption than preventive action. Militarily, however, preemptive attack forfeits some of the benefit of surprise that can be kept by a preventive strike.

The option of preemption was recommended by the JCS from the beginning of the postwar era. In September 1945 they argued "that the U.S. must be ready 'to strike the first blow if necessary,' " and two years later they "recommended that Congress be requested to redefine 'acts of aggression' to include 'the readying of atomic weapons against us,' and to

---

McNamara might have been confusing a November 1962 projected estimate for 1967 with a current estimate. See Draft Presidential Memorandum cited in Fred Kaplan, *The Wizards of Armageddon* (Simon and Schuster, 1983), p. 320. Also, some analysts criticized McNamara's calculations of this sort for erroneously assuming that all Soviet weapons surviving a U.S. first strike would be targeted on cities and that Soviet submarines could not be destroyed before launching their missiles.

74. See Betts, *Surprise Attack*, pp. 145–47.

authorize the President" to retaliate in anticipation. NSC 68 rejected preventive war but tentatively embraced preemption.[75]

SAC commander and later Air Force Chief of Staff Curtis LeMay is legendary for his enthusiasm for a first strike. His memoirs contain thinly veiled arguments in favor of preventive war and a book published in 1968, the year of his American Independent party candidacy for the vice presidency, endorsed first-strike capability, implicitly for preemptive purposes, as "absolutely necessary."[76] The most impressive claim about LeMay's attitude is a reported encounter between the general and Robert Sprague, deputy head of the Gaither Committee. LeMay allegedly told Sprague that he was not worried about SAC's vulnerability—about which Rand analyst Albert Wohlstetter was so concerned at the time—because if he received warning of Soviet massing from U.S. reconnaissance and signals intelligence, "I'm going to knock the shit out of them before they take off the ground." When the stunned Sprague replied that that was not national policy, LeMay responded: "It's my policy. That's what I'm going to do."[77] It is unclear how command and control arrangements could realistically have made a tightly coordinated attack in peacetime feasible without presidential authorization, but there are indications that authority may have been delegated for situations in which communication broke down. McGeorge Bundy warned Kennedy just ten days into his administration

75. Rosenberg, "Origins of Overkill," pp. 17, 25.

76. General Curtis LeMay with Mackinlay Kantor, *Mission With LeMay: My Story* (Doubleday, 1965), pp. 481–82, 559–61; General Curtis LeMay with Major General Dale O. Smith, *America Is In Danger* (Funk and Wagnalls, 1968), p. 63.

77. Quoted in Kaplan, *Wizards of Armageddon*, pp. 132–34. Sprague confirmed the essence of this account in a letter to Marc Trachtenberg. General Russell E. Dougherty provides another revealing anecdote: "When I assumed command of the Strategic Air Command on August 1, 1974, one of my most distinguished and admired seniors, General Curtis E. LeMay, pulled me aside during the reception that followed my swearing-in and asked me if I was fully aware of the implications of my command responsibilities. I assured him that I was. . . . Then General LeMay asked me point-blank, 'Whom do you remember from Pearl Harbor?'

"The question was so surprising . . . that I did not give a quick, direct response. When General LeMay pressed me to 'answer the question,' I gave him the only reply that came immediately to mind: 'Sir,' I said, 'I remember General Short and Admiral Kimmel.' I had been in my early twenties at the time of the attack and knew only the names of the responsible senior Army and Navy commanders in Honolulu who, in the extensive recriminations and investigations that followed the debacle, carried the brunt of the blame.

" 'You are exactly right,' he said. 'The responsible military commanders are the ones remembered in disasters and defeats.' " Dougherty, "The Psychological Climate of Nuclear Command," in Ashton B. Carter, John D. Steinbruner, and Charles A. Zraket, eds., *Managing Nuclear Operations* (Brookings, 1987), p. 407.

that a review of "existing papers" suggested the possibility of "a situation today in which a subordinate commander faced with a substantial Russian military action could start the thermonuclear holocaust on his own initiative if he could not reach you (by failure of communication at either end of the line)."[78]

At the beginning of 1958 Sprague told a few top State Department officials that the U.S. position relative to the USSR would be at its strongest during the subsequent two and one-half years. He spoke implicitly of U.S. first-strike capability: "During this period we can knock out the Soviet Union's military capability without taking a similar blow from the Soviet Union. Our present capability to do this is increasing. During this period the Soviet Union could in retaliation hurt the U.S., but could not put us out of action."[79] In 1960 Air Force Chief of Staff Thomas White testified in Congress against a U.S. policy of finite deterrence because it did not take account of "the possibility of reaction on our part to strategic warning."[80] Four years later Defense Secretary McNamara testified against a new manned bomber and in favor of emphasizing missiles because "the quicker our retaliatory force can reach the opponent, the more chance we have of catching a substantial part of his force on the ground."[81]

These examples of official support for preemption should not be astounding; they reflect general planning considerations, not geared to any specific crisis with all the attendant political confusion, uncertainty, and awesome immediacy. But what did commanders in chief, those most responsible for acting in such circumstances, think about a first strike? There is no way to know their most private thoughts, but there are other indications of their attitudes. Ironically, the clearest example of hesitation and moral reluctance was Truman's during the Berlin Blockade. At the time when the United States faced *no* Soviet retaliatory capability the nuclear signal in the crisis was among the weakest and most cautious of any discussed. For Kennedy, there is no public evidence of whether or how

78. Memorandum to the President, "Policies Previously Approved in the NSC Which Need Review," January 30, 1961, JFKL/NSF, Meetings and Memoranda Series, Box 313.

79. "Memorandum of Conversation," January 3, 1958, p. 2, in DDEL/John Foster Dulles Papers, General Correspondence and Memoranda Series, Box 1. Nevertheless, "Sprague pointed out that during the course of his work with the Gaither panel his resort to prayer had substantially increased." Ibid., p. 4.

80. Quoted in Robert Endicott Osgood, *NATO: The Entangling Alliance* (University of Chicago Press, 1962), p. 202.

81. Quoted in Robert Frank Futrell, *Ideas, Concepts, Doctrine: A History of Basic Thinking in the United States Air Force 1907–1964* (Aerospace Studies Institute, Air University, June 1971), vol. 2, p. 679.

he thought about a first-strike option in the two biggest crises of the Cold War that occurred during his administration.

Eisenhower, the president associated with the largest number of tacit U.S. nuclear threats, seemed to tilt in opposite directions at different times. In his private diary entry of January 23, 1956, reacting to one scenario in the air force briefing on likely damage to the United States, he wrote:

> The only possible way of reducing these losses would be for us to take the initiative some time during the assumed month in which we had the warning of the attack and launch a surprise attack against the Soviets. This would not only be against our traditions but it would appear to be impossible that any such thing would occur.[82]

On the other hand, when the Gaither Committee briefed him the next year he agreed that the Soviets should not be allowed to strike first, and records show that in his last year in office he was briefed by the JCS chairman on issues related to preemption after warning.[83]

Even if presidents could agree with military planners in principle, the actual circumstances of crises made a disarming first strike impractical because plausible assumptions about American intentions and capabilities were incompatible. The evidence of presidents' consideration of a first strike involved the preemptive variety, for a situation in which the Soviets, unprovoked, were preparing a nuclear attack of their own. For the best chance of effectiveness in destroying Soviet retaliatory capability, however, a first strike would have been preventive, undertaken before the Soviets got ready to fire.

In a crisis, realistically, political caution and common sense would delay even a decision for preemption. Thus U.S. capability to destroy Soviet forces would begin to decline as officials' willingness to launch a strike was rising. Moreover, none of the crises discussed in this book involved significant American fears of a Soviet nuclear first strike; rather the primary danger anticipated in each case was that Soviet or Chinese conventional forces might move alone.

Two sorts of actual situations put the dilemma in focus. First are the cases in which Washington had already used tangible nuclear signals to deter Soviet conventional action—for example, the limited SAC movements during the Suez and Lebanon crises of the 1950s and the 1973

---

82. "Jan '56 Diary," p. 2 (cited in note 51).
83. Herken, *Counsels of War*, p. 127.

Middle East War, or the awesome DEFCON-2 alert of October 1962. A real problem never arose, because the Soviets never countered such U.S. signals with comparable action. But if they had done so, U.S. leaders would have had two choices. They could have decided that Moscow meant to strike, and authorized preemption—thus fulfilling the worst fears of deterrence theorists about crisis stability and spiraling reactions. Or they could have recognized the Soviet alert as a precautionary counter to the American alert. The latter reaction is more probable; at the least, the fact that Washington had initiated the nuclear phase of the crisis would encourage debate among the highest-level decisionmakers.[84] It is not easy to imagine leaders, even in the dark days of the 1950s, resolving such an uncertainty in favor of preemption quickly enough to strike the Soviet nuclear force before Moscow's alert had modified its vulnerability.

A similar and ultimately more telling logical problem underlies the theoretical option for a disarming strike envisioned by some of the Berlin contingency planners in 1961, even if no prior U.S. nuclear threats would have been involved. The option implicitly assumed either that the Soviets would embark on conventional war without alerting their nuclear forces or that the Americans would launch a surprise preventive attack out of the blue. Neither premise is realistic, but in the absence of one or the other, it would have been difficult to bank on near-total effectiveness of a U.S. first strike.

To keep U.S. fatalities below 15 million, the reported plan was to catch the Soviet forces in their normal unready posture, with missiles and bombers separated from warheads, concentrated on regular bases, and screened by a faulty early warning network that U.S. bombers might be able to circumvent. But to provoke the U.S. strike in the first place, the Russians would have had to initiate military action to take West Berlin. Would Moscow conceivably start conventional combat without putting some reasonable portion of its nuclear force close to launch-on-warning status? The Soviets' own decision to go to conventional war would be the functional equivalent to them of strategic warning of U.S. nuclear attack. Thus primed and dispersed, the force would be unlikely to be caught flatfooted everywhere even if leaky radars let many U.S. bombers close to target before alarm. According to papers prepared for American participants in a NATO planning conference on September 8–11, "During an intense crisis period, some dispersal of the [Soviet] bomber force could be

---

84. See the arguments in Betts, *Surprise Attack*, chaps. 4–6.

expected. . . . In general, the Soviets could count on at least 30 minutes warning of high-level approaches to the Soviet border, degraded to ⅓ of this or less for low-level approaches. Permanent home bases of the long-range bomber force located in the interior might expect at least an hour of warning, while bases nearer the periphery and arctic staging bases would enjoy substantially less warning time." While about 10 percent of the Soviet bombers were kept on ground alert normally, at least double that "could be maintained" in a major crisis. "Estimated reaction time . . . of the ground alert aircraft is from 15 to 30 minutes."[85]

Under these circumstances, American missiles might have been more effective than bombers in catching alert bombers or soft ICBMs on the ground, since the Soviets were then only beginning to construct the Hen House radars for tactical warning of ballistic missile attack. But even the full U.S. single integrated operational plan (SIOP) could not have programmed ballistic missile warheads against all of the dispersal airfields in the vast expanse of the USSR. As of July 1961 the complete generated forces of SAC and the unified commands had only 188 ballistic missiles, and they were low in reliability; substantial cross-targeting would have been necessary to guarantee high damage expectancy. Of those 188 missiles, fully 80 were sea-based, which would have posed tougher coordination problems. The Soviets had an estimated 140 regular bomber bases, perhaps up to 200 suitable for dispersal. Even by the time of the Cuban crisis a year later, U.S. missile warheads still numbered only in the hundreds, and there were other high-priority targets for these launchers. The SIOP then in effect programmed the fastest warheads against peripheral defense sites to open corridors for bombers.[86] So even if only, say, 10 percent of the nearly 200 Soviet long-range bombers—not to mention any of the nearly 1,000 medium bombers capable of one-way missions, or the nearly 100 Soviet submarine-launched missiles—managed to escape the attack and penetrate U.S. air defenses, many megatons might still come down on American cities. Eight months before the Cuban missile crisis, Secretary McNamara testified secretly to that effect: "Soviet-inflicted

85. Declassified papers courtesy of Scott Sagan. These do not necessarily represent the final word in official assumptions, but the figures suggest that high confidence in catching nearly all the bombers on the ground after war has already broken out would rest on "*best*-case" rather than cautious estimates.

86. See Scott Sagan's commentary in *International Security* (forthcoming). On the SIOP then in effect, see "Briefing for the President by the Chairman, Joint Chiefs of Staff, on the Joint Chiefs of Staff Single Integrated Operational Plan 1962 (SIOP-62)," September 13, 1961, p. 12 (to be reprinted with Sagan commentary).

damage to the civil societies of the Alliance could be very grave indeed. Even if we attempted to destroy the enemy nuclear strike capability at its source, using all our available resources, some portion of the Soviet force would survive to strike back."[87] In short, a U.S. disarming preemptive strike after conventional war had begun would be infeasible, while a more effective preventive surprise attack before conflict erupted—an American Pearl Harbor—was politically unthinkable.

Some who believe that the first twenty years of the postwar era was a nuclear golden age would remain unconvinced by the foregoing argument because it rests on deductions from limited military data and on judgments about political instincts under unprecedented conditions. Emphasis on the significance of the U.S. first-strike option is sometimes sustained by several counterarguments. One is that even if disarming counterforce became problematic by the time of the Kennedy administration it had been viable during the 1950s, when the majority of crises occurred. Another is that even if the option was dubious in fact, Kennedy's advisers overlooked the reasons for doubt and offered the president some comfort in the option anyway.

The final argument is a sort of institutional conspiracy theory—that the air force had confidence in SAC's first-strike capability for reasons that, like a fraternal secret society, it kept to itself. The service distrusted civilian bureaucrats and politicians, fearing they would breach security. Estimates of appreciable U.S. population vulnerability, therefore, were produced by other government agencies not privy to the "real" story. The air force in turn abetted the erroneous estimates and indeed produced figures of its own that exceeded other estimates of prospective damage to the United States, because of a cynical budgetary motive: alarming estimates would support the allocation of more funds to air force programs.[88] None of these counterarguments hold up.

---

87. *Executive Sessions of the Senate Foreign Relations Committee Together With Joint Sessions With the Senate Armed Services Committee (Historical Series)*, vol. 14, 87 Cong. 2d sess., 1962 (GPO, 1986), p. 149. By that time, the administration estimated not only 200 Soviet bombers that could be launched for round-trip missions, but 30 submarines rigged to deliver 90 missiles. Ibid., p. 145.

88. Daniel Ellsberg claimed that as a Pentagon staffer in August 1961 he asked a SAC briefer how he could reconcile two air force positions: the private advice given to the president the week before about keeping American dead below 10 million with a U.S. first strike and the service's argument in the missile gap intelligence debate that the Soviets might have up to 800 unlocated and untargeted ICBMs. The briefer asked in " 'sincere mock horror'—whether it was being suggested that SAC had doctored its estimates to

U.S. attack capability grew through the 1950s, but, like air defense improvements, growth in offensive forces raced against growth in Soviet capacity. Splendid U.S. first-strike capability was often seen as almost within reach, never at hand. Revelations in recent years about the extraordinary quality of U.S. signals intelligence and substantial American and British aerial and balloon reconnaissance of the Soviet Union have underwritten nostalgia for the 1950s, since the revelations imply that there was greater ability to locate and target Soviet forces than has usually been assumed. But in fact high confidence and total coverage did not exist until the advent of satellite surveillance after 1960. Information yielded by the balloons was of negligible value. The U-2, which began flying in mid-1956, could not cover all of the Soviet interior; between early 1958 and April 1960 few deep-penetration flights were mounted.[89]

As early as March 1954, when U.S. superiority was scarcely in doubt, a Weapons System Evaluation Group (WSEG) briefing based on a projected war in July 1955 discussed a U.S. attack on Soviet bloc airfields. It noted that the counterforce target list was incomplete and that the projected U.S. attack would not cover even all *known* fields to which Soviet forces could be dispersed: "At least 240 unstruck and uncontaminated emergency airfields would be available to the Soviets. . . . even under the improbable assumptions that only 5 percent of the [Soviet] aircraft survived, *seventy-five weapons* could be lifted against the U.S." The briefing estimated that twice as many U.S. bombs as were then allocated would be needed to destroy "all known Soviet operational and staging bases."[90]

One might argue that such studies of U.S. first-strike coverage were artificially cautious or that they too often ignored Soviet operational constraints. According to a 1954 special national intelligence estimate, for example, the Soviets might need up to a month to deliver their entire nuclear stockpile.[91] The targeting assumed in the 1954 WSEG report, however, was "fundamentally the same" as the SAC offensive war plan of

inflate the Russian threat." Ellsberg deduced that of the two calculations the casualty figure was the true one, and that it had probably been estimated by adding the population of New York City "to that of one or two cities on the West Coast that might be struck by missiles on Russian submarines that survived SAC's disarming strike." Herken, *Counsels of War*, pp. 144–45.

89. Paul Worthman letter in Rostow, *Open Skies*, p. 193.

90. "Briefing of WSEG Report No. 12," reprinted in *International Security*, vol. 6 (Winter 1981–82), p. 32 (emphasis added); and David Alan Rosenberg, " 'A Smoking Radiating Ruin at the End of Two Hours': Documents on American Plans for Nuclear War with the Soviet Union, 1954–1955," *International Security*, vol. 6 (Winter 1981–82), p. 12.

91. Draft SNIE 11-8-54, cited in Rosenberg, "Origins of Overkill," p. 34.

the same year.[92] Three other considerations negate the notion that leaders would discount official estimates that indicated appreciable U.S. population vulnerability.

First is the simple point that numerous pessimistic estimates served as the currency of assessment and were not less widely purveyed at top levels than any confident views that could have prevailed within the inner sanctums of the Strategic Air Command. In 1955, for instance, the Technological Capabilities Panel reported, "Neither the U.S. nor the Soviets can mount an air strike against the other that would surely be decisive," with the definition of decisive including "ability to strike back essentially eliminated." The report did not foresee a U.S. capability to "mount a decisive air strike" until some time between 1956 and 1960.[93] And in 1956 a CIA contribution to the NSC Planning Board's report warned, "It is possible that the USSR, if it sought full strategic surprise, could launch an attack on the continental U.S. without undertaking any observable preparations which would provide strategic warning."[94]

Second, to discredit the relevance of pessimistic estimates, one would have to assume that the air force winked and whispered its closely held confidence in first-strike capability into the president's ear. But Eisenhower not only made numerous statements reflecting no confidence in low vulnerability; his January 1956 diary entry, mentioned earlier, shows that he took no secret reassurance from SAC's first-strike option. Moreover, any such assurance from the air force would have made a mockery of the service's own pessimistic estimates. If those estimates were disingenuous data games meant to support higher budgets, the ploy could not work unless the estimates were believed by the consumer who made the basic decision on budget trends, the president. And logically such a strategy could have backfired by encouraging diversion of resources from the offensive forces sought by the air force to air defense assets that it wanted much less. Indeed, at the end of 1956, Eisenhower reacted to damage assessments from the Net Evaluation Subcommittee by asking "why we should put a single nickel into anything but developing our capacity to diminish the enemy's capacity for nuclear attack" and stressed concentrating on better defenses and reduction of force vulnerability.[95]

It is impossible to prove a negative—that no president was ever told

92. Rosenberg, " 'A Smoking Radiating Ruin,' " p. 7.
93. TCP, "Meeting the Threat of Surprise Attack," pp. 72–73 (emphasis deleted).
94. NSC 5606, Annex B, p. 25.
95. Coyne, Memorandum, "Discussion at the 306th Meeting of the NSC," pp. 3–4 (cited in note 55).

that U.S. forces could execute a first strike that would prevent any significant Soviet retaliation. But there are ample positive indications to the contrary. During the 1961 Berlin crisis Kennedy was briefed directly on the SIOP, including preemptive options, by the chairman of the JCS, who said that the United States would "prevail" in nuclear war, but that even with U.S. preemption, "it would be expected that some portion of the Soviet long-range nuclear force would strike the United States."[96] There is no indication that the president was buoyed by the air force claim shortly before that a U.S. first strike could keep American fatalities down to 10 million. Kennedy's respect for Soviet capability is also reflected in his remark at the outset of the Cuban missile crisis that "they've got enough to blow us up now anyway." McGeorge Bundy, who sat at the president's right hand, later claimed that Kennedy believed in the simple notion of parity as mutual capacity to inflict unacceptable damage and believed that it already existed by 1960.[97]

Third, not until the advent of the Kennedy administration were the political leadership or war planners oriented to an absolute priority for counterforce in the first-strike option. During the mid-1950s, target planners compromised counterforce aim points in order to gain "bonus" damage against civil targets.[98] In December 1958, just after the Berlin Deadline crisis began, President Eisenhower questioned the need to strive for additional counterforce coverage given the overwhelming U.S. countervalue capability. He even doubted whether more U-2 flights were required to identify targets, since a sufficient number had already been located. The first SIOP was also based on an "Optimum Mix" of Soviet civilian and military targets. In 1960, Chief of Naval Operations Arleigh Burke criticized it as falling between two stools: "Counterforce receives higher precedence than is warranted for a retaliatory plan, and less precedence than is warranted for an initiative plan."[99]

Given the overwhelming percentage of weapons allocated to military targets during the 1950s, the limitations on counterforce optimization may seem trivial to some. But when McNamara arrived at the Pentagon, the air force had not yet been convinced of the desirability of maximizing counterforce in the terms envisioned by civilian analysts, and a WSEG

96. "Briefing for the President," p. 18 (see note 86).
97. McGeorge Bundy, "The Future of Strategic Deterrence," *Survival*, vol. 21 (November–December 1979), p. 269.
98. Kaplan, *Wizards of Armageddon*, pp. 211–12.
99. Rosenberg, "Origins of Overkill," pp. 7–8, 55.

briefing for the secretary argued against such a strategy by saying that nontargetable Soviet weapons would be able to deliver 1,000 to 2,000 megatons, killing half the American population.[100] It took time and effort by the new corps of civilian analysts to make counterforce the first priority in the early 1960s, and then it proved to be a fleeting priority.

Could one argue that none of the secret population vulnerability estimates mattered for crisis coercion, on grounds that U.S. leaders convinced Moscow that they were not intimidated by the prospective consequences of initiating nuclear war? Yes and no. That answer may be equivocal, but it lies at the heart of the peculiarly facile U.S. impulse to drop hints of nuclear blackmail. The threats were meant to communicate preference for nuclear war over conventional defeat. But presidents' statements never indicated any blithe ignorance of the probability that the U.S. homeland would suffer unimaginably. And if anything, prevalent discourse in the country, especially after Sputnik, projected a more devastating impression of nuclear war than that of secret government estimates. This was the era of popular apocalyptic literature like Nevil Shute's *On the Beach*, Walter M. Miller, Jr.'s *A Canticle for Liebowitz*, and Pat Frank's *Alas, Babylon*. The latter novel ends a year after nuclear war, as remnants of national authority begin to reestablish communication with surviving rural communities. Paul Hart, an air force officer landing in a Florida town, explains:

> "We're a second class power now. Tertiary would be more accurate. I doubt if we have the population of France—or rather as large as France used to be. . . ." Randy said, "Paul there's one thing more. Who won the war?"
>
> Paul put his fists on his hips and his eyes narrowed. "You're kidding! You mean you really don't know?"
>
> "No . . . Nobody's told us."
>
> "We won it. We really clobbered 'em!" Hart's eyes lowered and his arms drooped. He said, "Not that it matters."
>
> The engine started and Randy turned away to face the thousand-year night.[101]

---

100. Kaplan, *Wizards of Armageddon*, pp. 258–59. The principal air force resistance, however, was not to improving counterforce but to withholding strikes on urban-industrial targets. The WSEG report also was probably based on a projected situation a few years later.

101. Pat Frank, *Alas, Babylon* (Bantam Books, 1960), pp. 278–79.

Which was farther from the mark—the popular imagination or the belief of some professionals that Americans could weather nuclear war with consequences not radically worse than getting their "hair mussed"?

Did the Bomb Work "Both Ways"?

Why shouldn't the Soviets' retaliatory capability have deterred the United States from initiating nuclear combat? Were U.S. leaders in crisis decisions nonchalant about accepting tens of millions of casualties if U.S. nuclear threats failed to accomplish their coercive purpose and war broke out? No, but case studies of the crises concerned suggest that they refused to face this question decisively, banking that deterrence would not fail. For a strategist devoted to rationalism, certainty, and careful planning, the fit between U.S. doctrine, capabilities, and specific crisis initiatives appears uncomfortably loose. It is hardly surprising that confusion or hesitancy was magnified in political leaders' actual presentation of nuclear threats. And given the ambiguity of evidence about the logic that animated American presidents' thinking on these questions, speculation about Soviet thinking appears doubly adventurous. Some attempt is necessary, though, since a strategic equation has two sides.

Soviet Views?

So what were the Russians—the objects of crisis nuclear threats—to think? Were U.S. leaders foolishly blind to the risks of avoidable devastation of their society? Were they bluffing? Did Soviet leaders normally believe the latter about U.S. doctrine but suspect the former when faced with nuclear threats in crises? Were *they* bluffing about their retaliatory capability, believing it weaker than U.S. estimates did? Or was it all beside the point, because they did not intend to take the conventional military actions that the U.S. nuclear signals aimed to deter? The answer could be: all of the above.

The Soviets' rhetoric inflated their capabilities against the continental United States, but their defense policy as a whole reflected the logic of finite deterrence and the notion that even a limited nuclear capability should be able to deter U.S. escalation. Khrushchev justified his large planned cuts in conventional forces in the late 1950s on grounds that "the number of troops and rifles and bayonets is no longer decisive. . . . our ability to deter imperialist aggression depends on our nuclear and thermonuclear fire power." He also spoke often in terms of simple nuclear countervalue capability and overkill.[102] In 1960 he announced cutbacks in production of certain missiles because rockets "are not cucumbers, you know—you don't eat them—and more than a certain number are not required to repel aggression."[103] Although that sort of statement represented a bluff about existing ICBM capability, it reflected a belief in the adequacy of finite deterrence.

In the 1950s Soviet analysts often criticized U.S. nuclear doctrine not just for its offensive character, but because they saw an American failure to appreciate the prospect of Soviet retaliation if the Americans attempted a "blitzkrieg" by a nuclear first strike.[104] In 1959, for example, Defense Minister Rodion Malinovsky said in *Pravda*, "Playing down the effective capacity of the U.S.S.R. to deal a counterblow to the aggressor and exaggeration of their transoceanic capabilities . . . do not testify to the presence of common sense among the U.S. military."[105]

Moscow was relying primarily on its capability to destroy Western Europe. Claims about how much damage it could inflict on the U.S. homeland and against which targets, with what delivery systems, were only vaguely stated, but claims about damage to Europe were specific and frequent. Khrushchev's memoirs confess greater pessimism about Soviet intercontinental bomber capabilities than showed up in the American estimates.[106] Official rhetoric before the late 1950s did not explicitly suggest that the socialist camp would come out of war better off than the West, but it did claim that both Western Europe and the United States would receive unacceptable damage, and by the late 1950s the official view was clearly "that the *heartlands* of *all* states would suffer," so that "as a result, the West was deterred."[107]

Khrushchev's boldest bluffs did not come until after Sputnik was launched. He first mentioned that the USSR was producing ICBMs just two days after issuing the deadline that touched off the second Berlin crisis.

102. Talbott, ed., *Khrushchev Remembers*, pp. 516, 517.

103. Quoted in Arnold Horelick and Myron Rush, *Strategic Power and Soviet Foreign Policy* (University of Chicago Press, 1965), p. 72.

104. Raymond Garthoff, *The Soviet Image of Future War* (Washington, D.C.: Public Affairs Press, 1959), p. 81.

105. Quoted in Horelick and Rush, *Soviet Strategic Power*, p. 53.

106. Ibid., pp. 28, 49; Talbott, ed., *Khrushchev Remembers*, p. 516: "Our potential enemy . . . was so far away from us that we couldn't have reached him with our air force."

107. Zimmerman, *Soviet Perspectives on International Relations*, p. 173 (emphasis in original).

Several months later he boasted that the Soviet Union had " 'no less force and capabilities' than the United States." By 1960 Moscow was making the first claims of military superiority. In the most extreme variants, Soviet claims touted their air defenses as negating the U.S. bomber threat. Khrushchev took the downing of the American U-2 in May 1960 as evidence, he said, that "not a single bomber could get through to its target."[108] These bluffs energized debate in the U.S. body politic but did not worry Eisenhower, and in October 1961 the Kennedy administration brutally drove home its contempt for Moscow's deterrent. The reversal of fortunes was reflected that very month, when Marshal Rodion Malinovsky, in the first such statement by a major official since 1957, hinted that under some circumstances the Soviets might preempt.[109]

Implications

There may, conceivably, have been a golden age when U.S. leaders could be confident in their ability to limit damage from Soviet nuclear retaliation to a remotely acceptable level—say, total blast and fallout fatalities under 10 percent of the population. But it was an age that comprised, at best, only two brief periods: the years before the mid-1950s and a few years in the early 1960s. Evidence available today about the Soviets' lethargy in developing a bomber force in which *they* had confidence indicates that the United States was probably capable of limiting damage effectively throughout most of the first two decades after World War II. But the logic of deterrence rests not on reality but on beliefs about reality. Without dismissing most U.S. vulnerability estimates as hysterical eyewash—and his statements show he did not—Eisenhower may have had confidence in deterrence, but, during most of his presidency, he could not have had confidence that if he ever had to follow through on a nuclear threat, he would achieve more than Pyrrhic victory.

Leaving aside Soviet capability to destroy Western Europe, as well as the relevance of distinctions between a surprise preventive U.S. strike and a preemptive one, it is conceivable, though unlikely, that if forced to decide, U.S. authorities might have judged the death of up to 10 percent of the American people, as well as the serious injury of as many and the wreckage of a larger fraction of the economic and social fabric, a price worth paying to prevent the absorption of all Europe into Soviet dominion. The nuclear

---

108. Ibid., p. 175; Horelick and Rush, *Soviet Strategic Power*, pp. 50, 74; Khrushchev quoted on pp. 53, 75.
109. Zimmerman, *Soviet Perspectives on International Relations*, p. 187.

threats that came closest to being associated with such a prospective contingency were those over Berlin.

The reported civilian staff estimate in September 1961 of 2–15 million American fatalities if the United States struck first would be consistent with such a notion of acceptable damage, but the estimates during the late 1950s ranging upward from 25 million would not. Yet Eisenhower seems to have been more serene in his reliance on the nuclear threat in the second Berlin crisis than Kennedy was in the third. One explanation is that Eisenhower was willing to pay a higher price; another, apparently the correct one, is that he was not really worried that deterrence might fail. In either case, however, nuclear coercion was not based on a rationalistic cost-benefit computation of acceptable damage. The U.S. threats were directed not against a likely Soviet invasion of NATO territory, but against occupation of half a city. A domino theory—if today Berlin, then tomorrow, inevitably, Bonn and Paris—might be used to try to salvage the original rationale, but that logic was more persuasive in the early phase of confrontation than it would have been if war had ever been imminent. Is there really a good explanation for the logic of U.S. threats?

The balance of interests and balance of power hypotheses are the principal attempts to provide such an explanation. In opposite ways they seek to offer strong explanations; each cites a single major cause that is ostensibly calculable and a matter of substance—interests or power—rather than a slippery matter of style in diplomatic posturing. The balance of interests theory focuses on the incentives to make threats and draws its strength from the presumption that an asymmetrical propensity to risk flows naturally from defensive status, that the reason for the Soviets or Chinese to swerve first in a game of chicken was inherent in the stakes of the dispute. The balance of power theory focuses on the constraints against fulfilling threats—the logic of predicted outcomes if a conflict ends in war—and draws its strength from the presumption that however awful the result would have been, executing the threats might have been rational since the nuclear balance made the costs of nuclear war for the United States lower than the costs of conventional defeat.

As this chapter has shown, neither presumption was warranted, so neither explanation is really strong. Neither as it stands satisfactorily explains the logic both of U.S. nuclear initiatives and of Soviet responses, but both help to account for past outcomes if they are modified and combined. The modified arguments are weaker, however, because they are less parsimonious and based on more subjective factors. They are also less helpful for prediction and offer little reason to assume that the satisfactory results of the past would be repeated if similar confrontations were to occur in the future.

The persuasive aspect of the balance of interests thesis is that it accords with attitudes and assumptions of American leaders and thus with U.S. commitments and decisions to resort to nuclear threats. Its inadequacy is in regard to Soviet decisions to accommodate. It accounts for American risk propensity better than for Soviet risk aversion. For why the Soviets were sobered by U.S. resolve, explanation is forced back toward other grounds, more stylistic than substantive, for the Americans' manipulation of risk stratagem. Why should American blackmail prove any more credible or potent than the Soviets'? One plausible variation on the manipulation of risk theme is the "madman" image—that U.S. authorities successfully conveyed an impression of obliviousness to danger, or of willingness to accept what rational leaders would consider unacceptable damage, thus showing Moscow that finite deterrence would not work.[110] Conversely, Khrushchev's inflammatory nuclear rhetoric must have been unsuccessful in convincing American presidents that he was crazy enough to lean further over the brink.

This madman variant could be reinforced by other subjective explanations based on culture, ideology, and domestic political structure. For example, one could explain the differences in behavior by contrasts in national style and constraints. On the American side would be the traditional ethos of liberal absolutism, the religiously self-righteous confidence that "God's on our side," the cockiness bred by a history lacking any military catastrophe comparable to the Russians' 20 million dead in World War II, and democratic political inhibitions on leaders against appearing weak or backing down in international contests. Or one could argue that the personalities of American presidents, and their greater concern with reputation, lent credibility to their risk taking.[111] In contrast

---

110. Thomas C. Schelling notes, "Another paradox of deterrence is that it does not always help to be, or be believed to be, fully rational, cool-headed, and in control of oneself or one's country," and quotes the anarchist in Joseph Conrad's *The Secret Agent*, who prevented the police from capturing him by carrying nitroglycerin with his finger always on a detonator. Asked why the police would believe he would blow himself up, he says, " 'In the last instance it is character alone that makes for one's safety. . . . What is effective is the belief those people have in my will to use the means. That's their impression. It is absolute. Therefore I am deadly.' " *Arms and Influence* (Yale University Press, 1966), p. 37.

111. Richard Ned Lebow, "Misconceptions in American Strategic Assessments,"

would be Soviet sobriety, caution, and realism about the cataclysmic consequences of war, flowing from greater familiarity with national tragedy and instinctive feelings of inferiority, as well as greater freedom for unaccountable leaders to retreat in the face of a foreign challenge. In contrast to the American streak of religious confidence, Marxist materialism would also put more weight on the balance of power.

This study does not attempt to examine national styles or to compare the psychologies of presidents and politburos. Important as they may be in accounting for the past, these sorts of explanations cannot offer reliable comfort for the future. Culture and personality are hard to measure, subject to numerous interpretations, and tricky grounds for estimation. It would be a leap of faith to assume that such idiosyncratic influences on behavior would always apply in the same way or to the same degree; subjective factors in general are likely bases for miscalculation. Schelling himself doubts that American leaders can be convincing in a madman act.[112] Nor can real or apparent irrationality on the Soviet side be presumed away. Khrushchev certainly projected a reckless image. More than two decades after his ouster, he is often considered an adventurist aberration, but there is no automatic bar to another Khrushchevian personality reaching power in Moscow. Moreover, Khrushchev claimed to be more cautious during the Cuban missile crisis than his own military advisers, who appeared as much under the spell of political imperatives as American leaders and almost as loath to give in—and Moscow has not given in on a comparable crisis since then.[113]

Political Science Quarterly, vol. 97 (Summer 1982), p. 197: "The character and personality of the president is almost certain to be a more decisive factor in influencing the decision to launch a counterattack than any arcane calculations of relative military advantage offered by a military adviser. To the extent that Soviet leaders take such considerations into account ... their analysis of resolve is more in accord with the realities of human behavior than is the narrowly technical approach of their American counterparts." On the salience to American thinking of concern with reputation for toughness, and the lesser priority placed on it by the Soviets, see Glenn H. Snyder and Paul Diesing, *Conflict Among Nations: Bargaining, Decision Making, and System Structure in International Crises* (Princeton University Press, 1977), pp. 457–58, esp. p. 457n.

112. Schelling, *Arms and Influence*, pp. 42–43.

113. In a 1963 interview with Norman Cousins, Khrushchev said, "When I asked the military advisers if they could assure me that holding fast would not result in the death of five hundred million human beings, they looked at me as though I was out of my mind or, what was worse, a traitor. The biggest tragedy, as they saw it, was not that our country might be devastated and everything lost, but that the Chinese or the Albanians would accuse us of appeasement or weakness." Quoted in Schlesinger, *Robert Kennedy and His Times*, p. 529n.

The balance of power hypothesis in its strong form—that the United States could have executed nuclear threats at an acceptable price—appears insufficient to rationalize American risks or Soviet prudence. The Soviets' finite deterrent should logically have negated the probability that a U.S. first strike could protect either Western Europe or the United States from unacceptable damage. A modified version of the balance of power argument, if combined with the madman variation of the Schelling approach, is more persuasive. This weaker version is based on Eisenhower's notion, cited earlier, that even when Moscow had the capacity to cripple the United States, the American ability to inflict yet greater devastation on the USSR could still underwrite deterrence. In the contest of resolve, the prospect of unequal damage to the enemy could compensate for unacceptable damage to one's own nation; in the game of chicken the smaller car could be expected to swerve first, even if a crash would wreck both.

Although Eisenhower mentioned this notion in terms of all-out war, it overlaps what theorists later saw as the advantage in "escalation dominance."[114] It also made nuclear superiority if not a rational comfort, a visceral one; while relative advantage could not calibrate the costs of all-out war to the benefits of achieving objectives, it offered a diffuse sense of encouragement that the other side should blink first, either before confrontation turned into combat or before combat reached the all-out level. Soviet finite deterrence eroded American leaders' *confidence* in nuclear threats, but it did not prevent them from taking the *risk*, because U.S. nuclear superiority buttressed the emotional imperative to exploit the threats.[115]

---

114. See Herman Kahn, *On Escalation: Metaphors and Scenarios* (Hudson Institute, 1965), p. 290; and Paul Nitze, "The Relationship of Strategic and Theater Nuclear Forces," *International Security*, vol. 2 (Fall 1977), pp. 122–24.

115. "Then there is the puzzling question whether simple quantitative nuclear superiority does confer some bargaining advantage even when the nuclear balance is technically stable. Pure logic gives a clear negative to this question. . . . But perversely, the real world does not quite follow this logic. Many policy makers do seem to believe that simple 'superiority' somehow confers a crisis bargaining advantage. The belief may be explained in some cases as merely a lack of sophistication about nuclear strategic theory . . . [or] unconsciously, a higher sophistication . . . that political power in the nuclear age is a function more of 'psychological force' than physical force. It may be, for example, that in the tension of a crisis there is a tendency to regress to more primitive, naive thinking and feeling, to tacitly set aside the esoteric calculations of the strategic theorists, and to adopt and act upon the simple and deeply ingrained idea that he who is superior in physical force is superior in bargaining power. . . . The fact that the Cuban missiles would have been highly vulnerable to a U.S. first strike suggests that the Soviets were thinking not in terms of strengthening their position in the strategic balance as technically defined, but in terms of the psycho-political advantage to be gained by reducing the U.S. margin of absolute superiority." Snyder and Diesing, *Conflict Among Nations*, pp. 459, 461.

According to legend, when one of the top decisionmakers in the Cuban missile crisis was later asked whether U.S. nuclear superiority had anything to do with the outcome, he answered, "Hell no!" Asked whether he would have been comfortable going through the crisis if the nuclear balance had been reversed, he replied, "Hell no!"[116]

The modified version of the balance of power theory helps explain U.S. resolve in the past but does not provide a basis for resolve in the future. The disparity of prospective damage is long gone—and all American leaders since the Nixon administration have made clear that they recognized that fact. Yet they have not suggested that the old reliance on nuclear first use has been outmoded. The tension inherent in this combination of change and continuity has not been subjected to a severe test by crisis since 1962. While any reckoning in practice has been averted, the ever-present possibility in theory that such a crisis could recur has led to tense and frequently confused debates about doctrine and especially about the nature and measurement of the nuclear balance. Confusion has been abetted by other developments during the decade of the 1970s, which witnessed the transition of the nuclear balance into parity and the clash of hawkish and dovish arguments about the meaning of nuclear superiority. To understand the implications of that transition for future crises, it is necessary to sort out what happened—obviously, implicitly, and sometimes without notice at the time—in that period.

116. When I asked the individual about this story he did not recall it or deny it, but again downplayed the significance of the nuclear balance at the time.

CHAPTER FIVE

Parity:
Change, Continuity, Confusion

The Presidents of the nuclear age have recognized that the law of diminishing returns applies to strategic missiles. . . . But they have all rejected the gamble of limiting our strategic strength in terms of any absolute concept of what is enough. They have measured our strength against that of the Soviet Union and have aimed at strategic superiority; that superiority has had different meanings at different stages, but seen from the White House its value for peace has never been small. McGeorge Bundy, "The Presidency and the Peace," *Foreign Affairs* (April 1964)

The heavy rhetorical emphasis on continuing American superiority was misleading. . . . What we did not say so loud was that the principal use of this numerical superiority was in its value as reassurance to the American public and as a means of warding off demands for still larger forces. McGeorge Bundy, address to the International Institute for Strategic Studies, September 9, 1979

DID THE NUCLEAR BALANCE matter in the past? Will it in the future? The record surveyed so far suggests that it mattered in the past less than risk-minimizing strategists usually assume and more than risk-maximizing strategists believe. There is little evidence that presidents based their brinkmanship on confidence that decisive nuclear superiority could prevent unacceptable damage to the United States in the event of war. Rather, they seem to have valued marginal superiority as a prop for initiatives they felt compelled to take for political reasons. At first glance, past cases may seem poor guides to the future. Over the past twenty years the relationship between the United States and the Soviet Union has changed markedly, especially in three ways.

First, nuclear parity emerged between the superpowers. By the 1980s, U.S. superiority had disappeared as a fact and ostensibly as a value. After 1969 no American president, not even Ronald Reagan, endorsed the notion of regaining nuclear advantage. Throughout this latter period, however, politicians and analysts have disputed the nature and consequences of parity and whether it was giving way to Soviet superiority. Conscious

180

attention shifted from maintaining U.S. nuclear leverage to preventing Soviet nuclear blackmail.

Second, nuclear threats declined as a tactic in superpower disputes. Four times as many threats marked the first two decades after Hiroshima as the next two. When conditions similar to those that had evoked U.S. threats in the past arose, however, presidents did not shrink from resurrecting the tactic.

Third, the severity of crises declined. None of the disputes between Washington and Moscow after the early 1960s matched the worst confrontations of the earlier period, such as those over Berlin and Cuba. With the death of détente by the end of the 1970s, however, the recurrence of intense crisis seemed less unlikely.

Those three developments led many observers to assume that American leaders were reconciled to the passing of U.S. superiority and that facile hints of nuclear blackmail in disputes are things of the past. The qualifications noted in each instance above, however, leave grounds for doubt about the depth or durability of the differences that distinguished recent decades from earlier ones. Significant continuities were obscured by some of the circumstances of the transition through parity and détente. Moreover, top policymakers such as McGeorge Bundy, Robert McNamara, and Henry Kissinger, looking back from private life, have contradicted their old official statements in revealing ways. Such inconsistencies suggest three things to keep in mind for understanding the significance of confusion about these matters. First, political and strategic constraints are often contradictory, and for leaders in office the former almost always dominate the latter. Second, less may have changed than meets the eye: some leaders' loss of faith in the value of superiority occurred earlier than official rhetoric at the time indicated; others' apparent acceptance of parity masked a lack of resignation and an urge to find some way to square the circle and retain leverage they had attributed to the old U.S. nuclear advantage. Finally, official rhetoric should not always be taken at face value.

How much really changed? Why? And how permanently? Since the three developments noted above were in some respects mutually reinforcing, a shift in any of them could shake the apparent new pattern. What were the cause and effect relationships among the changes—particularly between the official acceptance of parity and the decline of nuclear coercion? The third change, the reduced incidence of major crises, makes that question harder to answer than it might otherwise be by now.

To get at these questions from the U.S. side, this chapter explores briefly the conceptual confusions and political evasions that attended the advent of nuclear parity, facilitated its formal acceptance, sublimated anxieties about the loss of superiority in debates about the measurement and maintenance of the nuclear balance, and contorted plans for preserving extended deterrence. The first section argues that although most of the vexing strategic debates during the transition into parity were couched in terms of the problem of basic deterrence—preventing a Soviet nuclear first strike on the United States—the more convincing aspects of prominent criticisms were to be found in a hidden or unconscious agenda of fortifying American first-use options as escalation dominance disappeared. The second section focuses on more overt yet still slippery attempts to grapple with escalatory commitments.

To get at the other side of the equation—the question of Soviet reaction to developments after the early 1960s—it helps especially to highlight the question of whether nuclear parity made the United States accept détente or détente enabled Washington to welcome parity. The former was the official Soviet view, but the latter is closer to reality. If parity logically compelled détente, one would also expect to see the United States giving up reliance on nuclear escalation and accepting Soviet "equal rights" in the politico-military sphere, as Khrushchev had expected when he tried prematurely to exploit claims of parity. In the early 1970s the trend did seem to be toward such American resignation, but by the end of that decade it had turned around, with the United States moving to reinvigorate extended deterrence and reverse the shifting "correlation of forces" by deploying new missiles in Europe while continuing to deny the Soviets the right to analogous nuclear developments.

This chapter is not a general discussion of diplomatic and doctrinal developments in nuclear policy after the early 1960s, but a review of the perplexing aspects of them that bear on the potential for nuclear leverage. The review will suggest that despite the important differences between the first twenty years of the nuclear era and the second, U.S. leaders could still find themselves reaching for their nuclear prop.

Equivocal Views of Equivalence

American leaders came to endorse nuclear parity, but with an embrace that for most was initially grudging, then careless, and finally nervous. They let go of superiority less because it appeared to lack value, than because there seemed no way to hold on to it. To some involved in the issue the problem was that keeping superiority was militarily impossible. Soviet force development caused diminishing returns from U.S. nuclear investment: the margins of advantage that could be preserved by a vigorous arms competition would be too narrow to matter. To others, keeping superiority was politically impossible. Foreign distractions and domestic resistance blocked efforts to compete actively enough to stay ahead. The beginning of the transition was eased all around by the exit of nuclear concerns from center stage.

Washington was preoccupied with a burgeoning war in Vietnam by the time it faced a rapidly expanding Soviet ICBM force in the late 1960s. The Johnson administration began implicitly to accept nuclear equality of the superpowers and to pursue arms control as the way to secure it. Richard Nixon's 1968 campaign rhetoric endorsed the aim of keeping American superiority, and the threatened advent of parity was the principal reason that General LeMay agreed to serve as George Wallace's running mate.[1] Within his first year in office, however, Nixon became the first president to accept parity openly. What acceptance meant was ultimately far from clear.

Definitions Loose and Tight

In theory parity is a nullity—the absence of advantage on either side. In practice the matter is less simple because there are several dimensions of the nuclear equation. Definitions of parity grew in complexity with the consensus that it had arrived. In the era of unquestioned U.S. superiority in the 1950s there was comparatively little discussion of what it meant, because those who worried about the loss of superiority did not yet have to face it.

The minimalist definition of parity is not equality of nuclear capability; rather parity means that even the weaker side has enough capability to inflict unacceptable destruction on the stronger. Reflecting the emergence of Soviet finite deterrence, that usage appeared in the West by the late 1950s.[2] It was half implicit in the term "sufficiency," used by Eisenhower,

---

1. See Richard K. Betts, *Soldiers, Statesmen, and Cold War Crises* (Harvard University Press, 1977), p. 254n.

2. For example, Hans Speier spoke of emerging parity and the mutual negation of nuclear threats just after the Suez crisis: "Soviet Atomic Blackmail and the North Atlantic Alliance," *World Politics*, vol. 9 (April 1957), p. 311. The assumed strength of Soviet finite deterrence underlay the early critiques of massive retaliation. See William W.

who himself foresaw eventual Soviet narrowing of the gap in capability. In a 1955 press conference he reflected, "There comes a time, possibly, when a lead is not significant. . . . If you get enough of a particular type of weapon, I doubt that it is particularly important to have a lot more of it."[3] But Eisenhower did not quite suggest what Khrushchev did before his frustration in the crises of 1961–62—that the United States and Soviet Union had equal deterrent capability. Eisenhower's sufficiency bowed to the inevitability of growing U.S. vulnerability, but still took comfort from persistence of greater Soviet vulnerability.[4]

Debate reflecting uncertainty about the meaning of sufficiency toward the end of Eisenhower's administration presaged the slipperiness of the term when Nixon revived it a decade later, when the disparity of vulnerability that had buoyed Eisenhower had waned.[5] When asked what it meant, Nixon's deputy secretary of defense, David Packard, replied, "It means that it's a good word to use in a speech. Beyond that it doesn't mean a God-damned thing." The president himself explained it in several senses, which could be seen by those anxious about the credibility of extended deterrence as inconsistent: "In its narrow military sense, it means enough force to inflict a level of damage on a potential aggressor sufficient to deter him from attacking. . . . In its broader political sense, sufficiency means the maintenance of forces adequate to prevent us and our allies from being coerced."[6] At another time Nixon explained parity as "a point in arms development at which each nation has the capacity to destroy the other. Beyond that point the most important consideration is not continued escalation of the number of arms but maintenance of the strategic equilibrium." In 1975 Henry Kissinger defined it as a balance in which "whoever may be ahead in the damage they can inflict on the other, the damage to the other in a general nuclear war will be of a catastrophic nature."[7]

Such statements reflect the focus on capacity to damage population and

Kaufmann, "The Requirements of Deterrence," in Kaufmann, ed., *Military Policy and National Security* (Princeton University Press, 1956), pp. 12–38.

3. *Public Papers of the Presidents of the United States: Dwight D. Eisenhower, 1955* (Government Printing Office, 1959), p. 303.

4. David Alan Rosenberg, "The Origins of Overkill: Nuclear Weapons and American Strategy, 1945–1960," *International Security*, vol. 7 (Spring 1983), p. 33.

5. See Jerome H. Kahan, *Security in the Nuclear Age: Developing U.S. Strategic Arms Policy* (Brookings, 1975), p. 43.

6. Packard and Nixon quoted in Lawrence Freedman, *The Evolution of Nuclear Strategy* (St. Martin's Press, 1981), p. 341.

7. Nixon and Kissinger quoted in Raymond L. Garthoff, *Détente and Confrontation: American-Soviet Relations from Nixon to Reagan* (Brookings, 1985), p. 57.

economy that predominated in assessments during the cold war, when the United States led in offensive forces, and during the heyday of détente, when fear of war between the superpowers was at the nadir. A related but distinct set of terms of reference for superiority and parity has been the quantitative ratio and relative quality of weapons systems. As massive countervalue capability became nearly equal, that secondary focus of strategic debate gradually became the primary one. The burgeoning of arms control forced this shift in focus, since weapons rather than targets constituted the currency of negotiation, but the trend had begun long before. It is unclear that the technical balance of forces—the "bean count," as it is known in Pentagon argot—has strategic significance in itself. Despite the drumbeat of alarm about the deterioration of the nuclear balance, for example, the United States had significantly more second-strike capability in terms of survivable warheads in 1980 than it did in 1964.[8] The deterioration was far clearer in terms of U.S. *first*-strike capability, but that concern was hardly ever discussed in the 1970s, although it was refracted in debate about second-strike counterforce. So how did such comparisons of the balance of forces come to dominate discussion?

By the mid-1960s McNamara had lost faith in the importance of counterforce and accepted the Soviets' acquisition of assured destruction capability. But he held resistance within the defense establishment in check by maintaining counterforce targeting as the priority in the SIOP, and he used the prospect of continuing U.S. superiority in the numerical balance of forces to hold his critics at bay. Speaking on the basis of intelligence estimates, he reported to Congress in 1965, "The Soviets have decided that they have lost the quantitative arms race, and they are not seeking to engage us in that contest. . . . There is no indication that the Soviets are seeking to develop a strategic nuclear force as large as our own."[9] The assertion appeared to assume that Soviet leaders shared McNamara's notions more than those of American hawks, that they recognized that forces beyond those needed for assured destruction were superfluous, and that they would not exaggerate the numbers required for it—in short, that

8. In terms of equivalent megatonnage, however, the 1964 force had more second-strike capacity. Warner R. Schilling, "U.S. Strategic Nuclear Concepts in the 1970s: The Search for Sufficiently Equivalent Countervailing Parity," *International Security*, vol. 6 (Fall 1981), p. 50 and 50n. Schilling's tongue-in-cheek subtitle reflects the convolution of official definitions, and the article is a cogent review of contradictions in the concepts.

9. Quoted in G. A. Keyworth, "Ganging Up on Star Wars," *Washington Post*, December 24, 1984. See also Fred Kaplan, *The Wizards of Armageddon* (Simon and Schuster, 1983), pp. 318–19.

they would proceed more wisely than the American decisionmakers of earlier years had.

Beginning in the following year, rapid expansion of the Soviet ICBM force invalidated McNamara's prediction in the terms that had predominated in U.S. measures of the weapons balance—the number of delivery systems—and critics cited the growing ICBM force as well as the large yields of Soviet warheads to question whether American superiority would endure. While McNamara cautioned about the dubious significance of numerical superiority in the face of Soviet assured destruction capacity, he continued to claim that the United States would preserve it. He supported the claim by shifting the focus of assessment to the number of warheads— an index in which U.S. forces would maintain a large lead through deployment of multiple independently targetable reentry vehicles (MIRVs). McNamara's successor as secretary of defense, Clark Clifford, reasserted the claim that superiority would be retained.[10]

The Strategic Arms Limitation Talks (SALT) required abandoning the objective of superiority, and Nixon's secure status as a conservative allowed it. Indeed, Nixon was driven to nuclear accommodation by the general collapse of support for international activism.[11] Hawkish criticism in Congress was outweighed by dovish criticism and temporary antidefense fallout resulting from the prolongation of the Vietnam War. By the time the SALT I treaty had been negotiated the new administration was claiming the U.S. warhead advantage not as a means to retain superiority, but as an assurance of parity, to offset the Soviet advantage in missile numbers and throwweight.[12]

The peculiar mix of reality, rhetoric, politics, diplomacy, and legislation surrounding SALT I, however, sowed the seeds for collapse of consensus about parity. Success in policy at the beginning of the 1970s was bought with a mortgage that ballooned at the end of the decade, when the Carter administration had lost the capital to pay. Two interacting evasions about the nature of parity were responsible. The evasions, perhaps not fully

10. Ted Greenwood, *Making the MIRV: A Study of Defense Decision Making* (Ballinger, 1975), pp. 77–78.

11. See the chronicle in Henry Kissinger, *White House Years* (Little, Brown, 1979), pp. 134–35, 195–96, 200–07, 212–15. On p. 196 he writes of the transition to nuclear parity: "This should have changed all the assumptions of our postwar strategy. Unfortunately, at the precise moment that our national debate should have concentrated on the implications of this new situation, *all* our defense programs were coming under increasing attack" (emphasis in original).

12. Greenwood, *Making the MIRV*, p. 79.

conscious and certainly abetted by the looseness of prevalent definitions, were the Nixon administration's premature declaration that parity had arrived and charges by critics that parity was about to be lost.

Parity had arrived by the early 1970s only in terms of population vulnerability, not in terms of the technical balance of forces. Thus loose notions of parity were acceptable for official purposes. In 1969 Secretary of Defense Melvin Laird's criterion was preventing the USSR from "gaining the ability to cause considerably greater urban/industrial destruction than the United States could inflict on the Soviets."[13] But when different official purposes competed, the looseness made it conveniently possible for administration figures to assume some residual advantage in the U.S. position. The initial Nixon strategy of "linkage" in arms control negotiations—the aim to secure Soviet restraint in political competition as the price for nuclear arms limitation—implicitly viewed nuclear equality as an optional concession to Moscow. And in the 1973 Middle East War crisis, Kissinger, who had presided over the diplomatic codification of parity in SALT, claimed to see marginal remnants of U.S. advantage within the bounds of rough parity as support for the DEFCON-3 signal. Still, the dominant notion of parity early in the Nixon presidency was based on rough magnitudes of urban-industrial vulnerability. The subsequent concern of critics that parity was giving way to Soviet superiority was exemplified in Public Law 92-448, Senator Henry Jackson's amendment to the SALT I interim agreement, which required that future negotiations achieve nuclear equality. Charges of emerging Soviet superiority cited the balance of forces, not civil vulnerability. Such charges about Soviet superiority, however, were valid only if forces were considered selectively, with components allegedly crucial for counterforce being cited and some elements favorable to the United States being disregarded.

The administration could not claim that any American superiority remained under the SALT I treaty without undercutting its bargaining position with the Soviets. The agreement, however, encompassed only ballistic missiles and submarines, while the United States held a huge advantage in the excluded categories of intercontinental bomber numbers and payload, not to mention so-called forward-based systems, which Moscow considered strategic since they could strike Soviet territory. (The Soviets had lacked comparable systems ever since their IL-28s and missiles had been forced out of Cuba.) Although the U.S. lead in warheads was

13. Quoted in Schilling, "U.S. Strategic Nuclear Concepts," p. 64.

large and increased markedly in the three years after the agreement, the treaty allowed the USSR larger numbers and throwweight of missiles. The legislative history of the Jackson amendment reflected the senator's definition of numbers of missiles and throwweight as the measures of equality.[14] The actual language of the amendment, however, left equality undefined, allowing the Nixon, Ford, and Carter administrations to negotiate it in terms of the full range of offsetting measures of intercontinental nuclear striking power.

The diverging implications in the early 1970s of two definitions of parity—the loose one based on the balance of population vulnerability and the tight one based on the balance of forces—went unremarked at the time. Both presidential statements and Soviet writings focused on the looser notion, mutual civil vulnerability, and thus dated parity from the end of the 1960s; they did not distinguish the balance of forces as a separate concern and a disparity that remained in American favor in the early 1970s. Nixon also evinced no special grasp of the political implications of either sort of parity. These oversights subsequently enabled hawkish critics to cite Soviet gains in the balance of forces during the late 1970s, which were to a large extent catching up in net technical indexes, as movement beyond parity existing at the beginning of the decade. For example, Senator Jackson grilled Secretary of Defense Harold Brown in SALT II hearings, noting that four years previously Brown had characterized the superpowers' forces as "fairly well balanced" and criticized the ongoing Soviet buildup. "If we were equal then and if you were concerned about Soviet deployment activities then," Jackson queried, "how can you continue to claim that we are equal after the unbroken continuation of those Soviet programs?"[15]

The sensitive question of whether parity was giving way to Soviet superiority thus depended on when one assumed parity had arrived, which in turn depended on which sort of parity one was talking about. If it meant mutual vulnerability to unacceptable damage, parity came in the mid-1950s; if it meant nearly equal levels of civil damage, it arrived by the early 1970s; if equality in missiles or delivery vehicles, by the mid-1970s; if the measure is the balance of forces as a whole or of counterforce capacity, by the late 1970s.[16] Doves focused on the first or second sorts, and hawks on

---

14. *Military Implications of the Treaty on the Limitation of Strategic Offensive Arms and Protocol Thereto (SALT II Treaty)*, Hearings before the Senate Committee on Armed Forces, 96 Cong. 1 sess. (GPO, 1979), pt. 1, p. 30.

15. Ibid., p. 31. See also Garthoff, *Détente and Confrontation*, pp. 57, 59, 796.

16. The USSR had surpassed the American total of intercontinental ballistic missiles

the third and fourth, but high political leaders rarely specified what sort they were talking about.

Imprecision at the top persisted as the decade progressed. In an early press conference President Carter blended the two dimensions of assessment in a somewhat muddled way, speaking of the U.S. position as both superior and equivalent:

> At the present time, my judgment is that we have superior nuclear capability. The Soviet Union has more throw weight, larger missiles, larger warheads; we have more missiles, a much higher degree of accuracy, and also, we have three different mechanisms which are independently adequate to deliver atomic weapons—airplanes, submarines, and intercontinental ballistic missiles. I think that we are roughly equivalent, even though I think we are superior, in that either the Soviet Union or we could destroy a major part of the other nation if a major attack was made with losses in the neighborhood of 50 to 100 million people if a large exchange was initiated.[17]

By the end of the decade, however, the SALT process and charges about emerging U.S.inferiority served to make the specialists' focus on the nuances of the force balance the dominant currency of debate, and the motive of reinforcing crisis leverage, which had been eclipsed by détente, began to come out of the closet.

The Esoteric Becomes the Essential

"Once you involve yourself in a lot of detail," Dean Rusk said presciently about arms control, "you are dead."[18] SALT I avoided that problem by striking a symmetrical bargain on antiballistic missiles and sticking to simple terms of reference on offensive weapons: the number of missile launchers and platforms. The natural dynamics of further arms control negotiations, together with growing discord about relative marginal advantage under rough parity, made the descent into detail inevitable.

Political and diplomatic imperatives, however, made some ambiguity

by 1970, the number of submarine-launched ballistic missiles in 1975, and the total of long-range delivery vehicles (including bombers) by 1973. Schilling, "U.S. Strategic Nuclear Concepts," p. 49. The number of warheads and their accuracy provided a U.S. advantage for a longer time.

17. *Public Papers of the Presidents of the United States: Jimmy Carter, 1977*, Book I (GPO, 1977), p. 95. The United States did not have more missiles at the time, but did have more warheads.

18. Quoted in John Newhouse, *Cold Dawn: The Story of SALT* (Holt, Rinehart and Winston, 1973), p. 45.

about definitions a continuing necessity. While Washington and Moscow could agree on nuclear equality in principle, translating the standard precisely into technical indexes for asymmetrical force structures was impossible in practice. Very precise criteria would preclude an equality that was negotiable simultaneously with Moscow and with American hawks. In the mid-1970s the Ford and Carter administrations responded to the Jackson amendment by articulating "essential equivalence"—semantically more malleable than stark "equality"—as the standard of adequacy for U.S. forces relative to the Soviets'.[19]

Successive secretaries of defense confirmed the flexibility of the standard by emphasizing different implications. Each also moved back in the direction of an implicit emphasis on extended deterrence, but without baldly focusing on U.S. first-use requirements. James Schlesinger, more in tune with Jackson, precluded any "major asymmetries" in "throw-weight, accuracy, yield-to-weight ratios, reliability and other factors that contribute to the effectiveness of strategic weapons." Donald Rumsfeld cited "roughly equivalent" forces that would negate any misconceptions that could "lead to pressure, crisis, and confrontation." Harold Brown defined essential equivalence as requiring U.S. advantages to offset "any advantage in force characteristics enjoyed by the Soviets," and said it should work to enhance crisis stability, prevent Soviet use of nuclear forces for coercion, and favorably affect perceptions of third parties.[20]

The Rumsfeld and Brown refinements point to the failure of peacetime doctrine to focus on what was the usual issue in crises. Their stated concern about nuclear leverage was to prevent the Soviets from attempting to use it. In most cases, however, it had been the United States that had relied the most on manipulating the possibility of first use—and thereby had implicitly sought to discredit the adequacy of the Soviets' retaliatory deterrent to prevent it. U.S. leadership remained concerned with the coercive political utility of nuclear forces in theory, but was not addressing very clearly the questions about it that had usually arisen in practice.

---

19. Conversation with David Aaron, October 14, 1984. Aaron, who worked on SALT policy, recalls that the term emerged when a draft using only the word "equivalence" was being discussed. When a participant wrung his hands because it sounded "too tight," Aaron added "essential" and the worrier said "Great!" because that made it ambiguous enough to allow room for maneuver.

20. Schlesinger, Rumsfeld, and Brown quoted in James L. Foster, "Rethinking the Unthinkable: The Strategic Dilemmas of the 1980s," in *Rethinking U.S. Security Policy for the 1980s*, Proceedings of the Seventh Annual National Security Affairs Conference, July 21–23, 1980 (Washington, D.C.: National Defense University Press, 1980), pp. 138–40.

By the end of the 1970s the ascendancy of the balance of forces concept of parity was complete, but the more alarming arguments about the state of the nuclear balance were more convincing if one was really concerned about what would inhibit American first use than if the only worry was about deterring unprovoked nuclear assault on the continental United States. As a result, the domestic analytical-political debates of the 1970s were often unusually indirect and obscure because some on both sides contending for support of the centrists or fence-sitters avoided explicit or full discussion of their principal concerns. The commitment to extended deterrence remained in principle but it receded as a prominent or overt factor in debate. If hawks made too much of it, or if doves openly rejected it, both risked alienating moderates from the constituency that could support their positions on nuclear force modernization and arms control. Contending schools of thought were driven to oblique arguments. Two examples of widely publicized calculations are illustrative.

In articles in the mid-1970s Paul Nitze projected that a counterforce exchange would leave the Soviet Union with a marked edge in surviving forces and thus escalation dominance in war. That prospect, in turn, according to Nitze's chess-like reasoning, would give the Soviets the capacity for blackmail in a crisis. Some analysts rebutted that argument by changing the terms of reference, shifting the focus from postexchange to postattack ratios and the impressive U.S. assured-destruction capabilities available after absorption of a Soviet first strike; they challenged the relevance of Nitze's calculations, but not the figures themselves.[21] Others challenged the data, suggesting that the projection was based on statistical legerdemain.[22]

21. Paul H. Nitze, "Assuring Strategic Stability in an Era of Détente," *Foreign Affairs*, vol. 54 (January 1976), pp. 207–32; Nitze, "Deterring Our Deterrent," *Foreign Policy*, no. 25 (Winter 1976–77), pp. 195–210; Jan M. Lodal, "Assuring Strategic Stability: An Alternate View," *Foreign Affairs*, vol. 54 (April 1976), pp. 462–81.

22. Two noted that fiscal year 1979 Defense Department calculations presented projections through 1987 more favorable to the United States. They also argued: (1) Nitze's data assumed that all U.S. bomber payload would be expended against Soviet Backfire bomber bases—lower-priority targets even if the Backfires were caught on the ground—although official testimony had acknowledged that B-52s would be used against silos as well as other targets; (2) assuming that defenses prevent U.S. bombers from attacking silos, Nitze ignored the possibility of using missiles to cut corridors through the defenses; (3) Nitze's model, contradicting the Defense Department fiscal year 1979 Annual Report, assumed minimal effectiveness of air-launched cruise missiles (ALCMs) against silos; (4) since the Soviets normally deployed only four missile-launching submarines (SSBNs) near U.S. coasts, the transit of more submarines (to increase the threat to bomber bases) would give Washington time to increase alert and disperse bombers to additional inland sites, yet Nitze's model assumed that 30 percent of alert bombers as well as all

By contrast, a 1978 Arms Control and Disarmament Agency (ACDA) study attempted to demonstrate not just a more even balance of strategic capabilities than suggested by analyses such as Nitze's, but a U.S. advantage. The manipulation of premises, scenario, and data was different, but no less dubious. The focus was turned back toward countervalue capability, which made the favorable implication more impressive. Although the predominant attitude in ACDA was that survivable assured destruction capacity should be the only relevant concern, by 1978 it was politically suicidal to dismiss the importance of counterforce ratios. The agency's study genuflected to the relevance of counterforce and escalation dominance but used computational assumptions that could dismiss the question by attributing marginal advantage to U.S. forces.[23]

---

those not on day-to-day alert would be destroyed; and (5) Nitze used inconsistent calculations in some of his articles. Garry D. Brewer and Bruce G. Blair, "War Games and National Security With a Grain of SALT," *Bulletin of the Atomic Scientists*, vol. 35 (June 1979), pp. 20–22. See also Joseph M. Grieco, "Paul H. Nitze and Strategic Stability: A Critical Analysis," Occasional Paper 9 (Cornell University Peace Studies Program, November 1976). In another paper circulated widely at the time, Nitze's calculations yielded alarming projections, but he assumed that ALCMs had a circular error probable (CEP) of 300 feet and that U.S. ICBMs would have identical CEPs in 1977 and 1985 while comparable Soviet CEPs would be cut in half during this period. Paul H. Nitze, "Current SALT II Negotiating Posture," unpublished paper, January 1979, p. 25. The figure for ALCMs was higher than some other estimates in open literature at the time, and it is hard to rationalize the lack of change in U.S. ICBM accuracy from 1977 to 1985, given the intervening deployment of the new NS-20 guidance system.

23. Assuming that differences in Soviet and American target systems were not significant, ACDA evaluated effectiveness of both nations' forces against a hypothetical common set of 1,500 hard targets and 5,000 soft targets. The analysis also relied on the trade-offs necessary to reach an "equal damage point" (EDP) against hard and soft targets. U.S. Arms Control and Disarmament Agency, "U.S. and Soviet Strategic Capability Through the Mid-1980s: A Comparative Analysis" (August 1978). But neither abstraction is relevant. The USSR has many more hard targets than the United States, so the ACDA calculations exaggerated U.S. counterforce capabilities. And if the Soviets strike first there is no reason to believe that they would seek to destroy as many soft targets as hard ones. Maximizing the incineration of civilians conceivably makes sense for a second strike, but offers no military payoff for the initiator of a nuclear war. (If desired, it could be accomplished in follow-up attacks with reloaded systems.) Stipulating the EDP as a goal, especially when the hypothetical number of soft targets was more than three times greater than the hard, understated Soviet counterforce capabilities by draining them away for other missions. Also, the ACDA model apparently assumed that U.S. forces are fully generated and that the soft targets are point rather than area targets, thus overrating the U.S. advantage in number of warheads and underrating the Soviet advantage in yield. Some of these points are made in Committee on the Present Danger, "An Evaluation of 'U.S. and Soviet Strategic Capability through the Mid-1980s: A Comparative Analysis'," press release, September 1978, pp. 3–4. On data problems in modeling separate target

Nitze's calculations did the reverse, focusing on counterforce and assuming data that suggested Soviet advantage. His argument, however, was couched in terms of *basic* deterrence, a scenario of a surprise Soviet first strike out of the blue. The most common criticism of his argument was directed against the plausibility of a Soviet gamble that a president would shrink from retaliation after thousands of nuclear detonations on military bases in the United States, or especially that a president might back down in a political confrontation when he thought ahead to the likely residual balance of forces after a counterforce exchange. If the Nitze argument appeared implausible for a situation that involved retaliation after an unprovoked Soviet surprise attack on the continental United States, however, it would seem less so in regard to extended deterrence. First, the analytical focus on a Soviet first strike was not necessarily disingenuous; U.S. interest in first use would be a salient ingredient even in a Soviet first-strike scenario. If one seeks a Soviet motive for a first strike, what reasonable one could there be apart from concern about the prospect that American strategic forces would eventually be launched in response to successful advance of Soviet conventional forces? A counterforce strike that spares other assets accomplishes nothing else beyond preempting a U.S. nuclear attack.

Second, the calculations of counterforce ratios that are expected to daunt a president contemplating his next move in a crisis would take the wind out of his sails more quickly if he were thinking about a prospective escalatory initiative of his own than if he were wondering about whether his survivable retaliatory forces would deter the Russians from starting a nuclear duel. The intuitive argument that nuclear resolve is independent of relative power is less persuasive in regard to first use than to retaliation after absorbing some nuclear damage.[24] And by portraying the postexchange balance in terms of a Soviet first strike, the calculations could also be conducive to an impression of the balance in general as less favorable to Washington than if the numbers were derived according to a scenario of an American first strike. Nitze alluded vaguely to the problem of extended deterrence, but the vivid graphs presented did not include a variant for U.S. initiative.[25]

---

bases, see Francis P. Hoeber, *Military Applications of Modelling: Selected Case Studies* (Gordon and Breach, 1981), pp. 170–71.

24. For counterargument see Robert Jervis, *The Illogic of American Nuclear Strategy* (Cornell University Press, 1984).

25. Nitze, "Deterring Our Deterrent," pp. 202–03, 206.

Finally, questions about Nitze's judgments in 1976 emerge with more clarity if one compares them with remarkably similar ones made in the same journal exactly two decades earlier. In a 1956 article he argued that purposely attacking cities in atomic warfare would make no sense for either side, that counterforce superiority would allow the victor "to issue orders to the loser and the loser will have to obey them or face complete chaos or extinction," and that even though the Soviets would narrow the gap, marginal U.S. superiority would remain a significant deterrent.[26]

Whether or not concerns about the option of deliberate U.S. escalation were meant to figure in the 1976 argument, it would have been politically maladroit to pose them directly. Commitment to strong basic deterrence was unquestioned while commitment to first use of U.S. intercontinental forces—often criticized as suicidal even before U.S. superiority waned—had become far less popular. It was not even respectable any more to cite escalation dominance as a requirement of U.S. nuclear strategy. After the early 1960s, many who accepted extended deterrence came to identify it only with tactical or theater nuclear weapons rather than with the full range of nuclear commitment formally embodied in the flexible response doctrine. Perhaps this mistake occurred because the discourse of professional strategic analysts dealt more often in terms of military logic than in terms of political compromise or diplomacy and emphasized the obvious strength of mutual deterrence at the central strategic level of intercontinental capability, as if the formal policy commitment to European allies was a disingenuous irrelevance.

For critics who wanted to fortify first-use options, real equivalence in the balance was less comfortable than at least some putative margin of advantage in force elements. For others who saw any notion of first use of strategic forces as dangerously destabilizing and sought progress in negotiated accommodation with Moscow, strict equivalence was not vital as long as basic deterrence through second-strike countervalue capability was preserved. The norm of parity occupied the center between hawks and doves, and to compete for political support both had to endorse it. A relaxed standard for measuring it threatened hawks' desire to preserve some margin of leverage against the Russians, while a stringent standard threatened doves' hopes for braking the arms competition.

Equivalence reigned in principle although it had no operational rationale. It offered either too much or too little, mandating a level of American

26. Paul H. Nitze, "Atoms, Strategy and Policy," *Foreign Affairs*, vol. 34 (January 1956), pp. 188, 191–93, 196; quotation on pp. 190–91.

capabilities that would be superfluous for assured destruction but deficient for escalation dominance, more than a risk-maximizing strategist would need to back nuclear coercion and less than enough to comfort a risk minimizer. The rationales for the norm of strict parity in forces were less strategic than political and diplomatic—a compromise on which domestic consensus could be forged from grudging agreement by both hawks and doves and international agreement could be negotiated between Moscow and Washington. The norm was so solidly established that it survived the political triumph of the hawks and the near-collapse of arms control. In 1984 President Reagan opposed inclusion of the goal of superiority in the Republican Platform as "counterproductive" and stated his preference for parity.[27]

Parity and Nuclear First Use

Confusion, whether genuine or studied, about the nature and implications of parity was virtually inevitable and even necessary, if normal peacetime policy was to bridge inherent contradictions among different aims and circumstances.[28] Contradictions were not difficult to live with when superpower relations were comparatively calm and the question of nuclear blackmail had receded into the realm of the abstract; they became more pressing as Moscow and Washington moved back into a more hostile relationship.

Academic analysts deal readily with questions of abstract consistency in policy and doctrine. Politicians tend to focus on issues in disaggregated terms—specific programs and parts of problems as they arise. Presidents seldom have time or inclination to ponder seriously the circumstances under which they would direct that nuclear weapons be used. Analysts or bureaucrats who grapple more intently with the question usually do so in terms of NATO contingencies. By the time the U.S. strategic nuclear edge countering Soviet conventional advantage in Europe had eroded com-

27. Lou Cannon and David Hoffman, "GOP Platform Being Fashioned as Political Weapon," *Washington Post*, June 24, 1984.

28. For elaboration of this argument and associated points see Richard K. Betts, "Compound Deterrence vs. No-First-Use: What's Wrong Is What's Right," *Orbis*, vol. 28 (Winter 1985), pp. 697–718; Betts, "Nuclear Weapons," in Joseph S. Nye, Jr., ed., *The Making of America's Soviet Policy* (Yale University Press, 1984), pp. 97–127; and Betts, "Solidarity and Security: NATO's Balancing Act after the Deployment of Intermediate Nuclear Forces," *Brookings Review*, vol. 3 (Summer 1985), pp. 26–34.

pletely, improvement in the political situation had muted the impact of the military shift so that political leaders were not pressed to face the doctrinal dilemmas that agitate professional strategic analysts.

Prolonged calm in Europe has coincided with changes in what the Soviets call the global correlation of forces—the relationship of military, political, economic, and social forces in the evolution of international class conflict. That coincidence points to different sorts of potential confrontation. With the conflict in Europe stabilized, a crisis that could raise the issue of nuclear threats again is more likely to originate elsewhere. But with the global correlation of forces linking developments in the center and periphery, a war between the superpowers anywhere could easily spread to Europe. Dilemmas about the viability of extended deterrence in a peripheral contingency would magnify those implicit in Europe-oriented doctrine.

Swords, Shields, and Stabilities

The massive retaliation doctrine cast NATO conventional forces as a shield to block a Warsaw Pact attack long enough for the American sword—the Strategic Air Command—to destroy the Soviet Union. For Moscow to try to negate the doctrine, the roles for the USSR would logically be reversed: nuclear forces would be a shield to deter U.S. escalation, so that the conventional sword could be decisive.[29] In the Cuban crisis, where perceived conventional advantages were reversed, U.S. nuclear forces also assumed a shield role—and did so more effectively than Soviet forces did in the two preceding Berlin crises. To the extent that resolve is linked to the balance of power, the end of nuclear imbalance favorable to the United States would paralyze the escalatory counter to conventional aggression and thus increase the tension between the stability of mutual nuclear deterrence and conventional military stability.

The arrival of parity of intercontinental nuclear forces after the mid-1960s was a more arresting development to American strategic analysts than it was to European political leaders, who had long been living as hostages to Soviet assured destruction capability resting in medium- and

---

29. This was the concern of Western critics of massive retaliation in the 1950s, but actual Soviet adaptation of military doctrine followed U.S. moves toward flexible response. The Soviets continued to see an American interest in escalatory threats for some time. See Andrew Goldberg, "Conventional Options and Escalation Control in Soviet Strategy," in Coit Blacker, ed., *Soviet Military Doctrines and Weapons Capabilities* (Stanford University Press, forthcoming).

intermediate-range forces. Disparities in prospective damage to the super-power homelands that buoyed U.S. strategists trying to cope with Soviet finite deterrence meant little to allies. European governments thus tended to place more emphasis on the psychological and political as opposed to material and military underpinnings of stability, making the codification of parity as part of détente a positive event. They had never had the option of playing nuclear chess; détente meant they would have less need to rely on roulette. The embrace of vague parity on both sides of the Atlantic muddled the implications for extended deterrence because détente damp-ened worries about deterrence altogether as politics took precedence over strategy.

Because European governments had also tended to view the biggest bang as the best deterrent, they never evinced enthusiasm for the limited nuclear options (LNOs) implicit in the flexible response doctrine foisted on them by Washington in the 1960s. Parity in the 1970s, however, did not drive U.S. policy away from flexible response to either extreme—onward to no first use or back to massive retaliation. The challenge to American strategy was to fortify graduated nuclear deterrence without a cushion of superiority and to maintain the credibility of first use of strategic forces without implying first-strike ambitions. This led to attempts to refine limited options for strategic forces, from Schlesinger's retargeting program in 1974 to the Carter administration's "countervailing strategy" and Presidential Directive 59 in 1980. In both cases the implications for first use were blurred. To justify his program in Congress, Schlesinger used calculations based on a scenario of a Soviet first strike, and argued that U.S. limited options would not lower the nuclear threshold. He also noted, however, that his adaptation of targeting doctrine "recoupled U.S. strategic forces with the security of Western Europe."[30] The doctrinal evolution under Carter was rationalized primarily as denying escalatory advantages to the USSR, but also as reinforcing the availability of strategic forces for the defense of allies.[31] American escalation dominance had been lost, so the fallback was a high premium on escalation equity. Such a standard did not clearly support the wisdom of first use; it simply made it less incredible

---

30. Schlesinger testimony in *Briefing on Counterforce Attacks,* Hearing before the Subcommittee on Arms Control of the Senate Committee on Foreign Relations, 93 Cong. 2 sess., 1974 (GPO, 1975), pp. 7, 41–42, 44.

31. Harold Brown, Secretary of Defense, *Department of Defense Annual Report, Fiscal Year 1981* (GPO, 1980), pp. 65–67; *Nuclear War Strategy,* Hearing before the Senate Foreign Relations Committee, 96 Cong. 2 sess. (GPO, 1980), p. 34.

than an imbalance in Soviet favor would. The blurring reflected the heightened tension between mutual nuclear deterrence between the superpowers and extended deterrence for allies.

That tension, latent as détente bloomed, emerged as it faded, and precipitated the 1979 NATO "dual track" decision to deploy and negotiate about new U.S. longer-range theater nuclear forces (LRTNF). That initiative too had quite confusing aspects. The impetus was assumed by many to be German Chancellor Helmut Schmidt's 1977 London speech, but that speech never mentioned the Soviet deployment of SS-20 intermediate-range missiles, later cited as the prime reason for the NATO initiative. Nor did the chancellor focus on the balance of nuclear capabilities within Europe. He focused on the parity of intercontinental strategic forces as the driving problem:

> SALT codifies the nuclear strategic balance between the Soviet Union and the United States. . . . SALT neutralizes their strategic nuclear capabilities. In Europe this magnifies the significance of the disparities between East and West in nuclear tactical and conventional weapons. . . . The principle of parity . . . must be the aim of all arms-limitation . . . and it must apply to all categories of weapons. . . . Strategic arms limitations confined to the United States and the Soviet Union will inevitably impair the security of the West European members of the Alliance . . . if we do not . . . achieve a conventional equilibrium as well. . . . Today we need to recognize clearly the connection between SALT and MBFR.[32]

Schmidt was criticized by other Europeans for this formulation because it tacitly accepted the sequestering of U.S. strategic forces from those available to implement the first-use commitment of flexible response. The subsequent decision to deploy Pershing IIs and ground-launched cruise missiles was officially justified only as providing a bridge or ignition circuit between tactical and strategic forces, not as a substitute for the latter. Indeed, in the Reagan administration the term longer-range theater nuclear forces was changed to intermediate-range nuclear forces (INF) in order to avert

---

32. Helmut Schmidt, "The 1977 Alastair Buchan Memorial Lecture," *Survival*, vol. 20 (January–February 1978), pp. 3–4 (MBFR refers to the Mutual and Balanced Force Reduction negotiations on NATO and Warsaw Pact conventional forces). Some European and American defense intellectuals had been promoting new Europe-based nuclear forces before Schmidt spoke. Fred Kaplan, "Warring Over New Missiles for NATO," *New York Times Magazine*, December 9, 1979.

the implication that their mission was segregated from that of intercontinental forces.

It was inconvenient to European governmental elites to question directly
the compatibility of parity with extended deterrence or the sincerity of the
Americans' continuing formal commitment to the full range of flexible
response. French President Charles de Gaulle had not shrunk from doing
so, but in the process he had shaken the alliance. While de Gaulle's view
about the credibility of the U.S. nuclear guarantee may have been wrong
in the early 1960s, it became harder to deny by the 1970s. Frank statements
by retired American leaders pointed starkly in this direction. On one hand
Robert McNamara repudiated the commitment he had made as secretary
of defense, and implied that it had not been genuine even at the time. In
1962 he had told the allied leaders in a secret speech at Athens that "the
most important implication" of what he was telling them was that "nuclear
superiority has important meanings. . . . The United States is also prepared
to counter with nuclear weapons any Soviet conventional attack so strong
that it cannot be dealt with by conventional means."[33] Two decades later
he claimed:

> *Nuclear weapons serve no military purpose whatsoever. They are totally*
> *useless—except only to deter one's opponent from using them.* . . . In
> long private conversations with successive Presidents—Kennedy and
> Johnson—I recommended, without qualification, that they never initi-
> ate, under any circumstances, the use of nuclear weapons. I believe they
> accepted my recommendation.[34]

Even more indelicately, in 1979 Henry Kissinger declared to a European
audience:

> I have sat around the NATO Council table in Brussels and elsewhere
> and have uttered the magic words which had a profoundly reassuring
> effect, and which permitted the Ministers to return home with a rationale
> for not increasing defence expenditures. And my successors have uttered
> the same reassurances and yet if my analysis is correct these words
> cannot be true, and . . . we must face the fact that it is absurd to base

33. "Remarks by Secretary McNamara, NATO Ministerial Meeting, 5 May 1962,
Restricted Session," declassified 1979, quoted in David N. Schwartz, *NATO's Nuclear
Dilemmas* (Brookings, 1983), pp. 158, 160. McNamara explicitly committed U.S.-based
strategic forces to this mission.

34. Robert S. McNamara, "The Military Role of Nuclear Weapons: Perceptions and
Misperceptions," *Foreign Affairs*, vol. 62 (Fall 1983), p. 79 (emphasis in original).

the strategy of the West on the credibility of the threat of mutual suicide.[35]

McGeorge Bundy in turn confessed in 1979, in another speech in Europe just a week after Kissinger's, that the views on nuclear superiority that he had promulgated in office had not quite matched his real thinking, but he softened the point by reaffirming the viability of extended deterrence.[36] He jumped ship a few years later, however, and virtually endorsed the notion of no first use.[37]

Nevertheless, the 1979 LRTNF decision and subsequent U.S. policy continued to affirm the full traditional scope of extended deterrence. Leaders in office today continue to affirm that the balance of resolve is equal to that in the earlier period of confrontations despite parity's alteration of the balance of power. But if not only professional analysts but leaders released from the strictures of official responsibility suggest that the commitment is disingenuous, in a future crisis how should Moscow assess the relation between nuclear resolve and nuclear balance?

The Soviet Union and Extended Deterrence

In 1982 Leonid Brezhnev formally announced the commitment of the Soviet Union to a policy of no first use of nuclear weapons, and the USSR joined the People's Republic of China as the only nuclear powers to declare such a policy. The Soviet announcement was denigrated by some Western analysts as simple propaganda, on grounds that the semantics of Soviet military definitions left a loophole to allow preemption: if an enemy was preparing a nuclear attack against the USSR, a preemptive Soviet launch would be only anticipatory retaliation against the Western first strike.[38]

35. Henry A. Kissinger, speech in Brussels, September 1, 1979, reprinted as "NATO: The Next Thirty Years," *Survival*, vol. 21 (November–December 1979), p. 266. The edited version of Kissinger's remarks that appeared in print actually softened his message; see p. 264.

36. McGeorge Bundy, keynote address to the International Institute for Strategic Studies conference in Villars, Switzerland, September 9, 1979, reprinted as "The Future of Strategic Deterrence," *Survival*, vol. 21 (November–December 1979), pp. 268–72. The McNamara, Kissinger, and Bundy admissions were an impressive sequence of punches to the credibility of official U.S. declarations.

37. McGeorge Bundy, George F. Kennan, Robert S. McNamara, and Gerard Smith, "Nuclear Weapons and the Atlantic Alliance," *Foreign Affairs*, vol. 60 (Spring 1982), pp. 753–68.

38. On a related matter, Arkady Shevchenko claims that in 1972 Foreign Minister Gromyko told him to "concoct a proposition that would permit us to use nuclear weapons against China and at the same time would not make it look as if we were abandoning our

Overall, however, Soviet no first use accords with a view common among Western strategists that, given the logic of geography and conventional military balance in the Eurasian heartland, mutual nuclear deterrence best serves Soviet offensive objectives in the event of war. Thus in negotiating the 1973 U.S.-Soviet Agreement on Prevention of Nuclear War the Soviets first proposed mutual renunciation by the superpowers of the use of nuclear weapons against each other. When the United States refused, they proposed restricting nuclear weapons fired in a NATO–Warsaw Pact war to targets in the territory of allies.[39] Although Western hawks have charged Moscow with seeking or achieving nuclear superiority, the principal danger hawks fear exists even with nuclear parity if it suffices to secure the Soviet deterrent shield against Western escalation. Soviet no first use does not stand in the way of Soviet retaliatory threats meant to deter American first use.

The issue is tied up in the overall global competition between the superpowers. It is easily forgotten that most past American nuclear threats were made in crises on the periphery rather than in Europe. In most third world crises U.S. leaders never thought nuclear threats were necessary or appropriate and relied on conventional military action, or else, as in the case of Indochina in 1954, considered a nuclear option but decided not to resort to any threat. Some Soviet analysts, however, linked the U.S. nuclear advantage before the end of the 1960s to freedom of action in the third world. As William Zimmerman describes it, when Washington countered the growing Soviet nuclear deterrent with the flexible response doctrine, "Russia's essentially passive deterrence posture placed it in the strategic bind from which the United States had just managed to extricate itself." In regard to the third world, Zimmerman continues, "How could the Soviet Union effectively deter the 'export of counter-revolution' . . . in areas not adjacent to itself?"[40] The Soviet spokesman Henry Trofimenko later charged American strategists with thinking that "the United States could assume that, from even marginal superiority, it could more boldly use its conventional armed forces. . . . 'on the periphery,' achieving partial military solutions in conditions when the other side would have no stake

position on the prohibition of these arms." The language of Gromyko's United Nations speech emphasized banning nuclear weapons but artfully left a loophole whereby "those who disobeyed the ban on using any kind of force might be punished by nuclear reprisals." Arkady N. Shevchenko, *Breaking with Moscow* (Alfred A. Knopf, 1985), pp. 166–67.

39. Henry Kissinger, *Years of Upheaval* (Little, Brown, 1982), pp. 275–77.

40. William Zimmerman, *Soviet Perspectives on International Relations, 1956–1967* (Princeton University Press, 1969), pp. 192–93. Quotations on p. 193.

in reversing local American victories through a broadening of the conflict."[41]

Viewing the Soviet-U.S. competition in this context makes three things less surprising than they would be if the focus were confined to Europe. First, Soviet observers seemed more impressed by the role of nuclear threats in the comparatively minor cases outside Europe than were American analysts, who pooh-poohed them. Second, it helps to explain the Soviet commitment to match American nuclear strength: to contest U.S. stratagems on the periphery, more than the minimalist finite-deterrent standard of nuclear parity was necessary. Third, Soviet rhetoric and analyses in the 1970s tended more than American to emphasize the evolution of nuclear parity in terms of its place within the overall global correlation of forces—political, economic, and social, as well as military. The principal Soviet argument was that military parity forced Washington to accommodate peacefully to the shifts in other elements of the correlation that were unfavorable to "imperialism," and that a lessened danger of military confrontation worked in Soviet favor since the natural historical dynamics of local class struggles moved in the direction of socialism. As Khrushchev had prematurely envisioned, Soviet nuclear power's capacity to prevent general war would "deprive imperialism of its capacity to impede artificially . . . processes taking place within states as a result of the disequilibriating tendencies inherent in a revolutionary epoch."[42] As William B. Husband characterizes the Soviet logic:

American confidence in military intimidation was so complete, the argument continues, that the U.S. underestimated the power of political and economic processes as vital historical forces. Only when the United States began to suffer international setbacks due to changes in the postwar political and economic order did the Americans reluctantly begin to assess more critically their exaggerated reliance on projecting military strength. . . . as long as the United States held a strategic advantage over the U.S.S.R., change came slowly. Not until 1970, when the Soviet Union is said to have achieved strategic parity and thereby nullified the military advantage necessary to make the positions-of-strength policy operable, did a more promising atmosphere for peaceful coexistence emerge. . . . The majority of Soviet writers state that the

41. Henry A. Trofimenko, "Counterforce: Illusion of a Panacea," *International Security,* vol. 5 (Spring 1981), pp. 35–36.
42. Zimmerman, *Soviet Perspectives on International Relations,* p. 279.

balance of strength and influence in the world is swinging toward the Soviet Union. . . . They therefore treat any reduction in the possibility of a serious military confrontation as a benefit accrued to the U.S.S.R.[43]

U.S. flirtations with "linkage," never officially explained with as much directness or clarity as Soviet views, implicitly agreed with some of that logic and resisted accepting the situation. For American conservatives détente and arms control were to go together with stabilization of areas of political competition. To the Soviets, détente and arms control should free the progression of local class struggles. "There is no contradiction in the maintenance of 'military-strategic parity' while 'the overall balance of strength in the world continues to change,' " as Raymond Garthoff cited from Soviet sources: "Peaceful coexistence based on strategic parity 'does not and cannot mean some kind of status quo between socialism and capitalism.' "[44]

The unresolved tension over the relationship between military parity and political competition was reflected in the superpowers' failure to make clear the specific meaning in practice of the general principles of détente and crisis prevention embraced in the U.S.-Soviet Basic Principles Agreement of 1972 and the 1973 Agreement on the Prevention of Nuclear War (Kissinger evaded Nixon's instructions to make the U.S. position on intervention clear during the negotiations). And whereas Khrushchev had been more or less roundly rebuffed in 1961–62 when he argued that the Soviets' military forces were equal to those of the United States and therefore that "there must also be equal rights and equal opportunities,"

43. William B. Husband, "Soviet Perceptions of U.S. 'Positions-of-Strength' Diplomacy in the 1970s," *World Politics*, vol. 31 (July 1979), pp. 496–97, 505. Another author quotes a "typical" Soviet statement: "The establishment of the dynamic balance of strategic forces between the USSR and USA substantially limits the military activities of imperialism in the international arena and compels it to take into account the peaceful policies of the socialist community of states. . . . Thus military power is and remains one of the most important instruments of foreign policy available to states." Julian Lider, *Military Force: An Analysis of Marxist-Leninist Concepts* (Westmead, England: Gower, 1981), p. 212. D. Tomashevsky wrote in the Moscow journal *International Affairs* in 1976 that "recognition of Soviet-U.S. parity in strategic armaments was a special factor behind the realization by Western ruling circles of the new realities of our day and the corresponding correction of their political line." In the same year A. A. Gromyko and B. N. Ponomarov said that new military parity "forced U.S. ruling circles to revise their foreign policy and military concepts." Quoted in Michael J. Deane, "Soviet Perceptions of the Military Factor in the 'Correlation of World Forces'," in Donald C. Daniel, ed., *International Perceptions of the Superpower Military Balance* (Praeger, 1978), p. 77.

44. Garthoff, *Détente and Confrontation*, p. 64.

the negotiation of the agreements of the early 1970s genuflected to the notion of superpower political equality while obscuring the fact that the Soviets took this point far more seriously than the Americans—and in a different vein.[45]

Such confusions are normal in politics and diplomacy and can be functional where clarity might preclude accommodations that could achieve less ambitious aims or buy needed time. The confusions were certainly useful in the U.S. domestic debate. Nixon and Kissinger's critics on both left and right faulted their tactics in the early 1970s, but the détente bought at the price of some confusion about terms served purposes of those closer to the center. For the center-left, it established norms and hopes for arms control that persisted remarkably even after the crushing victories of the right in presidential elections of the early 1980s. For the center-right, détente bought time in the early 1970s against ascendant antimilitary or "neo-isolationist" sentiments, until the domestic political tide shifted to allow revival of assertive foreign policies. Confusion was thus useful in the short term, however, precisely because it pushed the reckoning with unresolved problems into the future.

Which view of the relations between parity, détente, and nuclear blackmail carried the most freight between the superpowers? Did the U.S. acceptance of parity reduce the incidence of crises, as the Soviets saw it, or, as is more likely, did the absence of crises facilitate the U.S. acceptance of parity? Confusions about terms of reference functioned in the super-power relationship as they did in the American domestic debate. In smoothing over near-term negotiations and the transition to vague parity of the early 1970s, they set the stage for longer-term clashes, charges of bad faith, more exacting disputes over precise parity, and a highlighting by the end of the decade of U.S. resistance to Soviet views of "equal rights."

Although Soviet negotiators in the early phase of SALT I insisted on counting U.S. forward-based systems—aircraft that the United States viewed as theater weapons, but that had the technical capability to hit targets within the USSR—they eventually agreed to exclude them from the interim agreement. U.S. leaders, however, saw no strategic advantage

---

45. Alexander L. George, "Introduction," "Detente: The Search for a 'Constructive' Relationship," and "The Basic Principles Agreement of 1972: Origins and Expectations," in George, ed., *Managing U.S.-Soviet Rivalry: Problems of Crisis Prevention* (Westview Press, 1983), pp. 3, 22–24, 108, 115–16. Khrushchev quoted in Hannes Adomeit, *Soviet Risk-Taking and Crisis Behavior: A Theoretical and Empirical Analysis* (London: Allen and Unwin, 1982), p. 252.

accruing from the concession; to stanch hawkish domestic criticism they cited the exclusion as one consideration offsetting the Soviet advantage in the number of missile launchers allowed in the agreement.[46] One of the implicit benefits to the United States of excluding forward-based systems, despite their nuclear delivery role, was to obscure the relationship between the continuing NATO first-use doctrine and the codification of parity. That doctrine was protected, while the old agreement that had resolved the Cuban missile crisis remained in force, preventing the Soviet Union from extending deterrence in a comparable form to its ally in the shadow of American power. When Soviet construction of naval facilities at Cienfuegos in 1970 caused alarm, Washington secured assurances from Moscow that operational missile-carrying submarines would not visit Cuba. And the Carter administration insisted that MiG-23s deployed in Cuba in 1978 must not be models with rigging capable of carrying nuclear ordnance.[47]

In deploying INF in Europe in the 1980s, Washington played a conceptual double game with its allies and adversary. In dealing with the allies, the United States accepted the doctrinal principle that no separate "Euro-strategic" nuclear balance should be recognized, that the new forces were linked inextricably with U.S.-based strategic forces in the "seamless web" of flexible response. In dealing with the Soviets, in contrast, the United States maintained the diplomatic principle that the new forces *not* be deemed strategic and that they should count against Soviet theater forces— SS-20s, SS-4s, and SS-5s. Moscow agreed with the logic implicit in the official Western European rationale—that missiles based on the continent that could hit the Soviet Union were "strategic" forces. Therefore the U.S. deployment was a backdoor attempt to regain superiority by circumventing the parity codified in SALT treaty limits. In Washington the Soviet complaint was considered disingenuous. It is interesting to recall, though, that decades earlier Paul Nitze had argued that capitalizing on bases in Europe was the way to retain U.S. nuclear superiority in the face of declining advantage in force size. As the Soviets approach "roughly equivalent capabilities" in weapons and delivery systems, he wrote, "the significance of the geographic factor increases." Nitze continued:

The United States is vulnerable to direct attack only from bases on the

46. See Gerard Smith, *Doubletalk: The Story of SALT I* (Doubleday, 1980), pp. 90–93.
47. Gloria Duffy, "Crisis Prevention in Cuba," in George, ed., *Managing U.S.-Soviet Rivalry*, pp. 288–90, 296–97.

Eurasian land mass and from submarines. The U.S.S.R. is vulnerable to attack not only from North American bases but also from bases closer in on the periphery of the Eurasian land mass itself. . . . Given anything approaching equality in numbers and quality of planes, missiles and the other elements of modern delivery systems, the geographic factor should give the West the possibility of a continuing and decisive margin of superiority.[48]

When it came to negotiations on INF, Moscow also insisted on defining nuclear parity in terms of the opposing alliances, because Britain and France had nuclear forces, while no Soviet allies did. Western leaders insisted on defining it in terms of the balance between the superpowers' forces alone. The aim of the Soviets' demands to take account of allied missiles was less achieving precise equality of forces between East and West than stopping any U.S. missile deployment at all on the continent.[49] And as they had relented years earlier on the forward-based systems issue, by 1986 they were in effect offering to exempt British and French forces and accept the West's "zero" solution for removal of all INF missiles on both sides in Europe, which would reduce their relative position in theater nuclear forces below what they had earlier claimed was an existing parity and in any case below what it had been for a quarter century. The new Soviet SS-20s had replaced old SS-4s and SS-5s that had faced Western Europe since the 1950s, while most U.S. intermediate-range missiles had been withdrawn from the continent by 1963. The zero solution, therefore, would leave the Americans with no fewer of such missiles than they had had throughout the twenty-year interim, the Soviets with hundreds fewer than they had had.[50] Yet the West did not jump at the offer.

Perils of Parity

All of this points to two basic problems. First, the continuing belief within NATO governments that deterrence of Soviet conventional attack requires the threat of U.S. nuclear first use, combined with Soviet embrace of no first use, makes *rough* parity of forces easier for Moscow to live with comfortably than for many Western strategists. While the United States acceded to parity in principle, domestic debate pushed policy toward

48. Nitze, "Atoms, Strategy and Policy," pp. 191–92.
49. Leon V. Sigal, *Nuclear Forces in Europe: Enduring Dilemmas, Present Prospects* (Brookings, 1984), pp. 148–50.
50. American Mace-B cruise missiles had remained until the end of the 1960s, but these were scarcely noticed.

demanding standards of precision. And by excluding certain categories of forces from the calculus at times, Western definitions allowed what Moscow would cite as marginal U.S. superiority in the number of nuclear forces that could strike the superpowers' homelands. Second, except for the minority comfortable with a conscious reliance on the balance of interests, American strategic elites have been disinclined to recognize fully or resolve forthrightly the relationship between parity and extended deterrence. When they were emphasizing the desirability of parity, their rhetoric tended to ignore the commitment to first use; when they were emphasizing extended deterrence, their criteria for acceptable parity pressed harder against Moscow's definitional tolerance for roughness.

By the end of the 1970s the strategic debate in the West had come to echo the arguments of the late 1950s over massive retaliation. The similarity was reflected most curiously in the 1979 Brussels speech by Henry Kissinger, who as an analyst had participated in the earlier debates and as an official had presided over the sanctification of parity:

> the change in the strategic situation that is produced by our limited vulnerability is more fundamental for the United States than even total vulnerability would be for the Soviet Union because our strategic doctrine has relied extraordinarily, perhaps exclusively on our superior strategic power. . . . Even an equivalence in destructive power, even assured destruction for both sides is a revolution in NATO doctrine as we have known it.[51]

The limited vulnerability Kissinger mentioned was not a new problem: it had driven the alliance to flexible response many years earlier, well before the arrival of full parity. What had changed most significantly during the 1970s was not the military implication that parity inhibited threats of nuclear first use, but the political crumbling of the détente that had put the doctrinal dilemma on the back burner.

The Primacy of Political Imperatives

By the end of the 1970s intensification of American anxieties about the nuclear balance was partially due to the fight over the SALT II treaty, which focused attention on nuances and arcane measures of capability. Fundamentally, however, the salient anxieties were general, political, and visceral more than specific, military, and technical. The dominance of

---

51. Kissinger, "NATO: The Next Thirty Years," p. 266.

subjective concerns was obvious in the initiative to deploy Pershing IIs and cruise missiles. No gap in U.S. capability to cover Soviet targets had been cited; rather what the missiles were to fill was a symbolic gap in U.S. intent. And when proponents of strict standards for parity were queried about why nuances of relative inferiority in the static force balance should matter if they would not make a detectable difference in war outcomes, they often came back to the question of crisis coercion.

Concerned with applying U.S. nuclear leverage or with facing Soviet nuclear blackmail in a political confrontation, both critics and officials came to focus on the question of how others see nuclear forces. Secretary of Defense Harold Brown testified to the security of U.S. second-strike capability but worried about the influence of the balance "on international perceptions (Soviet, third party, and our own). . . . The advantage to the Soviets of a possible lead in the primary measures of comparative capability is ill-defined in terms of useful wartime capability. But it might have some political value during peacetime or in a crisis."[52] The political importance of perceptions was either cited as real, vital, and grounds for altering the design of military force structures,[53] or dismissed as phony, illogical, and of no genuine significance to policy.[54]

Beliefs on controversial and sensitive matters come not only from rational evaluation of clear facts but also from filtration of ambiguous data through predispositions. Beliefs about the nuclear balance are politically significant in themselves if they diverge from military reality, but the only proof of what that reality is would come from the test of war. And as Herbert Goldhamer has put it, "When no clear understanding of 'reality' exists in a given situation, the observation and discussion of people's perceptions are likely to be distorted because the investigator's own vague 'reality' differs from the vague 'reality' of his subjects and influences his perceptions of the subject's perceptions." For the aims of deterrence or coercion, the issue of perceptions is a game of mirrors—beliefs about what others believe. Assertions about the independent influence of perceptions may often be valid, but they elude proof because information on adversar-

52. 1977 House Armed Services Committee testimony, quoted in Thomas A. Brown, "U.S. and Soviet Strategic Force Levels: Problems of Assessment and Measurement," *The Annals of the American Academy of Political and Social Sciences,* no. 457 (September 1981), pp. 19–20.

53. Edward N. Luttwak, "Perceptions of Military Force and U.S. Defence Policy," *Survival,* vol. 19 (January–February 1977), pp. 2–8.

54. See Steven Kull, "Nuclear Nonsense," *Foreign Policy,* no. 58 (Spring 1985), pp. 28–52.

ies' or allies' perceptions is even more limited than it is on the views of critical American elites.[55]

Ironically, those most concerned with perceptions of the nuclear balance did little to change the balance itself. For several reasons, the intensity of professional debate on the subject subsided in the early 1980s. No arms control treaty that would energize critics' statistical gamesmanship was in sight; the Reagan administration's domestic problem was to subdue fears about adventurism, not, as was Carter's, to fend off charges of wimpiness; and debate was diverted to futuristic questions about the Strategic Defense Initiative. But as President Reagan's rhetoric, aura, and defense budgets were dispelling diffuse fears of Soviet superiority, his program was doing little to change the actual nuclear balance of forces from what was projected at the end of the Carter administration. The 100 B-1 bombers added by the Reagan program were offset by eliminating 100 of the 200 MX missiles planned by Carter and by placing the MXs in the same silos that had created the "window of vulnerability" for which Reagan had blasted his predecessor. For hawks most concerned with fast-moving counterforce capability, survivable MXs were more important than B-1s; and as of early 1987 it appeared that Congress would authorize no more than 50 MXs. By not securing ratification of the SALT II treaty the administration also avoided forcing the Soviets to dismantle 10 percent of their launchers, as the treaty would have required. At the same time, the administration retired delivery vehicles that could have been kept if treaty constraints were disregarded—B-52D bombers and Poseidon missile launchers. The only qualitatively new addition to American launchers is the deployment of several hundred nuclear-armed sea-launched cruise missiles, which are either canceled out by the undismantled Soviet launchers or matchable by comparable Soviet systems. In the view of some observers it was Reagan's inability to "fix" the problems in the offensive nuclear balance for which the Carter administration had been criticized that helped impel him to the Strategic Defense Initiative in 1983.

In short, political imperatives tended to dominate peacetime disputes about the nature of the balance of forces, just as they did past crises. In those cases, political pressures tended to override cold calculation of the relation between the intrinsic value of territorial stakes at issue and the

55. Herbert Goldhamer, "Perceptions of the U.S.-Soviet Balance: Problems of Analysis and Research," in Daniel, ed., *International Perceptions of the Superpower Military Balance*, p. 7. For a sampling of the roughness of data on foreign perceptions, see the other chapters in the volume.

potential risks embodied in nuclear threats, leading presidents to reach for nuclear leverage even though the prospective price of having to fulfill the threat exceeded the value of what was in dispute. Critics faulted Eisenhower's massive retaliation doctrine for its disproportionality, but, when in power, implicitly fell back, for political reasons, on similar tactics during the two biggest crises of the cold war in the early 1960s.

The Kennedy administration's vulnerability on its domestic right flank helped fuel its compulsion to risk war over a few missiles in Cuba. Similarly, the antidefense sentiment welling up on the Nixon administration's left flank in its first years in office encouraged it to accept loose standards for judging the nuclear balance. The dramatic alert in October 1973 helped screen U.S. pressure on the Israelis from domestic supporters of that country by shifting attention to the Soviet threat. Political incentives presented by international challenges and domestic pressure have rarely if ever taken second place to strategic constraints implied by the nuclear balance, yet leaders in office never suggest that the balance is not crucial. What do presidents really think, if and when they ever do think much about it, and what are Soviet leaders to believe that they think? Is there no potential for miscalculation in crisis, by one side or the other, in this confusion?

In the late 1970s, as détente was collapsing, the individuals who came to dominate the U.S. strategic establishment proclaimed the advantages that accrued to Moscow from the shift in the nuclear balance, yet once in power they developed no significant means, other than visions of strategic defense that at best might be achieved decades later, to rectify materially the situation they had characterized as so dangerous. Yet there is little indication that they would not attempt to respond to Soviet challenges comparable to the big ones of the cold war—ones mercifully absent during the past decade—more or less as earlier leaders did. The post-détente consensus in the strategic establishment was that the nuclear balance of power is crucial. If so, the tendency of a political imperative for action to override calculations about the balance could prove less benign in crisis behavior than in peacetime debate.

The danger of miscalculation brings back the question of how the implications of the nuclear balance are perceived. This study considers what U.S. leaders have thought of the nature and implications of the balance and speculates about what Soviet leaders may have thought. Herbert Goldhamer suggests what should be especially borne in mind in trying to connect assessments of the balance with the uses of nuclear threats:

Any attempt to convey perceptions of the U.S.-USSR balance . . . runs the danger of giving the description greater exactness and sharpness of contour than existed in the original perception. The exigencies of exposition and communication put a premium on reducing fuzziness or vagueness that may have existed in the original perception. In fact, this vagueness may be a more important characteristic of the perception than its substantive content. What is often required is an exact description of confusion. Confusion may lend itself to manipulation much more readily than precise or well-ordered knowledge and may provide a richer field, both in crises and in stable situations, for the political use of military forces.[56]

Confusion is the central reality of beliefs about nuclear leverage, the source simultaneously of potential political clout and potential military disaster. Confusion can be used against an enemy by increasing his uncertainty and encouraging caution, but it also widens the range for miscalculation. The confusions of political leaders that make them waffle, leave the record of their deliberations in past crises contradictory, and vex interpretations by analysts should be a warning beacon for the future. If confusions cannot be resolved at the political level more consensually than they have been by professional analysts—or if they are best not resolved because certainty would deprive statesmen of useful coercive stratagems— the beacon should at the least illuminate the need for more careful thinking and hedging before resort to nuclear threats than appears to have occurred in the past.

56. Ibid., p. 4.

CHAPTER SIX

Is There a Future
for Nuclear Coercion?

What in the name of God is strategic superiority? What is the significance of it, politically, militarily, operationally, at these levels of numbers? What do you do with it?
Henry A. Kissinger, news conference, Moscow, July 3, 1974

On at least one occasion I contributed to the existing ambivalence. After an exhausting negotiation in July 1974 I gave an answer at a press conference which I have come to regret. . . . My statement reflected fatigue and exasperation, not analysis. . . . If we opt out of the race unilaterally, we will probably be faced eventually with a younger group of Soviet leaders who will figure out what can be done with strategic superiority.
Henry A. Kissinger, hearings on the SALT II treaty, U.S. Senate, July 31, 1979

THE CONTRAST between Kissinger's 1974 and 1979 statements about superiority epitomizes the tension in strategic attitudes lying behind events considered in this study, the refractory nature of the issues involved, and the barriers to drawing unqualified conclusions about nuclear blackmail. Kissinger's remarks also point to the difference between the dominant issues in American strategic theory and those in crisis practice. Theory has focused on mutual nuclear deterrence and capacity to stand up to Soviet nuclear blackmail. Practice has more often involved the reverse: U.S. attempts to make deterrence asymmetrical, to advert to the possibility of first use in the face of conventional military provocation despite Moscow's retaliatory capability. Anxieties cast in terms of the danger of Soviet superiority mask the underlying reality that U.S. policy has traditionally rested on a more demanding role for nuclear deterrence than has Soviet policy. The switch in Kissinger's declarations also appears to be just the reverse of the shift represented in McGeorge Bundy's statements prefacing the previous chapter. Together these combinations typify the pervasive ambivalence in the attitudes of top U.S. leaders about nuclear leverage, documented in previous chapters. Chapter five explored the implicit ways in which the confused concepts and ambivalent attitudes bore on the issue

212

of potential nuclear leverage during the transition from an era of U.S. nuclear superiority to one of equality. This chapter summarizes and bounds the lessons that might be drawn for the future.

The Past

How often and why did leaders resort to nuclear threats, how useful were those threats in affecting the outcomes of crises, and how did the nuclear balance of power figure either in decisions to threaten or in the results? The answers need not all point in the same direction. The probability that threats will recur may not depend on whether they clearly "worked" before. Political leaders are rarely students of history beyond their own experience; even if they were, the pattern of evidence is too permissive to prevent them from conforming interpretations to predispositions.

The points immediately below summarize the fundamental patterns of decisions and outcomes that emerged from the case studies. The two sections that follow after them explore their implications further. As in the rest of the analysis, the focus is on American threats.

In crisis decisions the United States exhibited a proclivity toward nuclear coercion that was not strongly governed by the nuclear balance of power.

—In the first twenty years of the postwar era presidents had an almost facile inclination to introduce vague nuclear threats in military confrontations despite the apparent vulnerability of the United States to Soviet retaliation.

—Presidents and their principal advisers often appeared to make the threats without carefully thinking through whether they would be willing to initiate the use of nuclear weapons as implied by the signals or what the consequences would be if they did. They focused more on the political imperative of blocking the adversary's advance than on the danger of war if the enemy refused to desist and the dispute intensified.

—The logic in this pattern was most consistent with a risk-maximizing attitude toward coercion, reinforced by belief that the balance of interests favored the credibility of American resolve.

—U.S. nuclear superiority did not instill confidence in political decisionmakers, since they did not assume that it could prevent unacceptable damage, but it nevertheless cushioned their anxieties and made it easier to edge toward the brink; escalation dominance and the prospect of unequal damage was an ancillary support to credibility.

—The arrival of nuclear parity changed the behavior of leaders less than is often assumed; it fostered anxiety about whether first-use threats remained practical but did not prevent resurrection of the tactic when crises comparable to former cases occurred.

In the outcomes of crises, the nuclear balance appears to have played a moderately influential role when it was uneven and an uncertain one when it was equal.

—The effects on Soviet or Chinese accommodations in crises are uncertain, but overall there is more reason to believe that American threats impressed the communists than that Soviet threats impressed U.S. leaders.

—Soviet behavior following U.S. nuclear threats in crises through the 1960s appeared more consistent with a risk-minimizing attitude and sensitivity to the imbalance of nuclear striking power.

—In the early 1970s Moscow assumed that the arrival of parity compelled change in American behavior, making it more accommodating. Events of the decade did not confirm American reticence, but neither did they imply that the Soviets were as impressed by U.S. nuclear leverage as they had been in previous decades.

Decisions to Threaten

There were many East-West disputes in which nuclear coercion never entered. The one type of dispute in which the United States almost always brandished the specter was that in which it seemed to face a choice between leaving an ally to face Soviet or Chinese conventional attack or raising the ante. The same cannot be said of the Russians. Although Washington warned of escalation over Berlin and Quemoy and Matsu, for example, Moscow backed off from similar support of Cuba and did not even attempt it on behalf of clients in Grenada or Nicaragua.

Though American presidents were alike in their support of allies, their anxieties about relying on escalation differed. Eisenhower's nuclear doctrine in principle and his action in practice were fairly consistent, but the doctrine would have proved dubious at best if crisis posturing had failed to avert the actual test of war. Kennedy's problem was the reverse. Flexible response, especially with its greater emphasis on bolstering conventional capacity for combat against Soviet forces, was a less worrisome doctrine than Eisenhower's massive retaliation in terms of its implications for war because it rested on more of a proportionality between military means and political ends. In this sense, however, peacetime doctrine and crisis practice under Kennedy appeared less consistent than they did under Eisenhower. On Berlin, Kennedy's military signals reinforced the reliance on escalation despite the lack of a ready option for graduated or limited use of strategic forces.

It is also well to remember that assessing the probability of future nuclear threats requires attention not only to the circumstances of crisis and the wisdom of general doctrine, but to the possibility of nuclear threats *unintended* by political authority. The several past examples—Truman's foot-in-mouth performance at his press conference of November 30, 1950, and the straying of the U-2 over Soviet territory and the SAC commander's uncoded message in October 1962—may have been as impressive to adversaries as the other purposeful signals discussed. Given the substantial alert authority delegated to commanders, positive action by an extraordinarily active and operationally informed executive could be required to avoid making an apparent nuclear threat.[1]

All in all, the record suggests that U.S. leaders were reasonably quick to hint at nuclear blackmail in crises, but the incidence of threats is clustered in the first half of the postwar era. Does that mean that the nuclear balance of power indeed was a major influence on willingness to invoke such threats? No. The Soviets made several nuclear threats during the Khrushchev years, when the USSR was markedly inferior in nuclear power, but they have made none since they attained clear parity. And there is no known case in which an American president wanted to apply nuclear leverage but refrained because the balance did not seem favorable.

The only good test of whether parity in itself constrained nuclear blackmail after the mid-1960s would have been a case in which political circumstances resembled those that had provoked threats in the past, but hints of escalation were held back. No such case arose. There were only two instances in which direct Soviet or Chinese attack on a U.S. ally was feared or U.S. conventional options were assumed inadequate—in 1973 and 1980—and in those cases American leaders did not hold back from nuclear signaling.

---

1. See Scott D. Sagan, "Nuclear Alerts and Crisis Management," *International Security*, vol. 9 (Spring 1985), pp. 99–139; Bruce G. Blair, *Strategic Command and Control: Redefining the Nuclear Threat* (Brookings, 1985); Paul Bracken, *The Command and Control of Nuclear Forces* (Yale University Press, 1983). Another unintended signal discussed by Sagan, a 1960 SAC alert of larger proportions than Secretary of Defense Gates understood when he directed it, did not occur in the midst of crisis.

Nor was the propensity of presidents to send nuclear signals calibrated to the degree of U.S. advantage in the balance. Truman was more hesitant about exploiting superiority when it was absolute or nearly so than his successor was when it was declining. Eisenhower's inclination did not shift between the beginning of his administration, when possible damage to the United States might have been deemed acceptable, and the later period, when estimates ranged upward from tens of millions of fatalities. Kennedy was less comfortable than Eisenhower with reliance on escalation although estimates during his administration temporarily offered the possibility of lower damage. The Nixon and Carter administrations did not avoid the tactic when they faced vulnerability at unprecedentedly high levels.

An important qualification is that evidence of the seriousness of intent to follow through with nuclear escalation if threats failed to deter did decline as U.S. nuclear superiority did. Truman ultimately declared his readiness to use the atomic bomb if war came. Eisenhower evinced the clearest interest of any president in actual use of nuclear weapons as opposed to diplomatic bluff, the most impressive examples being his prodding in several NSC meetings in the spring of 1953 and his statements in secret meetings with congressmen in spring 1959. Kennedy exploited nuclear leverage, but there is less available evidence of what his thinking was about what he would do if the crunch came. There is no available evidence of Nixon's or Carter's real views on whether they would have followed through on escalatory threats if the Soviets had moved into the Sinai or Iran. Erosion of nuclear superiority did not prevent presidents from trying to use nuclear leverage, but it did seem to dent their interest in thinking seriously about the moment of truth.

Outcomes of Threats

Without reliable data about decisionmaking in Moscow or Beijing the effects of American threats can be inferred only from circumstantial evidence and correlations between the threats and the two sides' concessions. Any such inferences must be extremely tentative, for two basic reasons. First, many elements besides nuclear blackmail were involved in these confrontations; any might have determined Soviet or Chinese behavior. Second, it is not possible to be sure exactly what the initial objectives of the Russians or Chinese really were. It is only possible to know what they *said* their objectives were.

In the sense that whichever side backed further away from its initial position may be said to have lost more than the other, there were no absolute or lopsided victories in the crises discussed in this book. The complexity and ambiguity of objectives in many cases means that the evidence can be cited or emphasized selectively to support different verdicts—that threats were effective, irrelevant, or counterproductive.

One could argue, for example, that American nuclear threats were generally effective. After they entered the equation in the three crises over Berlin, two over the Chinese offshore islands, the end of the Korean War, and Cuba in 1962, the Soviets or Chinese backed off from demands that had precipitated or prolonged the confrontations. In each case, Washington made fewer significant concessions from its opening position than its adversaries did. And if one could assume that Moscow had intended more aggressive action in the crises over Suez in 1956, Lebanon in 1958, the Middle East War in 1973, and the Persian Gulf in 1980, U.S. leverage in those instances would appear effective as well.

It is almost as easy, however, to deprecate the significance of many of those U.S. threats. The Russians did not seriously indicate an interest in interdicting the Berlin airlift before U.S. B-29s were sent to Europe. The Chinese stood up to anticipated nuclear pressure when they intervened in Korea in 1950, so the resolution of the war in 1953, as well as the Taiwan Straits crises, might be attributed to other considerations.[2] The West's acceptance of the Berlin Wall in 1961 was nearly as big an embarrassment as the Soviets' retreat from plans for a separate peace treaty. And Moscow did not give up any announced objectives in the Suez, Lebanon, October War, or Persian Gulf cases. Arguments in chapters two and three suggest that the threats were more effective than irrelevant, but the verdict is a close call.

Finally, one could argue that long-term negative results for the United States from the most crucial cases rivaled the significance of short-term benefits from all of them combined. During the 1950s Khrushchev was satisfied with finite nuclear deterrence and even initiated significant conventional troop reductions; reverses in the Berlin and Cuban crises might easily be credited as the spur to the impressive Soviet military buildup that so agitated American leaders by the 1970s. The prospective change in the balance of nuclear power that brought Washington close to war over missiles in Cuba looks trivial compared with the change to full parity that occurred within a decade.

Judgments about the effect of Soviet threats on U.S. leaders are easier

---

2. The extent to which China was not intimidated by U.S. nuclear power during other Asian crises of the 1950s and 1960s may be as impressive as the indications of prudence in the cases studied here. See Lawrence Freedman, "Strategic Superiority," *Coexistence,* vol. 21 (1984), p. 15.

than those about the effect of American threats on Soviet and Chinese officials. From the record of American deliberations during past crises, it is hard to argue that any of the Soviet threats were effective; indeed, they provoked more than deterred. In 1956 even a thoroughly elliptical hint by Moscow led Eisenhower to gesture with SAC and to support the allies from whom he was alienated over the Suez issue. On Berlin, Khrushchev's rhetorical fulminations about rockets flying automatically were taken in stride, and the concrete deployment in Cuba brought American nuclear striking power to the edge of action. Both the weakness and strength of Soviet nuclear moves in the crises involving China hurt Soviet interests in the long run. The tepidness of counterthreats against the United States in 1958 helped to drive the wedge in the Sino-Soviet alliance, and threats against China in 1969 pushed Beijing closer to Washington's embrace.

Although the evidence as a whole cannot sustain a firm and consistent conclusion, it appears that U.S. threats up through the 1960s were more effective than the two later ones. Soviet threats, in turn, impressed London and Paris more than Washington in 1956. Against China in 1969 they were effective in the short run. Thus to the extent that a case can be made for the effectiveness of past threats, success does seem to correlate with superiority in the nuclear balance of power, although, as in the decisions to make the threats, not with the degree of superiority.[3] Failure coincides more often with inferiority.

What might a decisionmaker in a world of parity infer if he were to consider this simplistic tally? If he were predisposed against nuclear risk he could find points in the record to confirm his instinct, but no more easily than one with an incentive to try nuclear blackmail could find support. Attempts to exploit nuclear leverage in the past seem useful at best and not costly at worst, unless a country is operating from the inferior position. The question of long-term costs is more complex, but political leaders facing immediate challenges in crises rarely subordinate near-term chances for success to uncertain future costs. At any rate, there is scant reason to assume from the record of high-level deliberations in chapters two and

3. Using a somewhat different sample, Barry Blechman and Stephen Kaplan reach a similar conclusion in their book, *Force without War: U.S. Armed Forces as a Political Instrument* (Brookings, 1978), pp. 128–29; see also pp. 47–49. The authors measure the degree of superiority according to U.S.-Soviet ratios of nuclear warheads and delivery vehicles. Although their interpretation implies slightly less significance in superiority, they note that the outcomes in their sample were "favorable in nearly every one of these fifteen incidents in short term, and in three-fourths of them over the longer term" (pp. 99–100).

three that the nuclear balance would be the prime consideration in a decision about whether to resort to nuclear coercion.

Implications

Comparative analysis can provide positive or negative conclusions. The positive sort resolve ambiguity and confusion, make reality clearer and simpler than it had appeared, and offer a better basis for prediction by identifying causes and effects. The negative kind make things that had seemed clear and simple look more complex and less certain, and propositions about cause and effect more conditional than they had been. Positive conclusions are intellectually exciting and satisfying, because they bring order out of chaos, but negative conclusions can be as useful for policy if they highlight false bases for confidence.

This study's conclusions are obviously more negative than positive. They suggest less which explanations of past cases make sense than which ones are inadequate, less about what can be expected in future cases than about what possibilities cannot be foreclosed. More positive conclusions would require more procrustean analysis. The negative conclusions are useful, however, because they provide a caution against assumptions that grew up on both sides of the U.S. strategic debate about the importance of nuclear superiority. It appears that superiority was less of a comfort to earlier American leaders in deciding whether to make a threat than is usually assumed and that parity was less of a restraint on later ones. The incentives imposed by the perceived balance of interests seem a better predictor of American attempts at nuclear leverage than do the constraints imposed by the balance of power.

The influence of superiority on the outcome of a crisis is more ambiguous. The last real test of U.S. threats occurred a quarter century ago in Cuba, when American superiority was at a peak. The outcome was a success for the United States, but also yielded Vasily Kuznetzov's oft-quoted line, "You Americans will never be able to do this to us again."[4] That view implies a greater significance for the balance of power. The indeterminate results of the American threats in 1973 and 1980 thus are less interesting than others if one looks backward, but rather disturbing if one looks forward. Those threats did not discredit Kuznetzov's warning: Nixon and Carter did not "get away" with anything Moscow was committed to prevent. But neither did the outcomes discredit the U.S. tactic by showing

---

4. Charles E. Bohlen, *Witness to History: 1929–1969* (W. W. Norton, 1973), p. 523.

presidents that they could not get away with it. The latter cases proved that nuclear parity had not changed American willingness to threaten escalation; they did not test whether parity had changed Soviet willingness to bend to U.S. pressure. These last cases thus demonstrate no reason to assume that U.S. nuclear threats will not recur or that the Soviets' reactions will not differ from those in the past if they face a choice of backing off or calling the American hand.

Future Cases?

The principal danger in using the past to predict the future is that differences in circumstances will be ignored.[5] For this study the caveat cuts in two directions, depending on whether the military or political context is the focus. Considering probabilities for the future involves integrating inferences from the period of U.S. superiority covered in chapters two through four and the period of parity discussed in chapter five. Relevance of the first period may be overestimated if the difference in *constraints* implied by the balance of power in the second period is overlooked. Parity does not preclude threats, but might still inhibit them, and certainly reduces the interest of leaders in contemplating whether they would follow through on them. If one focuses on differences in the political context of *incentives* for threats during the second period, however, relevance of the earlier cases for the future could be greater. Parity coincided with the decline of crises and thus of the sorts of incentives that used to provoke threats. For the foreseeable future, parity is likely to endure. Whether the superpowers will be able to continue to avoid direct confrontation is more uncertain.

Crises: Types and Probabilities

If parity itself caused the reduced incidence of intense crises after the early 1960s—as the Soviets officially explain U.S. acceptance of détente—one must implicitly buy the Soviet line that the United States was the aggressive party causing crises earlier in the cold war. Otherwise, one must assume that the Soviets' risk propensity is inversely proportional to their strength. Not surprisingly, more persuasive explanations are available.

5. See Ernest R. May, *"Lessons" of the Past: The Use and Misuse of History in American Foreign Policy* (Oxford University Press, 1973); and Richard E. Neustadt and Ernest R. May, *Thinking in Time: The Uses of History for Decision-Makers* (Free Press, 1986).

Conflicts after 1962 occurred on the periphery rather than in the core security zones of the superpowers, and through proxies not formally integrated in alliances, rather than between Washington and Moscow directly. Cuban interventions in Angola and Ethiopia were in support of local revolutionary regimes. Without the prospect of Soviet or Chinese conventional action against a U.S. ally or vital territory, the ingredients to precipitate a U.S. nuclear threat were absent. In one close exception, the October War of 1973, Washington did not keep the nuclear element out of play. Moscow continued to be cautiously abstemious and did not interpose itself against American attacks on friendly governments, such as Grenada and Libya, outside the central sphere of Soviet interest.

U.S. activism in contesting challenges to containment in the third world ebbed temporarily in the 1970s, in part because the earlier tendency to inflate the stakes in peripheral conflicts was arrested by the Vietnam experience. By the end of the decade the tide had reversed, and what began as a crisis the Soviets seemed to consider peripheral to U.S. vital interests (the invasion of Afghanistan) became central to the American government and prompted the Carter Doctrine. By the advent of the Reagan administration the old domino theory was already resurgent.

Two other changes, both of which have endured, are the stabilization of the political equilibrium in Europe, the central source of cold war crises, and Sino-American détente in East Asia. The comparative solidity of the European accommodation, reflected in agreements on the status of Berlin and the Helsinki accords, has not affected abstract debate about the role of nuclear escalation in military doctrine—perambulations in strategic theory continue around scenarios of war in Europe—and the durability of U.S.-Chinese accommodation is less reliable than is stability in Europe. But the developments do diminish the probability of major crises comparable to those over Berlin and Cuba or even the Taiwan Straits. If direct confrontations recur, they will probably be over peripheral areas that become central or over local conflicts that spill into more crucial arenas. The two exceptions to the decline of nuclear signals during the transition into parity, the October War and the Carter Doctrine, point in this direction.

The Near East was for many years on the borderline between center and periphery in American interests. With the intensification of U.S. alignment with Israel (a notable contrast to the 1956 Suez case) and the formalization of U.S. military commitment to defend the Persian Gulf, the region moved closer to the center. It is also more volatile than Europe and has fewer buffers than do points of tension in Asia to keep the superpowers from being drawn into military entanglement on behalf of local clients.

Elsewhere in the third world, changes of regime have led to greater interpenetration of superpower interests and commitments. In the first two decades of the postwar era Moscow had Marxist clients only in Eastern Europe, East Asia, and Cuba. Since then revolutions or coups have involved the Soviets on behalf of more Marxist governments in Asia; Angola, Ethiopia, and others to a lesser degree in Africa; Afghanistan and South Yemen in the Near East; and Nicaragua in Central America. The challenge to governments by insurgent movements identified with the opposing superpower, so often a problem for Washington in past decades, now faces Moscow. If the so-called Reagan Doctrine of aid to anti-Marxist insurgents were to prove effective in a few cases, it would raise the specter of "rollback" in the third world. The U.S. invasion of Grenada already symbolizes the potential of direct U.S. overthrow of Soviet clients. The prospect of widespread counterrevolution could increase Soviet incentives to think in terms of their own domino theory and to inflate the stakes of a small conflict as the United States did in earlier decades.

To date the USSR has remained discreet in avoiding overcommitment to friendly but exposed regimes and may indefinitely avoid risky action on their behalf; official Soviet positions in the mid-1980s emphasizing self-reliance by such clients point in this direction. It is often asserted that the Soviets are especially cautious by tradition and more sober about the danger of war because of the searing impact of their devastation in the 1940s. They did not, however, consistently avoid adventurist risks in the cold war. Khrushchev's initiatives may be atypical, but there is no guarantee that Kremlin behavior will always be "typical," especially given a new generation of leadership less annealed in the experience of war and more accustomed to taking superpower status and nuclear parity for granted. Insistence that equal military power mandates equal political rights might be less readily compromised in the future than it was in the Khrushchev period. In any event, it would be uncomfortable if U.S. policy had to bank on the adversary being more prudent about political commitment and threats of military escalation than American leaders have sometimes been.

Threats: Probability and Advisability

Prevalent views about the wisdom of U.S. reliance on nuclear threats cut across general ideological divisions. Those who support first-use commitments include hawks who believe that U.S. superiority—which made them viable in the past—might be regained and doves who believe that the balance of interests supports U.S. resolve in a contest of risks, irrespective of relative power. Those who criticize continued reliance on first use include hawks who worry that its incredibility under parity would be exposed in a crunch and doves who believe it has always been too dangerous and can be replaced by conventional deterrence.

Analysts least troubled by reliance on first use are those who dismiss the relevance of the nuclear balance and those whose arguments are advanced in terms of abstract doctrine for deterrence of Soviet attack on NATO nations. Few political leaders, however, have ever agreed, at least when in office, that the balance of nuclear power is not crucial, and specific occasions that evoked actual threats in the past, or might again, involved challenges whose relation to NATO defense was only indirect. At the same time, those most worried about the adequacy of the nuclear balance tend to be the ones with the most ambitious notions of containment and least willing to contemplate concessions or compromises of objectives in crises.

Taken together, these tendencies suggest continuing tension between officials' general attitudes toward military doctrine in peacetime and their specific political incentives in time of crisis. The former reflect increasing concern with the constraints imposed by Soviet power, while the latter encourage risky resorts to threats as tactics in bargaining. More than in the first two decades of the postwar era, recent peacetime rhetoric about capabilities undermines options that might be desired in crises. Since the mid-1970s official rhetoric has hammered three themes: the delicacy of the nuclear balance and the need to prevent a U.S. slide into inferiority, the continuing dominance of Soviet conventional military power, and the need to contain and contest Soviet political pressure around the globe.

The first theme undermines the prospective credibility of nuclear threats and the utility of the risk-maximizing approach to crisis maneuvering, at least for objectives less central than defense of NATO territory. Hand-wringing in Washington about the nuclear balance of power implicitly validated the Soviet détente-era line about how military parity compelled U.S. accommodation. (In much the same way, perhaps, the domestic debate in the United States during the late 1950s over the "missile gap" may have misled Khrushchev about American resolve.) Moscow has since charged Washington with trying to regain superiority, but neither U.S. statements about the present or prospective balance nor the actual balance evolving as both sides continue to deploy new weapons supports any potential American pretension to having an exploitable nuclear advantage.

As to the second theme, the U.S. military buildup beginning in the late 1970s improved conventional power, but not to the point that traditional concerns about the need for escalatory options in past crises would be overridden. Some academics have debunked the traditional assumptions about NATO's conventional inferiority but have not shifted the consensus in political circles.[6] Nor has the Reagan program improved forces in NATO proportional to the increase in overall defense spending, which has been concentrated in the navy. In terms of measures likely to figure in politicians' minds, relative ground force capabilities appear no greater, and in some respects less, than they were in the earlier era of frequent nuclear threats.[7]

The third theme reflects the continuity or reinvigoration of political imperatives to back commitments, despite the net shift in the aggregate military balance toward the East. There is no evidence that lesser U.S. confidence in the balance underwriting nuclear leverage will yield comparably greater caution in crisis maneuvering; if the cases of 1973 and 1980 point either way, it is in the other direction. Even in the earlier era, as chapter four argued, American presidents' resolve was governed more by political imperatives to act than by confidence about whether it would be reasonable to implement military threats. In that period, however, when Khrushchev undertook initiatives thinking that his finite nuclear deterrent should compel U.S. accommodation in the face of Soviet conventional power, he backed away when Eisenhower and Kennedy dismissed that view of the balance.

It appears that trends cast more doubt on the wisdom of future nuclear threats than on the probability that presidents may be tempted to make them. Can it any longer be responsible to endorse such threats? Either of two risky assumptions could provide grounds. If the Soviets see American

6. Grounds for optimism remain questionable analytically as well. See the works cited and criticized in Richard K. Betts, "Conventional Deterrence: Predictive Uncertainty and Policy Confidence," *World Politics*, vol. 37 (January 1985), pp. 153–79.

7. Sophisticated calculations of firepower that take more account of qualitative differences and logistical advantages may yield different assessments from simplistic quantitative "bean" counts of manpower and weapons. Irrespective of which is analytically more revealing, though, the latter indicators dominate political debate. Despite large increases in the U.S. defense budget, the numerical ratio of such basic weapons as tanks, artillery, and aircraft did not change much in the 1980s. Active U.S. army and marine corps manpower since the end of the Vietnam War has remained about 20 percent lower than it was under the flexible response buildup of the early 1960s, which had been designed to reduce reliance on nuclear ordnance, and is even below the levels existing under the massive retaliation doctrine in the 1950s. The switch in China's role in threat assessments reduced U.S. military requirements, but the Soviets met their new requirement by fielding additional forces rather than diverting any from other commitments.

peacetime rhetoric about the tenuousness of the nuclear balance as disingenuous, meant only to beat the domestic political drum for stronger nuclear force programs, and no reflection on U.S. leaders' confidence in a crisis, Moscow might be unwilling to push Washington to the brink. Or if Moscow shares Washington's view of the balance of interests at stake in a confrontation, if Soviet protestations about equal political rights are not only illegitimate in U.S. eyes but disingenuous in theirs as well, the balance of resolve will favor the U.S. position and lessen the likelihood that the Soviets would stand up to a U.S. threat. Otherwise, avoidance of a nuclear showdown would rest on one of various possibilities:

(1) No intense crises involving central interests will arise;

(2) If an intense crisis occurs, American leaders will have confidence in conventional deterrence or will be willing to concede and so will refrain from escalatory warnings;

(3) If the United States can stand fast without relying on the nuclear crutch, the Soviets will be prudent and refrain from nuclear first-use threats of their own;

(4) If either side issues a threat, it will not be called to the test, because the conflict will be settled, as in 1973, on mutually acceptable terms or, as in 1980, will fester rather than intensify;

(5) If either side makes a threat that is called, it will back down and accept exposure as a bluffer, as Moscow did occasionally but Washington did not in the era before parity;

(6) The United States will escape from parity and reestablish some nuclear advantage to repeal the change in the balance of power that marked the past two decades.

The first three possibilities would define the problem away, and the fourth would avert disaster from miscalculation of enemy resolve by precluding the need for any concession. For such cases there is less reason for concern with crisis management altogether than in cases where either side has to back down. To the extent that crisis management does remain a concern, relying on the fifth possibility is troublesome. There is no precedent for Washington making a greater concession than Moscow after going to the brink for strong demands, while there is ample precedent, especially in the Cuban missile crisis, for risky moves closer to the brink being driven by fears of domestic and foreign reaction to weakness.[8]

---

8. See Graham T. Allison, *Essence of Decision: Explaining the Cuban Missile Crisis* (Little, Brown, 1971), pp. 187–190; Roger Hilsman, *To Move a Nation: The Politics of*

There is also no guarantee that the vague and tentative quality of nuclear threats that represented leaders' desire for flexibility in past cases would necessarily work the same way in the future if options for political settlement do not offer both sides a graceful exit. Casting a threat ambiguously might make the risk appear still manageable to Washington, but in the context of some greater margin of security felt by Moscow because of the equal nuclear balance, American hesitancy might make the Soviets feel safer in ignoring the threat or responding with a nuclear signal of their own. With leaders' egos and reputations more fastened to commitments at that point, the premium on truncating an escalatory spiral would be higher at the same time that it had become harder to pay.

The sixth possibility—to escape from parity—appeals only to a political minority and appears feasible to fewer people still. One way to strive to regain some form of escalation dominance is through competition in offensive forces. Although many experts see such a competition as futile pursuit of overkill, some believe that despite the survivable retaliatory capabilities existing on both sides for the past decade or more, regaining a discernible edge in counterforce capability might offer political advantage. It would be hard to accomplish, however, given domestic constraints in the United States: even the Reagan administration, the most hawkish in decades, has continued to pursue arms control negotiations. The other barrier is Soviet capacity to compete in the offensive force expansion from a base of hot production lines and a larger number of developed systems from which to choose. Under current circumstances, in any case, a margin of advantage in the balance of forces would not recreate the appreciable disparity in vulnerability to civil damage that endured until the late 1960s.

The other way to strive for superiority would be through unilateral deployment of effective population defenses. President Reagan's vision of the Strategic Defense Initiative (SDI) has been to develop defenses that could prevent unacceptable damage—in effect, like so much of what he has cherished, a return to life in the early 1950s. Reagan has also claimed the intention to share defenses with the USSR, however, thus making nuclear weapons "impotent and obsolete," thereby negating their utility for blackmail rather then regaining it. Reagan's intention would not bind a decision by a future president, and the aim of superiority is certainly a gleam in the eye of some of the program's enthusiasts. But few experts

---

Foreign Policy in the Administration of John F. Kennedy (Doubleday, 1967), p. 197; and Barton J. Bernstein, "Was the Cuban Missile Crisis Necessary?" Washington Post, October 26, 1975.

believe that a high degree of effectiveness for protecting population is possible. Most SDI advocates focus on its possible utility for more limited purposes, such as complicating a Soviet counterforce strike by defending American ICBMs and select military bases and command centers. It is conceivable that heavy investment in partially effective population defenses that could not prevent "unacceptable" damage might, if not matched by Moscow, reestablish some disparity of vulnerability that would offer a rationale akin to Eisenhower's "sufficiency"—inability to prevent very grave damage to the United States, but ability to inflict appreciably worse damage on the USSR.[9] That prospect, in tandem with the opportunity costs of competing in massive new military investments, appears to be the principal Soviet concern about SDI. In view of the futility of U.S. attempts to move toward highly effective air defense in the 1950s and of the likelihood that the Soviets would respond with their own missile defenses, the hope of thus restoring U.S. nuclear leverage appears possible but dubious.

Balance of Risks and Choice of Tactics

Attempts at nuclear coercion during the cold war were ambiguous in execution and uncertain in effect, but they were prevalent. Politicians, especially American politicians, repeatedly showed themselves willing to exploit the military risks when they came under intense political pressure. The advent of strategic parity after the mid-1960s coincided with, but does not seem to have caused, a reduced incidence of nuclear blackmail. Since the mid-1960s, American leaders have apparently resorted to the tactic less frequently only because challenges of the sort that used to evoke nuclear threats have arisen less frequently. There is no reason, however, to assume that the decline in the number of such challenges will be permanent.

The nuclear threats in 1973 and 1980 show that the political imperatives

9. Critics argue that the absolute number of warheads precludes this. For example, even a 90 percent effective defense intercepting 10,000 warheads would still not prevent the devastating impact of 1,000. To illustrate a counterargument, however, consider that Soviet cross-targeting would have to assign on average ten warheads per target for each one they expect to penetrate. Since defensive effectiveness might vary, or U.S. priorities for preferential defense might not be known, some targets might be destroyed by multiple detonations while others might escape or absorb a single hit that would leave some of the area intact. In other words, for example, the attack might leave Cincinnati obliterated, Los Angeles partially damaged, and Hartford unstruck. But the probability that defense effectiveness could approach anywhere near 90 percent is low. Even then, if deployment of defenses provoked Soviet multiplication of long-range warheads, to, say, 20,000 or more, the odds of significant damage limitation would be low.

that overrode caution about nuclear vulnerability *before* the advent of parity continued to take precedence for U.S. leaders afterwards as well. Soviet leaders, in contrast, appear to have let military prudence override political interests whenever the two came into significant conflict, as long as the nuclear balance favored the United States. Khrushchev's embarrassing retreats after making rhetorical nuclear threats also seem to have cautioned the Kremlin against facile use of the tactic. But neither the possibility that nuclear equality affords Moscow better grounds for standing up to nuclear coercion, nor Soviet willingness to make disproportionate political concessions in a severe crisis since the arrival of parity, has yet been tested. These facts add up to a worrisome background for any major contest of wills in the future.

What are the implications for U.S. policy? Some interests are great enough to justify their continued protection by nuclear threats even at significant risk. Others can be handled by nonnuclear military capabilities. And some may not be great enough to warrant dangerous military commitments.

The persistent first-use commitment in U.S. peacetime nuclear doctrine has been oriented to deterrence of attack on Western Europe.[10] That commitment is worth keeping, despite doubts about its credibility. The European situation has been comparatively stable, perhaps in part because of the commitment. The stability also reduces the chance that the threat will be called to a test. And if it were, the balance of interests that would obtain if Moscow contemplated attack would be clearly in U.S. favor, making that argument for U.S. credibility more applicable than it would be in the different sorts of crises that constitute the past record.

Most of the past crises and the least unlikely future scenarios involve areas that have not figured much in the theoretical evolution of formal strategic doctrine. For these, the risks of drawing lessons from the satisfactory outcomes of early cases and overlooking the possible effects of the Soviets' overcoming of their nuclear inferiority are greater than in the case of Europe. And in contrast to Europe, the relationship between competing political and military risks is more dangerous. American political stakes in the third world are lower than they are in Europe or Japan, which reduces

10. Extended nuclear deterrence also covers Japan in principle, but a large buffer of water and the limits of Soviet amphibious and airborne capabilities leave the islands less vulnerable to conventional attack than NATO is. Combined with the fact that most Soviet military forces are arrayed against Europe and China, this makes the U.S. nuclear commitment to Japan an untroublesome issue.

the credibility of U.S. nuclear threats in peripheral conflicts, which in turn increases the risk that any such threat might be called to the test. Compared with conflicts over central interests, nuclear threats over peripheral territories involve higher risks for lower stakes. Leaving nuclear threats out of the diplomatic toolbox would raise the marginal risk of failing to deter an adversary's advance, but using them would raise the risk of a choice between humiliating retreat, which would in turn depreciate the credibility and utility of the nuclear commitment to Europe, or an unpredictable course of escalation, which would be questionable even on behalf of the most central values, but certainly unwarranted for more peripheral ones. Reserving the nuclear threat for central alliance contingencies should also inhibit tendencies for third world confrontations to spill over into Europe. There is no need to invite a challenge by *declaring* that the United States would never escalate outside the defense of Western Europe or Japan, if leaders can remember to keep equally quiet and avoid reaching for threats if a challenge does come.

What then should be done to cover contingencies such as those that raised the issue of nuclear blackmail in the past? In some of those cases the assumption that U.S. conventional capabilities could not handle the situation was unwarranted. Escalatory gestures or plans in those instances were less a matter of necessity than of maximizing deterrence signals, as in Lebanon in 1958 and in the 1973 October War, or prospective military efficiency, as in Korea in 1953. For similar cases in the future, reliance on conventional instruments would be prudent. Although not exploiting nuclear risks might marginally reduce the strength of deterrence, the lower importance of the territorial stakes does not warrant even a slightly increased risk of backing presidents into a nuclear corner by having them make threats they would be embarrassed to admit were bluffs. The most difficult cases in the past were those such as Quemoy and Matsu or Berlin, where no credible option for conventional defense against determined attack existed, or those such as the Persian Gulf, where the chance of conventional defense was at least very doubtful.

Since normalization of U.S. relations with the People's Republic of China and withdrawal of recognition of the Republic of China government in Taipei in 1978, the United States no longer has a defense commitment to Taiwan, let alone the offshore islands. In any case, the use of nuclear threats in the straits crises of the 1950s was reckless and undesirable even then, given the disproportionality of risks to stakes, as critics at the time argued, and should have been avoided. The favorable results evident only in hindsight do not validate the wisdom of the decisions to take such risks. If for some reason an American government wished to defend the Taipei regime against attack, it could do so with conventional forces. Like England and Japan, Taiwan is blessed by a large buffer of water between it and the mainland, and the PRC has weak naval and amphibious capabilities. There would be no strategic or political reason to go as far as reinstating the old commitment to defend the little offshore islands. Letting them go would be a compromise equivalent to the evacuation of the Tachens in 1955.

West Berlin presents harder choices. Its historic symbolism, intrinsic value, and political significance to the solidarity of the Western coalition would preclude simply acquiescing to its annexation by the East German state. West Berlin cannot be defended, but is valuable enough to protect with deterrence. Deterrence by threat of nuclear escalation, however, is now too risky. It was risky already in the first two decades of the postwar era, when U.S. nuclear superiority was overwhelming. If Moscow for some reason decided to underwrite another challenge to the city's independence, after the chastening experiences of 1961–62, the crisis would be a sign that Soviet leaders had decided that real parity provided them the deterrent insurance against U.S. escalation that Khrushchev's premature declarations of parity did not.

Given this balance of stakes and risks, the Berlin case may be one of the few that recommend a deterrent strategy of horizontal conventional escalation—the threat of retaliation by U.S. attack on territory that is both more valuable to the Soviet Union and more vulnerable to American power. Reprisal by invasion of Cuba might be the least undesirable alternative to doing nothing, mounting futile and dangerous attempts to fight through to Berlin on the ground, or courting suicide by beginning the escalation process envisioned in the old National Security Action Memorandum 109. In a major war between the superpowers in Europe or the Near East, invading Cuba would be a dangerous gambit, diverting American forces that might otherwise spell the difference in odds of defense on the central front or in the Gulf. Cuba is a highly militarized society; invasion and occupation would be a massive undertaking.[11] Moreover, the diversion would not threaten an asset more valuable than the stakes—all Europe or big chunks of territory and oil in the Near East—at the initial scene of

11. Cuba has standing conventional forces of more than 160,000 men, double that number when reserves are included, a militia force of 1.2 million, and over a thousand tanks (though mostly old). See International Institute for Strategic Studies, *The Military Balance, 1986–1987* (London: IISS, 1986), pp. 184–85.

battle and would increase the risk of vertical escalation by broadening the conflict and increasing pressures on leaders' ability to control it or consider a truce.[12]

To deter a grab of Berlin alone, however, the threat against Cuba would not pose the same prospective choices. In terms of risks, without a large engagement raging elsewhere, concentration of U.S. forces against Cuba would not be a dangerous diversion. And if it raised risks of vertical escalation it would still be short of nuclear escalation itself, the other alternative to impotence in the face of losing Berlin. In terms of stakes, Cuba is by now more valuable to the USSR than is West Berlin, and is also more valuable to the USSR than West Berlin is to the United States, however much officials in Washington would not like to admit that to friends in Bonn. Cuba has about four times the population of West Berlin; it still symbolizes for Soviet policy the promise of revolution and the positive trend in the world correlation of forces; it has absorbed billions of rubles in subsidies over the years and now represents a fantastic sunk investment for Moscow; and it has been a major force in promoting Marxism-Leninism and Soviet interests in the third world. As a deterrent, such a threat is also highly credible, given the long history of extreme American irritation, and occasionally undignified preoccupation, with the threat posed by the Castro regime.

What about the Near East? Although both stakes and risks are high, risks are higher. The superpowers have well-established entanglements in the Arab-Israeli dispute and a substantial interest in the Persian Gulf region, but reliance on nuclear blackmail is too dangerous, because Moscow and Washington are less likely to be able to control the development of a crisis in that region. Compared with other areas, the local actors in the Near East are too volatile internally, too reckless externally, too numerous, and have political hooks buried too deeply in the superpowers' capitals to warrant any assurance that a one-on-one U.S.-Soviet duel near the brink could be managed.

American conventional military options in that region vary significantly, depending on the exact venue of conflict. For intervention in Egypt, Israel, Jordan, or even Saudi Arabia, the Soviet geographic advantage does not outweigh the U.S. advantage in capability for long-range projection and sustenance of ground and air forces to the extent that it does in Iran. And the situation in Iran—where the radical regime is no friendlier to Washing-

12. For related arguments see Joshua M. Epstein, *Strategy and Force Planning: The Case of the Persian Gulf* (Brookings, 1986), chap. 3.

ton than to Moscow—gives planning for U.S. intervention there, under anything like recent circumstances, an air of politically sterile unreality.[13] A confrontation in Iran is less improbable than many others and could be the most dangerous, given the congeries of actors, interests, and animosities. The combination of probability and danger make it a case where the intensity of risks should compel a reassessment of axiomatic assumptions about U.S. stakes and a compromise of objectives or commitments. If diplomatic skill proves insufficient to avert a Soviet military challenge there, or to arrange some sort of compromise division of spoils, it should not be unthinkable that the United States could accept defeat rather than lurch toward nuclear escalation.

Outside of Europe and areas close to Soviet borders, the United States has little reason to fear the need to substitute nuclear capabilities for conventional. American military forces are still superior to the Soviets' in capacity to apply force at long distances from the homeland, an advantage that has been accentuated in the Reagan buildup. So if the pattern of recent U.S. priorities in improvement of conventional military forces continues, it supports the reservation of nuclear threats for NATO contingencies. With naval, air, and light ground forces for projection of power having been improved more than heavy ground forces, U.S. capacity for conventional military action has grown for peripheral contingencies more than for the central one. Finally, underlining the distinction between central and peripheral commitments would help the cause of solidarity in the Western coalition, which is the biggest source of overall strength and deterrent capacity. When Truman and Eisenhower sent nuclear signals in Asia, their biggest problem was allied anxiety about Soviet nuclear blackmail in return. In that period the United States dominated the Western coalition politically and economically more than in recent times, and the alliance cohesion problem was more manageable then than it would be if Uncle Sam seemed to be swaggering around the nuclear brink again for the sake of secondary interests.

Because few nuclear threats have been made in recent times, whether because of military parity or the venues of crisis, U.S. leaders are not in the habit of resorting to them. They should thus find it easier to consider dispensing with that tactic in some circumstances that used to evoke it.

To those most ardently committed to containment, reserving nuclear

13. For elaboration of these points and recommendations for adjustments in military planning priorities, see Richard K. Betts, *Surprise Attack: Lessons for Defense Planning* (Brookings, 1982), pp. 262–73.

coercion for the most crucial commitment might smack of defeatism, a preemptive concession. It would be hard to reconcile a nonchalant attitude about nuclear risks, however, with a consistent view of the seriousness of the Soviet threat. If the USSR's malevolence and power are indeed awesome, it would be foolhardy to assume that it is a paper tiger. If the Soviets' military buildup of the past quarter century is as significant as generally acknowledged, it would be peculiar if their options for contesting American nuclear initiatives have not improved; if it is not, it is less certain that nonnuclear tools in the American inventory for bargaining will be inadequate.

The one way for either hawks or doves to avoid the question of evaluating the relevance of past threats is to dismiss their significance, to point to how vague, muted, hedged, and awash among other important considerations they were in the thinking of those who made or faced them. That argument would debunk not only their utility, however, but the excuse leaders had for invoking them at all. In crises, rhetoric about nuclear forces or changes in their readiness status are not good for fun and games. If a whiff of nuclear blackmail enters at all in the midst of conflict, the action should have a purpose. If the purpose is not serious, why depreciate the nuclear currency, and why tempt fate?

Index